Orchids

Orchids

by
ALICE SKELSEY
and
the Editors of TIME-LIFE BOOKS

TIME-LIFE BOOKS, ALEXANDRIA, VIRGINIA

Time-Life Books Inc.
is a wholly owned subsidiary of
TIME INCORPORATED

FOUNDER: Henry R. Luce 1898-1967

Editor-in-Chief: Hedley Donovan
Chairman of the Board: Andrew Heiskell
President: James R. Shepley
Vice Chairman: Roy E. Larsen
Corporate Editors: Ralph Graves, Henry Anatole Grunwald

TIME-LIFE BOOKS INC.

MANAGING EDITOR: Jerry Korn
Executive Editor: David Maness
Assistant Managing Editors: Dale M. Brown, Martin Mann,
John Paul Porter
Art Director: Tom Suzuki
Chief of Research: David L. Harrison
Director of Photography: Robert G. Mason
Planning Director: Thomas Flaherty (acting)
Senior Text Editor: Diana Hirsh
Assistant Art Director: Arnold C. Holeywell
Assistant Chief of Research: Carolyn L. Sackett
Assistant Director of Photography: Dolores A. Littles

CHAIRMAN: Joan D. Manley
President: John D. McSweeney
Executive Vice Presidents: Carl G. Jaeger (U.S. and
Canada), David J. Walsh (International)
Vice President and Secretary: Paul R. Stewart
Treasurer and General Manager: John Steven Maxwell
Business Manager: Peter G. Barnes
Sales Director: John L. Canova
Public Relations Director: Nicholas Benton
Personnel Director: Beatrice T. Dobie
Production Director: Herbert Sorkin
Consumer Affairs Director: Carol Flaumenhaft

THE TIME-LIFE ENCYCLOPEDIA OF GARDENING

EDITORIAL STAFF FOR ORCHIDS:
EDITOR: Robert M. Jones
Assistant Editors: Sarah Bennett Brash, Betsy Frankel
Text Editor: Margaret Fogarty
Picture Editor: Jane Jordan
Designer: Albert Sherman
Staff Writers: Dalton Delan, Susan Perry
Researchers: Diane Bohrer, Marilyn Murphy,
Susan F. Schneider
Art Assistant: Edwina C. Smith
Editorial Assistant: Maria Zacharias

EDITORIAL PRODUCTION
Production Editor: Douglas B. Graham
Operations Manager: Gennaro C. Esposito
Assistant Production Editor: Feliciano Madrid
Quality Control: Robert L. Young (director),
James J. Cox (assistant), Michael G. Wight (associate)
Art Coordinator: Anne B. Landry
Copy Staff: Susan B. Galloway (chief), Elizabeth Graham,
Lynn Green, Florence Keith, Celia Beattie
Picture Department: Barbara S. Simon

CORRESPONDENTS: Elisabeth Kraemer (Bonn); Margot
Hapgood, Dorothy Bacon (London); Susan Jonas, Lucy T.
Voulgaris (New York); Maria Vincenza Aloisi, Josephine du
Brusle (Paris); Ann Natanson (Rome). Valuable assistance
was also provided by Anne Angus (London); Diane Asselin
(Los Angeles); Carolyn T. Chubet, Miriam Hsia (New York).
The editors are indebted to Margaret M. Carter, Michael
McTwigan, Jane Opper, Maggie Oster, Wendy Rieder and
Anne Weber, writers, for their help with this book.

THE AUTHOR: Alice Skelsey, journalist and gardener, inherited her green thumb from her mother, whose Oklahoma garden flourished despite drought and grasshopper plagues. Mrs. Skelsey is the author of *Farming in a Flowerpot* and co-author of *Growing Up Green* and *Every Room a Garden*. She has also written a syndicated column about working women. Her Virginia home has a skylit garden room where she grows orchids, ferns, begonias and cacti.

CONSULTANTS: James Underwood Crockett, author of 13 of the volumes in the Encyclopedia, co-author of two additional volumes and consultant on other books in the series, has been a lover of the earth and its good things since his boyhood on a Massachusetts fruit farm. He was graduated from the Stockbridge School of Agriculture at the University of Massachusetts and has worked ever since in horticulture. A perennial contributor to leading gardening magazines, he also writes a monthly bulletin, "Flowery Talks," that is widely distributed through retail florists. His television program, *Crockett's Victory Garden*, shown all over the United States, has won countless converts to the Crockett approach to growing things. Dr. Ronald W. Hodges, an entomologist with the U.S. Department of Agriculture in Washington, D.C., grows hundreds of orchids at his home in Adelphi, Maryland, most of them miniatures he has collected in the wild. Merritt W. Huntington is a professional orchid grower and owner of Kensington Orchids, Inc., Kensington, Maryland. Dr. William Louis Stern is Professor of Botany at the University of Maryland, College Park. Dr. Carl Withner is a Horticultural Specialist at the New York Botanical Garden and Professor of Biology at Brooklyn College, New York City.

THE COVER: Three phalaenopsis blossoms cascade along a single stalk. Sometimes nicknamed moth orchid, because of its resemblance to certain tropical moths, phalaenopsis produces flowers that remain perfect for months. This particular plant is a hybrid called Grace Palm.

Library of Congress Cataloging in Publication Data
Skelsey, Alice Fulton, (date)
    Orchids.
    (The Time-Life encyclopedia of gardening; v.22)
    Bibliography: p.
    Includes index.
    1. Orchid culture. 2. Orchids. I. Time-Life Books. II. Title.
SB409.S58   635.9'34'15   78-18249
ISBN 0-8094-2593-9
ISBN 0-8094-2592-0 lib. bdg.

CONTENTS

Pl. 24

ODONTOGLOSSOM GRANDE.

Publ.d by J. Ridgway & Sons, 169, Piccadilly, Sept.r 1st 1840.

The bewitching world of the orchid 1

"I can always tell when someone is coming down with orchid fever," says a longtime orchid expert who has helped hundreds of beginners to get started. "The first symptom is pure amazement. The person will repeat over and over again 'I didn't know that' or 'I always thought. . . .' And I say to myself, 'You're hooked, friend. You'll never recover, and you'll never stop being astonished. Welcome to the orchid world.' "

Anyone who has fallen under the spell of orchids knows that the expert is absolutely right. Once an amateur has grown his first plant or two, he usually finds it all but impossible to stop. The magic lies in many things, but most of all in the endless variety and fascination of the flowers themselves. Their range of beauty is unsurpassed in horticulture, from the exquisite purity in an arching spray of moth orchids to the bold sensuality in a single bloom of a lady's slipper, from the extravagant flowers of some *Cattleya* species that measure almost a foot across to tiny, jewel-like *Pleurothallis* blossoms that are scarcely larger than the heads of pins. Many species are so fragrant that a single flower can perfume an entire room. Most orchid flowers, moreover, are notably long lasting, as are the plants themselves, staying in bloom for periods that range from several weeks to several months (one species, *Grammatophyllum multiflorum,* holds the floral record, remaining in flower for a full nine months). And since different species bloom at different times, a well-chosen handful of orchid plants can provide a continuous display of blossoms in the home year round.

Who could take a reasoned approach to flowers such as these?

Not William George Spencer Cavendish, one of the earliest orchid hobbyists and the sixth Duke of Devonshire. While attending a Royal Horticultural Society exhibition in 1833 he succumbed at the first sight of a butterfly orchid, *Oncidium papilio,* its spritely yellow flower banded in brown. The Duke indulged his new-found

The tiger orchid (Odontoglossum grande) is still popular—and vastly more available than it was in 1840 when this drawing first appeared in James Bateman's Orchidaceae of Mexico and Guatemala.

In 1640, when this drawing of "the male Neapolitane Foolestones" appeared in John Parkinson's Theatrum Botanicum: The Theater of Plants, orchids were thought to influence virility because their tubers resembled testicles. The "Foolestones" orchid, which Parkinson described as having flowers shaped "like bodies with short armes as it were hanging downe," was considered particularly potent. A man who ate the larger of the plant's two tubers, reported Parkinson, would "beget men children."

passion and housed the collection that followed by building a glass conservatory 60 feet high and roughly the size of a football field.

Not Nero Wolfe, famed fictional detective whose exploits first appeared in print in the 1930s. Through more than 80 mystery tales spanning 40 years, the fat, flamboyant private eye created by Rex Stout confounded everyone by deliberately suspending work, even on the most urgent and baffling cases, so he could devote his accustomed four hours a day to tending the 20,000 orchids that flourished in the "plant rooms" atop his Manhattan town house.

And certainly not today's legions of orchid fanciers, who in far more modest circumstances can grow plants that a few years ago were the province of the privileged and the professional—and who can choose from thousands of new hybrid orchids whose beauty, and low prices, would astound the detective and the Duke alike.

Thanks to the remarkable nature of these plants, moreover, the end of orchid fever is not even remotely in sight. Today orchids constitute the single largest and most varied family of flowering plants, and one that is being added to every year. The Orchidaceae, as the family is known to botanists, include some 30,000 known species, classified into 88 subtribes and 660 genera (more than the Compositae, once thought to be the largest floral family and including all the asters, daisies, chrysanthemums, zinnias and myriads of other flowers, vegetables and wayside weeds like dandelions and goldenrod). No other plants have given birth to so many hybrids, many involving three-, four- and even five-way crosses. More than 75,000 man-made hybrids have been registered in the last century and a quarter and the total continues to grow by hundreds every year; such crosses now far exceed the naturally occurring hybrids and provide most of the orchids sold for house plants and cut flowers. Today orchid blooms come in every imaginable combination of size, shape and color—except black. There are dark brown, dark maroon and dark blue orchids, but Nero Wolfe and certain comic-strip characters notwithstanding, a pure black orchid remains a myth.

More important to orchid culture are other widespread and persistent myths about the plants. One popular notion is that "it's too bad such beautiful flowers have to be parasites." Many orchids grow on trees in the wild, but they are not parasitic in the least, merely using the branches for support. Nor are they carnivorous, as some people believe; though they lure pollinating insects by a variety of devices, they do not feast on them like flytraps and pitcher plants.

Another myth is that all orchids are "jungle plants." Actually, species of orchids are found all over the world, from sand dunes and bogs in temperate zones to barren tundra above the Arctic Circle, and from sea level to altitudes of 14,000 feet. Three Australian species even manage to grow underground.

A third misconception is that orchids are fragile "hothouse plants," extremely difficult to grow and requiring expensive equipment and constant care. Though their blooms often do look delicate and do require specific conditions to come into flower, the plants are in reality quite tough and resilient. Many, if not most, orchids can be raised quite satisfactorily without a greenhouse—in a sunny living room window or in a basement under artificial lights—though many amateurs sooner or later resort to some kind of greenhouse structure as a matter of convenience and space.

As newcomers to orchids begin to get deeper into the subject, they may be in for some other surprises. One is that the widespread cultivation of orchids is a relatively recent pursuit. Wild native orchids figure in the art and legends of ancient China and medieval Europe—sweet-scented cymbidiums were especially prized by the Chinese, and Western herbalists believed that the *Orchis* heightened sexual powers—but with the exception of extracting vanilla flavoring from the vining orchid *Vanilla planifolia,* orchids for centuries remained of little importance, commercial or otherwise. A few orchids were brought back from far-off lands by British sea captains and explorers in the 18th Century, but they remained curiosities for a handful of botanists and wealthy amateurs.

In the year 1818, however, all that changed when a spectacular tropical orchid flowered in a hothouse in England. That it bloomed at all was a matter of considerable good luck. Gardeners of the day knew very little about orchids or how to care for them, and it was only by accident that the plant had found its way to England in the first place. In a shipment of plants sent to him from Brazil, William Cattley, an eminent horticulturist and importer, came across some strange foliage that had been used as packing material. Intrigued by the unfamiliar bulbous stems, he potted some of them and put them in his hothouse. That November he was rewarded for his pains when a flower unfolded—a gorgeous lavender bloom with purple markings. The plant immediately caused a sensation. Dr. John Lindley, a leading botanist of the day, conferred on it the name *Cattleya labiata autumnalis,* honoring not only its discoverer but the flower's beautifully ruffled lower petal, known as the *labellum* or lip, and the fact that the plant had bloomed in the fall.

The flower world still feels the impact of that single plant. What other flower but the *Cattleya,* the corsage orchid, has appeared on so many speakers' rostrums, made so many anniversaries and Mother's Days memorable, attended so many high-school proms? In the early

Early herbalists believed all orchids, including the "Stinking Goates Stone" shown in this drawing from Parkinson's Theater of Plants (opposite), were seedless plants that sprang spontaneously from the seminal secretions dropped from mating animals. The "Goates Stone" orchid was specifically thought to come from the semen of goats. "Not onely [do] they have a strong foule s[c]ent like a Goate," wrote Parkinson about the plant's blossoms, "but most of them have long tailes like beards."

1800s a single rare specimen, if it could be obtained at all, might have cost an eager lord or lady the equivalent of thousands of dollars. Today any amateur can buy one of hundreds of *Cattleya* hybrids, even more beautiful than the original, for less than ten.

Motivated by Cattley's discovery, commercial growers and wealthy fanciers immediately launched searches not only for more plants of the original *Cattleya* species but for other orchids. At the time, orchids were nearly impossible to propagate—many horticulturists actually believed them sterile—and the only way to obtain a number of new plants was to take them from the wild. Professional plant hunters were engaged and sent off to comb South America, the Far East and other reaches of the globe. The hardships they encountered—and the devastation they visited upon the natural habitats of many plants—are unmatched by any botanical adventure before or since. Entire forests were stripped of millions of orchids, and protests by naturalists and others had little effect. An English botanist wrote as late as 1878: "Not satisfied with taking 300 or 500 specimens of a fine orchid, they must scour the whole country and leave nothing for miles around. This is no longer collecting; this is wanton robbery." That same year a commercial grower announced the arrival of two consignments of orchids and estimated the total number of plants at no less than two million.

Many of the plants never survived the long journeys to their new homes, and those that did found a hostile, often lethal, environment awaiting them. Hothouses or "stove houses" such as William Cattley's were just that. They were heated from fires fueled by coal or wood; no ventilation was provided, and frequent drenchings with water created a steamy, stifling atmosphere. For years it never occurred to the growers that their orchids would have thrived on some fresh air and a lot less heat. To them orchids meant jungles, and jungles meant steaming hot. Many of the plants, it was true, had come from tropical or semitropical latitudes, but frequently they grew not in the dank sea-level jungles but high upon cool, cloud-brushed mountainsides.

THE AIR DWELLERS

Early orchid growers also made another major mistake. The limited success with orchids they had had up to that time was mostly with those types known as terrestrials, plants whose roots grow in the ground. Most of the new tropical and subtropical orchids, however, were not terrestrials but epiphytes, plants that attach themselves to tree limbs for support and live on the moisture and organic debris that settles on them in their habitats. When collectors sent back plants still attached to bits of branches, it was first assumed that epiphytic orchids must be parasites, but it eventually became evident that they absorbed nutrients from the air, from rain water and from bits of decaying leaves caught in the branches. It also became evident that they were not suited to the "hard potting" accorded to ground-growing plants. Gradually a few perceptive gardeners began to use a looser, airier potting medium that allowed the roots of the epiphytes to range freely, and results began to improve. Still, so many plants failed to flower, or died after flowering only a season or two, that orchid growers nearly gave up.

Partly because of the intense competition and secrecy surrounding orchid hunting, horticulturists were deprived of the very knowledge they needed to domesticate the plants. Actually orchids, even those within a given region, grow under a wide range of climatic conditions, including variations in temperatures, humidity, rainfall and breeze; even on a single tree some species grow near the top of the forest canopy in full sunlight and wind, others closer to the humid forest floor where less light and moving air filters through. Gradually trial and error revealed the plants' needs. Led by Joseph Paxton, the talented head gardener of the Duke of Devonshire, growers began to open up their hothouses to circulate fresh air, and to maintain different conditions of light, temperature and humidity for different kinds of plants. Cool-climate orchids like odontoglossums, which almost invariably had died under the jungle treatment, soon began to thrive. As more was learned, orchid species came to be identified with the temperatures that were best for them—cool,

MANY IDIOSYNCRACIES

Crates shipped from South America to Europe during the orchid-collecting frenzy of the early 19th Century often carried insect stowaways. Cockroaches, which feasted on the orchid blossoms en route, were especially maddening to English collectors, as shown in this sketch by caricaturist George Cruikshank. Bemoaned one collector: "It is indeed a cruel thing to expect Epiphytes and receive only Cockroaches!"

11

intermediate and warm—and are still classified that way to help amateurs as well as professionals in caring for them.

Despite such progress, however, orchids even at the turn of the century still remained beyond the reach of those who could not afford a greenhouse or a gardener, not to mention the price of the plants themselves. Wholesale collection from the wild had begun to slacken, partly because of the mounting protests and partly because in many areas there simply were no plants left. New plants could be obtained by dividing old ones into two or more sections, but this did not dramatically increase the supply, and the divisions often required years to reach flowering size. Above all, new plants could not be grown consistently from seed like other plants, no matter how hard growers tried. The mystery of the orchid persisted as scientists sought to unlock the final secret: how to get the seed to germinate.

For a long time the answers lay hidden within the structure of the flower itself, which is unique in the floral world. The outer part of the flower is made up of three petals and three sepals. Two of the petals, called the laterals, flank a third petal, the lip, which differs dramatically from them; usually the showiest part of an orchid flower, with brilliant colorings and markings, it varies in shape from the gracefully ruffled lip of a cattleya to the pouchlike cup of a lady's slipper. The three sepals, which make up a whorl behind the petals, serve as a protective cover for the flower bud; as the flower opens they enlarge and take on coloring. In some species the sepals look almost exactly like the lateral petals, in others quite different; the top, or dorsal, sepal may also be as showy as the lip.

A STRANGE STRUCTURE

Within this floral envelope the mystery deepens, for the inner workings of the orchid bear no resemblance to the vast majority of plants. The reproductive parts are not separate as in other flowers but are fused together in what is called the column, the chief characteristic by which a species is assigned to the Orchidaceae. At the top of the column is the male part, or anther, which bears its pollen in little bundles called pollinia. Below this is the stigma, a female part with a shallow, usually sticky cavity in which pollen must be placed to make seed production possible.

In the mid-19th Century, orchid flowers, like other intricate structures in nature, were widely regarded as beauty fashioned solely by the Creator for the delight of man. One who doubted this notion was the great English naturalist Charles Darwin, who felt there must be logical reasons why orchids had evolved in ways that called so much attention to themselves. Not far from his country house in Kent he came upon what he called the Orchis Bank, where a variety of native orchids grew among the trees, and he began to

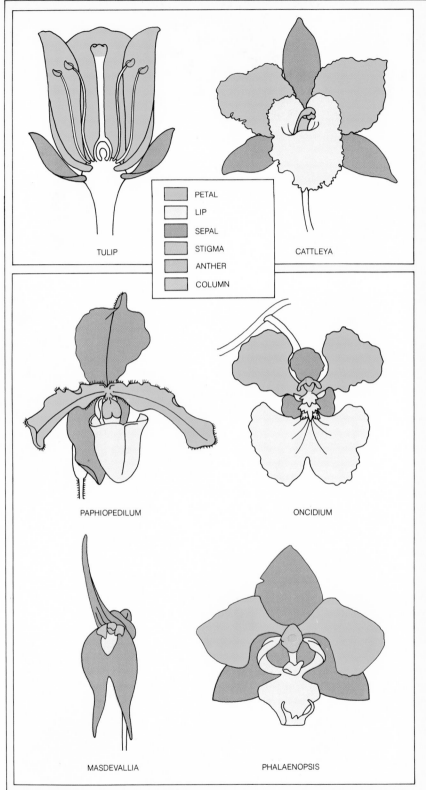

PETAL
LIP
SEPAL
STIGMA
ANTHER
COLUMN

TULIP

CATTLEYA

PAPHIOPEDILUM

ONCIDIUM

MASDEVALLIA

PHALAENOPSIS

Unique anatomy

Orchids possess the most highly developed flowers in the plant kingdom, for their male and female reproductive organs are fused together into a single cylindrical structure in the center of the flower, called a column. Most plants, such as the tulip, have separate male and female organs.

At the tip of the orchid's column is the male anther, which holds two to eight waxy pellets, called pollinia, each containing millions of grains of pollen. Just beneath the anther is a sticky convex surface, the female stigma, which catches the pollinia during pollination. And underneath the stigma is the ovary, from which the seed pod—the capsule—develops.

The column is surrounded by three sepals that cover the flower bud during its formation and three petals. One petal, called the lip or labellum, is usually larger and showier than the others.

An orchid's sepals and petals are not always easily distinguishable. On some flowers the petals are overshadowed by the sepals, and the two lower sepals may be fused, as they are on the paphiopedilum, or all three may be fused into a single cup, as on the masdevallia. On others, the lip is decorated with fanciful crests, tails, horns, fans or teeth, as on the oncidium and the phalaenopsis.

There are three basic types of orchid leaves. Plicate, or pleated, leaves can be found on orchids native to moist, shady regions where sunlight is not intense. They are generally wider and thinner than leaves of the other types, presenting more surface to capture sunlight. But they lack the capacity to store water or resist drying. A second leaf type, soft and fleshy, is found on orchids native to dry, cool, partially shaded areas. Although these leaves can store water, they dehydrate when sun or heat is strong. The third type, found on orchids native to dry areas with bright sunlight, are hard and leathery with excellent water-storing abilities.

THE FIRST HYBRIDS

study the ways in which insects pollinated the flowers. As his studies progressed, he excitedly enlisted help; the botanists John Lindley and Joseph Hooker sent him rare specimens, which he dissected, and his family and others took to orchid watching, even catching pollen-bearing moths at night. The result of years of labor was a masterly treatise that appeared in 1862 and to Darwin's surprise and gratification, became a bestseller not only among his fellow scientists but also the public at large. Titled *The Various Contrivances by Which Orchids Are Fertilised by Insects,* it eventually earned Darwin the Royal Society's coveted Copley Medal and provided Darwinists with one of the finest test cases for the theory of adaptive evolution.

Darwin demonstrated that orchids are almost perfectly adapted to specific pollinators, whether bee, fly, mosquito, butterfly, moth, hummingbird or bat—and that the pollinators in turn have evolved with the precise instincts and structures to obtain food from specific flowers, thus ensuring, not incidentally, that each orchid species will perpetuate itself *(pages 16-21).* Probably the most striking of Darwin's examples was that of the Star-of-Bethlehem orchid, *Angraecum sesquipedale,* a snowy star-shaped flower native to Madagascar that is equipped with a curious whiplike pendant spur 11½ inches long. On examining a specimen sent to him, Darwin noted that the lower 1½ inches of the spur were filled with nectar and predicted that in the orchid's native region there must be some kind of sphinx or hawk moth with a tongue at least 10 inches long. Prominent entomologists ridiculed the idea, but Darwin stuck to his guns. Four decades later such a moth was indeed found on Madagascar and, appropriately, *praedicta* became part of its name, though it remains for some future scientist to catch it in the act.

As botanists poked into the private lives of orchids, they gained enough knowledge to begin hybridizing them, crossing two parent plants with different characteristics to create new plants with the traits of both. The first man-made hybrid—a cross of two *Calanthe* species made by an English professional gardener, John Dominy— flowered in 1856. From a plant once considered sterile, new breeds could be created. And it turned out that orchid crosses could be made not only between related species within a genus, but between species of different genera, almost unheard of in horticulture until then—like creating an entirely new bird by crossing a cardinal with a goldfinch. Over the years hybridizers learned how to include as many as five genera in the cross-pollination process. With thousands of species to choose from, the number of combinations possible was astronomical. As the orchid scientist John Lindley exclaimed to Dominy on viewing his creation: "You will drive the botanists mad!"

Despite their discoveries in crossing orchids, growers still had one final, major hurdle to overcome: growing new plants reliably from seed. The only method that had met with much success was to place ripened seed at the base of the mother plant in a bed of moist sphagnum moss and hope for the best. Though this worked sometimes, disappointment was more often the case. The obstacles were formidable. Orchids produce among the smallest of all plant seeds; scientists once counted more than three million in a pod of *Cycnoches ventricosum* var. *chlorochilon*. The seeds are light enough to be wafted high on air currents, and there are enough of them so that a few will come to rest in spots where they have a chance to survive. They are as fragile as their size might indicate, and they have no tough seed coats to protect them and no food reserves to nourish them until they germinate. To keep going, they must land where they can coexist with a specific fungus that helps to nourish them.

When growers discovered this they tried introducing into the seedbed specific fungi found in association with the parent plants. But this was a tricky business because the fungi, or invading bacteria, often destroyed the seeds. In 1917 a breakthrough finally came. Dr. Lewis Knudsen, a scientist at Cornell University, believed that the real role of the fungus was to produce sugars that the germinating seed could use. After many experiments he came up with a new medium: basically a sugar, mixed with mineral nutrients, in a jelly-like extract of algae called agar-agar. Greatly increased numbers of seeds could be germinated using the agar-jelly method, though it still required care, sterile conditions and the sowing of the seeds in little incubators made out of stoppered glass flasks.

It took one more discovery, in the 1960s, to bring orchids truly within mass-market reach. A French scientist, Georges Morel, found that a laboratory technique called tissue culture could be used to produce thousands of plants from a single orchid's growing tip, called the meristem. The implications were staggering. In the United States, the first mericlone—a plant grown from a bit of tissue taken from a meristem—bloomed in 1966 in a commercial greenhouse in Kensington, Maryland. It was an exact duplicate of its parent plant, and so were other mericlones that followed. Today, thanks to the meristem method, some of the most famous species orchids of the past, as well as thousands of new hybrids, are widely available in quantity and at prices almost any gardener can afford.

A hundred years ago, or even 25, it would have been unthinkable that exotic orchids could become everyday house plants. Yet that is exactly what they are—and to those who catch orchid fever, plants that become more fascinating and more beautiful every year.

A SUGARY MYSTERY

Survival of the trickiest

Though orchids may appear ingenuous and gentle, many are actually unscrupulous deceivers and mimics—masters at making a host of creatures do their bidding to ensure the survival of the species. Almost exclusively dependent upon insects and birds for pollination, orchids have evolved elaborate designs and devices for luring unsuspecting visitors and pressing them into service as pollen-bearers.

Most orchids employ odors and visual cues that hold out the prospect of food, but often this promise is hollow, for many species bear little or no nectar. Once a potential pollinator—most often an insect—is attracted, the orchid's landing-pad lip guides it inside the flower. On the way in, the insect brushes against a gluey surface; on backing out, glue that adheres to its body picks up overhanging bags of pollen, called pollinia, which get carried away to be picked up in turn by the sticky stigma of the next flower.

Orchid trickery can take even more startling forms. Some orchids, especially those pollinated by notoriously unreliable flies, use the lip like a drawbridge or spring-loaded trap door to force the fly into a tunnel. There it is led past the glue and pollinia before it finds its way out. In coryanthes, bees intoxicated by a chemical in the lip stumble into a bath of water, wetting their wings so they are unable to fly and instead must climb past the pollinia. Species of catasetum shoot self-sticking pollinia at any insects that touch their hairlike antennae, which act like triggers to set off the process.

When the father of evolutionary theory, Charles Darwin, first described the rifle approach of catasetum, naturalist Thomas Huxley scoffed, "Do you really think I can believe all that?" Huxley's further reaction was not recorded when Darwin went on to analyze the orchids' most astonishing means of deception: mimicry. Several orchids disguise themselves as female insects so males will attempt to mate; the seduced insects succeed only in picking up pollinia. Other orchids are even more devious: they sway in the breeze like swarms of bees, inciting real bees to attack them; once again, the outcome profits only the wily orchids.

The honeydew-like scent of Epipactis gigantea (top) tricks a syrphid fly (bottom) into expecting aphids for its young to eat. Leaving an egg, the fly has picked up pollinia.

Getting the drop on insects

The fastest draw in the orchid world, a male Catasetum saccatum employs a musky odor to attract a bee, then fires sticky pollinia at the insect when it touches the flower's hair-trigger. The female flower, with its own aromatic scent, has the less violent task of catching the pollinia as the bee probes it in turn, searching for food. Neither actually produces nectar.

Slippery both in name—lady's slipper—and action, Cypripedium acaule specializes in inducing insects to take pollinating pratfalls. An insect, lured by an aroma of food, lands on the smooth, oily edge of a trap and drops into it. To get out, the insect must climb a series of hair-steps that lead past the sticky pollinia and out a narrow side exit.

Bartending is a fine art for
Stanhopea wardii, which profits from
pollination by besotted bees.
Attracted by Stanhopea's fragrance, a
bee scratches the surface of the
flower and absorbs an intoxicating
chemical. The drunken bee slides
down a chute, brushing past a column
where it picks up pollinia to take to
the next orchid.

A master of deception, rosy
Calopogon pulchellus proffers a feast of
what appear both in color and in
shape to be a mass of pollen-bearing
stamens. But when a bee touches
down to sup at the disguised hairs, the
hinged lip fails to support its weight
and it is unceremoniously thrown
against a column where it is stuck
with the plant's real offering of pollinia.

19

Mimics: pollination by proxy

The Cupid of orchids, Trichoceros antennifera bears an uncanny resemblance to a female fly—even to a stigma that mimics the fly's genitalia. Fooled into love at first sight, a male fly picks up pollinia as it attempts to mate and, unchastened by experience, pollinates the next proxy lover that catches its eye.

Actively soliciting the assaults of angry bees, Oncidium stipitatum relies on the wind to set its brazen mime show in motion. A light breeze turns the flowers' basic physical similarity to bees into the frenetic appearance of a swarm. To protect their territorial rights, real bees attack the flowers repeatedly, pollinating as they strike. With a margin for error of less than a millimeter, the bees seldom miss.

Narrowing the choices in a forest of flowers 2

Gardeners new to orchids are sometimes overwhelmed by the feast of flowers set before them. "I knew I was in trouble by the time I reached page nine of my first orchid catalogue," says one experienced gardener who thought she had been immunized after years of reading nursery catalogues. "I had already made three choices, and I still had 151 pages to go."

While it is easy to be dazzled by the beauty and variety of orchids, a beginner should follow a few common-sense rules. First, narrow the field to types that not only appeal to you but are suited to your region—and more particularly to the conditions that you will be able to provide in your home. Certain vandas, for example, are undeniably gorgeous, and they will grow splendidly outdoors in such warm areas as southern Florida and Hawaii. But they need so much sunlight and grow so robustly—some reach a height of 6 or 7 feet— that they are poor choices for indoors, particularly in northern climates where winters are cloudy. On the other hand, orchids that need lower temperatures, like some of the smaller cymbidiums and odontoglossums, are almost impossible to grow in semitropical areas without artificial cooling, yet they do well on breezy sun porches in the cool, damp Northeast or Pacific Northwest.

When you consider buying a particular orchid, then, first find out if it is classified as "cool," "intermediate" or "warm." Ideal growing temperatures for specific plants are given in the encyclopedia *(page 89)*. Generally speaking, cool-growing types such as cymbidiums, odontoglossums and some species of paphiopedilums and cattleyas (affectionately known as "cool catts") grow and flower best when night temperatures are between 50° and 55° and day temperatures are between 60° and 70°, although they will tolerate higher or lower temperatures for short periods. Intermediate-temperature types—the largest category, including most cattleyas, epidendrums, oncidiums, dendrobiums and laelias—thrive in night

A group of phalaenopsis species and hybrids surrounds a greenhouse fountain. Requiring a night temperature of only 65° and no direct sunlight, long-blooming phalaenopsis is an excellent house plant.

temperatures of 55° to 60° and day temperatures of 65° to 75°. Warm types like vandas and phalaenopsises prefer 60° to 65° at night and 70° to 85° during the day.

In all categories, the night temperature is most critical, especially in winter when the plants receive less light and make less food. Unless they can be provided with a 10° to 15° drop in temperature at night, which they normally experience in nature, the constant warmth will induce them to grow without rest, forcing them to draw on food reserves and resulting in weaker plants less likely to bloom.

A COMFORTABLE WARMTH

Fortunately, the intermediate range of most orchids—55° to 60° at night and 65° to 75° during the day—is close to what most people find comfortable. You can get a general idea of room temperatures from a wall thermostat, but more accurate readings can be made by placing a separate thermometer close to the plants and checking it from time to time. Best of all is a thermometer of the maximum-minimum type, available at many garden-supply centers and hardware stores. In this device a U-shaped column of mercury not only indicates the temperature but also records on one side the high for the day and on the other the low during the night. With its help, you can determine the best location for the orchids you are growing and adjust night and day temperatures closely to their needs. While intermediate orchids are the best to start with under average conditions, you may find that you are able to grow other types as well. The temperature groupings overlap; some warm and cool orchids can be grown under intermediate conditions.

When you choose any orchid make sure that you can provide it not only with suitable temperatures but also with the amount of light it needs. Most orchids, though not all, benefit from as much sunlight as you can give them. The best indoor location in winter is close to an unobstructed south-facing window. An east-facing one will generally receive enough morning sun to do the job; a west-facing window is also acceptable, although you may have to shield some plants from hot afternoon sun. A north exposure does not provide enough natural light for most orchids, though some coelogynes, stanhopeas and phalaenopsises will survive. Keep in mind that most orchids can also be grown under artificial light, used either as a supplement or to supply all of the required illumination.

HOW HIGH THE HUMIDITY

Orchids require a rather high degree of humidity, along with good circulation of air. Most will get along with relative humidity of 40 to 60 per cent, which you can achieve in your house, even in winter (Chapter 3). But if you are not prepared to go to great lengths to create a closely controlled environment, avoid species that require relative humidity in the 70 per cent range.

Finally, in choosing orchids, consider when you want your plants to bloom. Some gardeners like to have all their plants in flower at the same time. "It makes a stunning display," says one, "especially in winter with the flowers massed at a living room window. You get the same sort of lift that you get in the spring when daffodils and tulips appear outdoors." Other orchid growers select plants that bloom at different times, so that something will always be in flower, or choose varieties that bloom more than once during the year. You can plan a calendar of bloom with the types of orchids suited to your house conditions by consulting the encyclopedia and the chart of characteristics on pages 150-153. You could, for example, have *Paphiopedilum fairrieanum* coming into flower in fall, *Laelia autumnalis* in early winter, *Phalaenopsis stuartiana* in late winter, *Cattleya mossiae* in spring and *Chysis aurea* in summer.

If you are trying a few orchids on a window sill for the first time, specialists suggest that you start with types that flower in late fall and winter. Says one expert, Terry Pogue of Rockville, Maryland, "These plants can spend all summer outside where they get plenty of light and fresh air; when they are moved inside they will be vigorous and ready to do their blooming best." In contrast, she points out, spring and summer bloomers in most of the United States have to build strength and flower buds indoors in winter. Weak sunlight or

Cymbidiums, with their lush foliage and tall arching spikes of long-lasting flowers, repay in beauty the extra care they demand: a cool greenhouse where the night temperature can be monitored year round.

prolonged overcast skies may deny them enough light to produce good flowers when their appointed times come around.

As you narrow your choices according to orchid types, growing conditions and flowering periods, you will still be faced with a generous number of varieties and hybrids available in any given group. You will need to assess particular plants as they are labeled in a greenhouse or listed in a grower's catalogue. The names are formidable, but they contain precise information. Orchid specialists are perhaps more consistent than any other horticultural group in using botanical rather than common names: "moth orchid" may be used to refer loosely to a general class, but a multipart Latin name, such as *Phalaenopsis parishii,* is needed to identify a particular plant. If this seems like one-upmanship, it is not. With a family the size of the Orchidaceae it is essential that plant identifications be exact.

Many Latin names, like *Aerangis, Aeranthes* or *Aerides,* add to the pleasure of orchid gardening, once you have mastered them, for they have a lovely, lilting music of their own. Do not be overly concerned about pronunciation. In many cases more than one version is acceptable. Just get the spelling correct on your order and your plant tags, and you will be all right.

ORCHID NOMENCLATURE   As in all plant names, those of orchids have at least two parts: the first part refers to the genus in which the orchid has been classified. This generic name is always capitalized and can be abbreviated according to rules established by the International Orchid Commission. The abbreviation for *Paphiopedilum,* for example, is *Paph.;* for *Cattleya,* a single *C.* is used. Names following the generic name describe a particular species, hybrid or variation of the species. *Paphiopedilum bellatulum,* for example, identifies a particular species within the genus *Paphiopedilum,* a name from the Greek for "slipper of Venus." *Paph. bellatulum* var. *album* is a white variation of the purple-spotted species.

Among the many man-made paphiopedilum hybrids available is a cross (represented by a multiplication sign) between two species, as in *Paph. bellatulum* × *Paph. niveum (niveum* means "snow-white"). For convenience this cross is called *Paph.* Psyche, the name given the first hybrid and all subsequent hybrids of its kind. The name of such a particular hybrid is not italicized; it may be almost anything—the name of the hybridizer or one of his friends, a Greek god, a president, an opera star. Psyche was the princess in Greek mythology whom Cupid loved. When *Paph.* Psyche was crossed with another species, *Paph. insigne,* the resulting plant was christened *Paph.* Astarte in honor of an ancient Middle Eastern goddess; mating *Paph.* Astarte with another hybrid, *Paph.* Actaeus, produced the well-known *Paph.* F. C. Puddle, for many years one of the most dependable of hybrid parents. (F. C. Puddle was head gardener for an English lord when the hybrid was named after him in 1932.) Often an outstanding new plant, called a clone because it cannot be propagated sexually, appears among the offspring of a crossing made previously. To signal its special characteristics, such as notable variation in flower color or markings, a selection name is often added in single quotation marks, as *Paph.* F. C. Puddle 'White Majesty.'

Although hybrid orchids are rare in the wild, a large number of them can be crossed artificially. Many crosses have been made among cattleyas and members of other genera in the so-called cattleya alliance to combine valued flower qualities and other desirable traits such as compact growth, repeated blooming, plant vigor or multiple growing tips. Epicattleyas are hybrids of epidendrums and cattleyas; brassolaeliocattleyas are hybrids of brassavolas, laelias and cattleyas. When as many as four genera are used in the creation of a single new hybrid, the new genus established will have a name ending in "ara." *Kirchara,* for example, denotes a crossing of epidendrum, sophronitis, laelia and cattleya plants. *Potinara* replaces what otherwise might have been *Brassosophrolaeliocattleya*—for which all growers can be grateful. Crosses between two or three genera, the bigeneric or trigeneric hybrids, are often written as abbreviations. *Sophrolaeliocattleya* appears as *Slc.,* as in the hybrid *Slc.* Jewel Box. Outstanding clones of this hybrid are *Slc.* Jewel Box 'Dark Waters,' with flowers a dark red, and *Slc.* Jewel Box 'Scheherazade,' with an improved flower form that is colored orange-red.

You will sometimes see other notations after particular orchid names. Both the above plants, for example, won awards from the American Orchid Society (AOS). 'Dark Waters' earned the Highly Commended Certificate (HCC), receiving a score from orchid judges of between 75 and 79 points out of a possible 100; any plant propagated from it is entitled to carry the pedigree and its tag may read *Slc.* Jewel Box 'Dark Waters' HCC/AOS. Its cousin 'Scheherazade' scored even higher, earning between 80 and 89 points and an Award of Merit (AM) from judges of both the AOS and England's Royal Horticultural Society. As a result, its name may be written *Slc.* Jewel Box 'Scheherazade' AM/AOS-RHS.

Occasionally you may see other initials denoting special awards of the AOS: CBM, the Certificate of Botanical Merit; CCM, the Certificate of Cultural Merit; JC, the Judges' Commendation; and AD or AQ, the Award of Distinction or the Award of Quality.

The highest award of either the American Orchid Society or the Royal Horticultural Society is a First Class Certificate (FCC); it is

THE EYES HAVE IT

Going sightseeing is one of the most gratifying ways of becoming familiar with uncommon orchid species that you may want to add to your collection. Many public botanical gardens have sizable orchid displays, and of the 200-odd orchid clubs affiliated with the American Orchid Society, some have regular shows. A calendar of such shows is available from the American Orchid Society at the Botanical Museum of Harvard University in Cambridge, Massachusetts 02138.

INITIALS OF HONOR

given by the AOS to orchid selections that score 90 points or more. It is not earned easily; of as many as a thousand plants receiving AOS awards in a single year, rarely are more than half a dozen accorded an FCC. So when you see that designation, you can be certain that orchid is among the finest of its kind.

CATALOGUE SHOPPING

The easiest way to become familiar with currently available orchids and their pedigrees is to send for the catalogues of one or more major growers, who advertise in orchid journals and gardening magazines. Some catalogues are free and others cost as much as several dollars, though the charge is often applied against the first order. Orchid catalogues are sources of information on orchid culture and trends in hybridizing, and they give descriptions and current prices of available plants. Catalogues also display an array of potting and mounting materials, containers and equipment that may be hard to find. Many mail-order growers guarantee plant arrival in good condition, except during the coldest months to addresses in the North; some guarantee safe arrival regardless of weather.

Whether you buy in person or by mail, begin your collection with mature specimens close to flowering size or actually in bloom. Then you can see what you are getting and you will not have to wait months or years for flowers; furthermore, mature plants are better able to survive the change from the greenhouse to your home, not to mention any mistakes you may make while learning to care for them. Avoid plants sold with bare roots or those recently harvested from the wild; they may require more time and trouble than you can give them. Seedlings are cheaper, of course, and experienced amateurs often buy them to fill out collections. But they too require more care and you may run out of patience during the several years before they bloom. A larger plant will give you immediate pleasure and can be divided after flowering to yield still more plants *(Chapter 4)*.

CHECKING LEAF COLOR

When you shop at a greenhouse that specializes in orchids, examine individual specimens carefully. While handsome foliage is not the hallmark of all orchids, it still should pass inspection from a standpoint of health. In general, light green leaves indicate that a plant is healthy. A dark green, attractive in other house plants, means that an orchid has not been receiving enough light, while a pale yellowish green indicates too much light.

Also look for buds that promise flowers or future growth. Cattleyas and many other orchids commonly grown as house plants are of the sympodial type *(page 29),* with successive growths sprouting from the rhizome—a thick stem that creeps gradually across or slightly under the surface of the potting mix. New growth comes from pale green buds at the growing end of the rhizome; generally one bud forms a new lead, but sometimes two buds become separate growing points, and the rhizome branches. A large plant with as many as a dozen upright leaf-bearing stems may produce three or even four leads, each capable of branching again. Such a plant will not only bear several flower stalks but it can also be divided later into several plants. (Some orchids are monopodial—meaning "one-footed"—and grow upright with a single stem.)

Next examine the plants for signs of insect infestation or disease. Orchids are as tough as any plants, and import regulations have largely banished pests like the cattleya fly and the dendrobium beetle that prey on species in their natural habitats. But some common garden pests afflict orchids. Look for brown or black mottling or streaking that may signal a fungus disease; glistening droplets around pits caused by bacterial parasites; chewed places or small, dark depressions left by aphids, thrips, slugs, snails, weevils or beetles; cottony white fluffs in leaf joints that betray colonies of mealy bugs; shiny little domes that cover sucking scale insects; speckled undersides of leaves that may be evidence of spider mites. Though such afflictions can be controlled *(page 48),* there is no point in starting with a plant that could spread the problem to other plants in your house.

Finally, inspect the plant's roots. The roots of epiphytic (tree-growing) orchids are usually visible on the surface of the potting mix; they should have a thick, whitish coat of velamen, a protective corky substance that absorbs moisture and nutrients, and the root tips should display points of fresh green growth. If you can, look at roots

PESTS AND DISEASES

ONE UP OR MANY ACROSS: SINGLE AND MULTIPLE STEMS

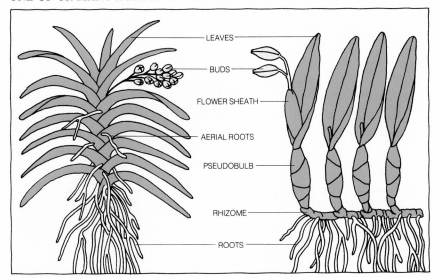

LEAVES

BUDS

FLOWER SHEATH

AERIAL ROOTS

PSEUDOBULB

RHIZOME

ROOTS

Orchids have two patterns of growth, one vertical, the other horizontal. The vertical, or monopodial, orchid (left) has a single stem that grows continually taller. Flowers appear between the leaves near the top of the plant; aerial roots sprout along the lower part of the stem. A horizontal, or sympodial, orchid (right) produces new growth from its rhizome, which elongates each year to form a succession of thickened upright stems called pseudobulbs; these "false bulbs" look like true bulbs but do not contain plant embryos. From each pseudobulb emerge the leaves (generally one or two) and then the sheath that protects the flower buds.

below the surface too, by gently pushing some of the potting material aside or even tapping the plant out of its pot. If there are many brown or blackish roots, the plant has received too much water and is succumbing to rot; if roots are densely packed or winding around inside the pot, the plant may be overdue for repotting.

Once you have bought a greenhouse plant, there are several things you can do to ease its transition. If the weather is cold, have it enclosed temporarily in a plastic bag or several layers of newspaper stapled loosely at the top. This should provide enough protection while you move the plant from the warmth of the greenhouse to the warmth of your house. Whether you carry a plant home or receive it by mail, a good first step is to immerse it, pot and all, in tepid water for 15 or 20 minutes. This will remedy any drying that may have occurred and leach out excess fertilizer salts. The water will also float out insects hiding in the potting mixture. Let the plant drain thoroughly, then set it out of direct sunlight and withhold further water or fertilizer while it adjusts. Keep it away from other plants in case it harbors an undetected disease or pest. After a week or two, if it seems healthy, you can remove it from quarantine.

WELCOMING THE SUN

If you are growing orchids by a window, remember that a southern exposure, where the plants get direct sun for a maximum number of hours each day, is usually best. To assure maximum light, use curtains that can be pulled back so the entire glass area is exposed. Some indoor orchid growers eliminate curtains entirely or install wood shutters that fold back on either side of the window frame. To increase light at an orchid window you can also paint the room's walls a light-reflecting white or line the window opening with mirrors. If the plants need to be screened from afternoon sun in summer, as many do to prevent sunburn, hang light mesh curtains that can be drawn during the hottest part of the day.

Set orchids needing the most light closest to the glass, but do not let the foliage touch the glass; it can become hot or cold enough to harm the plants. Species demanding less light can be placed farther back. If your window sill is not deep enough you can extend sill space into the room by building a shelf, or make multilevel plant stands to display a number of plants while assuring that no plant blocks another from the sun. Such stands are especially suited to floor-to-ceiling windows. Some enthusiasts curtain window walls with orchids, with some plants grouped at floor level, others set on stepped stands, still others suspended in hanging baskets. If the wall is equipped with sliding glass doors, so much the better. As the weather warms in spring you can open the doors to give the plants fresh air during the day; in summer they can be moved outside.

The growth cycle of a pseudobulb

Cattleya orchids follow a growth and flowering cycle that is typical of other sympodial (many-stemmed) orchids. The cycle begins when a vegetative bud called an eye begins to swell and form roots at the base of the previous year's growth (1). The bud soon develops into a lead which creeps horizontally for an inch or so, becoming an extension of the plant's rhizome or ground stem.

The lead then curves upward to form a thickened upright stem called a pseudobulb (2). This false bulb stores food and water.

When the pseudobulb is 3 or 4 inches tall, one or two leaves, depending on the species, emerge from its tip (3). Initially folded flat through the middle, the leaf unfolds as it grows, and a green flower sheath, approximately 1 inch across and 4 inches tall, becomes visible at the junction of the leaf and pseudobulb. The sheath encloses the developing flower buds; some cattleyas have two sheaths, one inside the other.

It takes about six weeks for the flower buds to push up from the base of the sheath to its tip and three more weeks for them to reach full size and open. On some cattleyas, the buds develop along with the rest of the new growth; on others, the buds do not begin to grow until several months after leaf and pseudobulb have matured.

In maturing, the pseudobulb hardens and its leaflike outer covering dries to the texture of tissue paper (4). The leaf also becomes hard and thick, and will eventually wither and die. After flowering, the plant goes into a dormant period and the bulb ripens. Then a new eye bursts from the old pseudobulb and the cycle begins again.

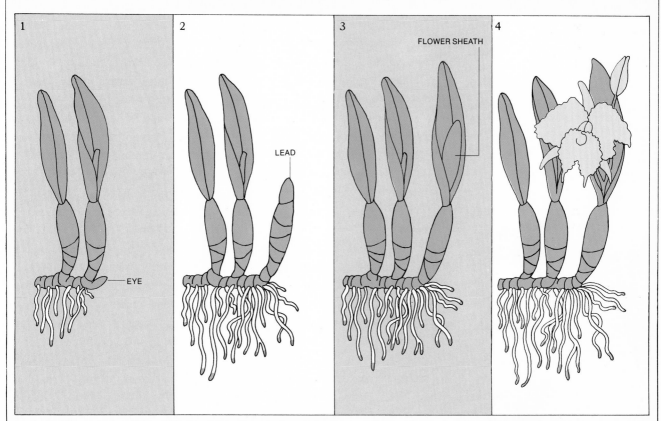

From the swelling of the eye (1) to the opening of the flower (4), a cattleya takes five or six months to mature.

Where window-sill space is at a premium, orchids in small pots can be suspended along a vertical strip of ¼-inch mesh hardware cloth 2 inches wide, hung from a ceiling swivel hook so plants can be rotated for even lighting. Attach pots with rustproof metal plant hangers (inset) sold at orchid greenhouses, or use pliers to fashion hangers from 12-gauge wire. The hanger should clip under the lip of the pot so that the pot's weight will provide enough pressure to keep it from slipping loose.

A greenhouse, of course, provides maximum sunlight from the top as well as the sides. By easing temperature and humidity control, a greenhouse also allows orchid growers to raise a greater number of plants, including the more demanding species, and to produce large, healthy specimens with superb blooms. Manufacturers offer greenhouse structures of almost any shape and size, including modest lean-to models that attach to house walls.

If your orchid collection is not large, but your indoor space and light are inadequate for it, you may want to consider a miniature greenhouse that mounts in an ordinary window and projects outside. The smallest models are fabricated of glass and aluminum and are equipped with adjustable shelves and top-opening vents to admit fresh air and control the temperature. The regular windows can be removed so the plants are clearly displayed and easy to tend; sliding glass panels can be installed for closer control of the environment inside—a practical feature if you intend to grow species that require high humidity or especially low night temperatures. The minigreenhouse climate is more difficult to control than that of a full-scale greenhouse, but it can be regulated with electric heating cables connected to a thermostat in cold weather, screening of split bamboo or shade cloth that can be rolled down against hot sun, and water-filled trays to keep the atmosphere moist. You can even mount fluorescent tubes beneath the shelves, creating a brilliantly lighted showcase at night for orchids not sensitive to day length.

Artificial lighting can dramatize any display of orchids. It will also brighten an indoor garden on short winter days and during overcast periods. In fact, with the proper choice and location of fixtures you can grow orchids almost anywhere in your house or apartment without need for windows. Many orchid enthusiasts have found that they can grow plants quite satisfactorily—even more reliably, some insist—under lights mounted in bookcases, tea carts, stair wells, utility rooms, even closets, basements and attics as long as good air circulation and adequate humidity are provided. With the flexibility afforded by plant lighting equipment and techniques, gardeners are free to mix their methods of indoor growing. Larger plants can be set at living-room windows where they get direct sunlight, while smaller plants are placed under lights away from windows. Seedlings, plants that have not reached flowering size, and mature plants not particularly attractive after they have bloomed can be removed to basement areas where they can receive intensive care and be easily watered, repotted and otherwise tended. Since they must be close to the light source, however, the best orchids for growing under lights are those that do not exceed a foot in height, including the compact hybrids of taller species and the miniatures.

If you have only a few orchids, you can start growing under lights with ready-made pieces of equipment designed for the purpose, from small tabletop rigs that resemble desk lamps to multi-tiered stands or roll-around carts that accommodate several levels of plants and have lights, reflectors, plant trays and timers built in.

Whatever kind of artificial light you choose, make sure it is mounted close enough to the plants to keep them growing. Many indoor light gardeners use basic modules of four 40-watt fluorescent tubes 48 inches long, combining warm-white and cool-white tubes. The fixtures can be hung on chains so the height can be adjusted over plant tables. The tops of plants that need a lot of light, such as cattleyas, oncidiums and epidendrums, should be no more than 3 or 4 inches below the tubes. Less demanding genera like *Paphiopedilum* and *Phalaenopsis* can be placed as much as 12 inches below the fixture. The light intensity from a fluorescent tube drops off toward the ends, however, so the plants that need the most light should be given center stage. Since tubes produce less light as they get old, it is also a good idea to replace them at least once a year.

To make up in time what fluorescent tubes lack in sunlike candle power, you generally will need to keep the lights on 14 to 16 hours a day, letting the plants rest in darkness during the night. An inexpensive timer will turn the lights on and off automatically at the hours you choose. Note, however, that some orchids like *Cattleya percivaliana* and *C. trianaei* are sensitive to seasonal day lengths and will not bloom satisfactorily unless you reduce the light to 11 or 12 hours a day during the period when they are forming flower buds. When you start to grow any plants under artificial light, do not be dismayed if some seem sickly at first; it may take a year or more for them to adjust to the new conditions.

The possibilities for growing orchids indoors under lights are almost endless, and seem to attract more devotees every year. One is David Perrin of Springfield, Virginia, who started at age 14 with a single cattleya. Soon he owned more than a dozen different species, which flourished in his bedroom under a bank of fluorescent tubes concealed in an overhead redwood frame. For humidity and air movement he rigged up lengths of terry cloth behind the plants and carefully wet it down every morning before turning on a small electric fan. As one of the youngest members of the National Capital Orchid Society, he saved his allowance for a long "want list" of alluring species and hybrids. Now that he is "into orchids," as he puts it, he has found, like many another convert young and old, that getting in is a lot easier than getting out.

GROWING UNDER LIGHTS

CONTROLLED DAYS AND NIGHTS

A shapely variety show

Few flower fanciers would care to dispute the overall beauty of the orchid family. But if asked what defines this beauty, gardeners will give as many different answers as there are orchids. For some admirers, the quintessential orchid is a delicate miniature perused through a magnifying glass; others may choose a spectacular giant. Whatever the species, orchids offer a variety of shapely, colorful flowers and foliage unmatched in the plant world, with hundreds of new hybrids being added every year. Small wonder that orchids have continued to fascinate diverse cultures from ancient days to the present.

In the Orient, where orchid blossoms have long been considered a symbol of nobility and elegance, the great Chinese sage Confucius ordained the orchid "King of Fragrant Plants." Two millennia later, in the 16th Century, German botanist Hieronymus Bock first noted that some species of the plant bore an uncanny resemblance to birds and animals. Many gardeners since have been astonished by such oddities as a tiny pleurothallis whose brown and purple sepals gape like the jaws of a crocodile, and an oncidium with the shape and markings of a whimsical butterfly *(page 39)*.

Some of the greatest flights of orchid fancy are to be found in the 19th Century musings of John Burroughs, father of the American nature essay, who wondered of a forest cache of blossoming lady's slippers, "Were they so many gay bonnets rising above the foliage? or were they flocks of white doves with purple-stained breasts just lifting up their wings to take flight? or were they little fleets of fairy boats, with sail set, tossing on a mimic sea of wild, weedy growths?"

Even more surprising than the dramatic images they conjure up is the fact that few non-corsage orchids bear much resemblance to the large, ruffly cattleyas that have set so many hearts aflutter. A number of orchids that grow in the wild have small blossoms, often with spidery shapes. Others might pass for daisies—the *Coelogyne ocellata*—or tulips *(page 45)*. Moreover, many orchids are grown for the interesting shapes and patterns of their foliage alone.

Resembling a thin flamingo, a Scaphosepalum gibberosum flower appears to take flight from the stem, whose zigs and zags show where earlier blossoms grew.

The delights of fanciful forms

Famous for their staid splendor as corsages, orchids actually include an astounding range of strange forms more at home dancing breeze-blown upon their stalks than pinned to evening gowns. Whether suggesting the delicate grace of a ballet dancer, hovering like a formation of helicopters, or encircling a stalk like acrobats, some orchid flowers appear less like plants than entertainers.

Dangling wraithlike petals make a Phragmipedium hybrid one of the largest of orchid flowers.

The waxy orange lip of Epidendrum pseudepidendrum hovers as if held up by propeller-like sepals.

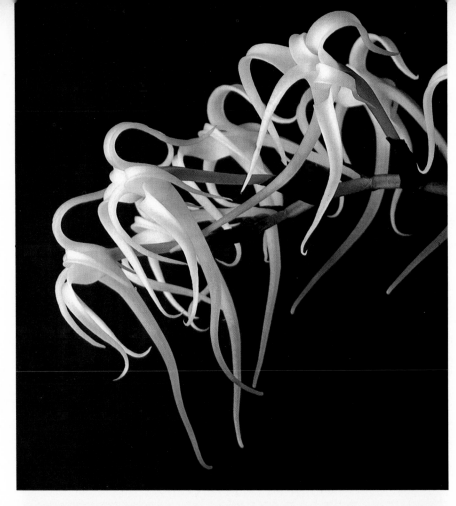

The fragrant white blossoms of an African Cyrtorchis arcuata seem to swoon in a classical ballet.

The snow-white beard and bloodshot eyes of Dendrobium pulchellum appear the work of a whimsical painter.

Like aerialists, Schomburgkia undulata blossoms swing, dive and catch one another in a spectacle of color.

With sepals as antennae and mottled petals for wings, Oncidium sanderae bears a resemblance to a butterfly.

Leaves worth another look

In their understandable infatuation with beautiful blossoms, some gardeners overlook a second commendable feature offered by many orchids: their foliage. Leaves and stems that may be braided, bulbous or dappled not only delight the eye when plants are not in bloom, but in the case of some species the foliage entirely supersedes flowers as the year-round focus of attention.

Especially prized for its unusual foliage, the stems of Lockhartia acuta carry overlapping leaves that appear braided.

Shoehorn-shaped leaves and a flower spike sprout from glossy water-storing pseudobulbs of Epidendrum atropurpureum.

Long, curling leaves, staggered pseudobulbs and flowers combine to give Maxillaria variabilis a sculpted appearance.

A 9-inch forest of waxy foliage is created by the huddled stems and paddle-shaped leaves of Brassavola digbyana.

Luxuriant sprays of dappled leaves show off the varying
shades of three species of Paphiopedilum. At bottom is the
original hybrid, Paph. harrisianum, created in 1869.

Solitary oval leaves of Phalaenopsis veitchiana, a natural hybrid, spread in near-perfect symmetry. At upper left, a flower spike extends from beneath the mottled foliage.

Blossoms that fool the eye

Although the more ostentatious orchid blossoms, such as *Cattleya* hybrids, are readily identifiable as orchids, many smaller species that occur naturally may fool the untutored eye with their unorchid-like shapes. Some appear simpler than the way most gardeners expect orchids to look. Others, because of the shape of the blossoms or their arrangement on the stalks, resemble entirely different kinds of flowers.

Little resembling the larger hybrids, a young Cattleya aurantiaca spreads its unruffled, flamelike blossoms.

Starry white but for a yellow lip, Dendrobium infundibulum flowers beam atop a hirsute stem.

A crown of fragrant flowers in pink-to-purple shades surmounts the stubby stem of a Central American Epidendrum endresii.

Surrounded by sepals and petals that mimic leaves, the lips of Brassavola cordata blossoms seem to be separate flowers.

Strings of tiny, quarter-inch blossoms dangle from stalks that stretch from the base of a Brazilian Pleurothallis rubens.

Opening only a bit more when in full bloom, the large solitary blossom of Anguloa ruckeri looks like a tulip.

Supplying the needs of a sturdy breed 3

"Orchids are so easy to grow it almost takes a genius to kill one." So says an expert who may be allowed some slight exaggeration because his own orchid career was launched when he found an abandoned phalaenopsis in the basement of a vacant house. Repotted, watered and gradually given an increasing amount of light and fertilizer, the plant has repaid its rescuer with magnificent blooms.

Orchids are indeed easy to grow—if only you follow a few basic guidelines. In addition to meeting their light and temperature needs, the most important thing to remember is that orchids, like most of their owners, thrive in an atmosphere that is fresh and not too dry, with good air circulation. The ancestors of most of today's popular varieties came from tropical or semitropical regions, where they were accustomed not only to ample light and warmth but to high humidity, to rain showers that periodically soaked their spongy roots and to almost constant breezes that dried them off quickly.

While you will not be able to duplicate this natural environment precisely, you can come close enough to grow orchids well. In a greenhouse, you could maintain relative humidity as high as 70 or 80 per cent, but you do not need that for the orchids that you can grow on a window sill or under lights. However, you will have to increase the level well above the desert-dry 20 per cent or less found in many homes where the environment is artificially conditioned all year long. If you raise the humidity around the plants to between 40 and 60 per cent, you will benefit not only them but yourself. You will be less likely to experience dry skin or nasal passages, and in winter you will feel warm at a lower temperature, thus saving fuel.

There are many ways to increase humidity around your orchids. One is to group plants closely, so moisture transpired from the leaves of one raises the humidity in the air near another. In addition, you can set the plants on water-filled trays that increase humidity by evaporation into the air above. If you have a large collection of

To receive optimum light, two ascocendas hang in baskets near the umbrella-like ceiling of an octagonal greenhouse. In bloom below are many cattleyas, including a white Elizabeth Carlson hybrid (right).

To provide orchids with the humidity they need, but without risking root rot, fill a 3-inch-deep plastic or rustproof metal tray, at least as wide as the spread of the foliage, with 2 inches of gravel or pumice. (The latter, being porous, is preferable since it increases the amount of evaporation.) Add an inch of water and maintain this level. For extra insurance, raise plants off the bed on upturned pots, saucers, bricks or a platform of wire-mesh hardware cloth bent at the edges to fit the tray.

MECHANICAL MOISTURIZERS

plants, build a wide, shallow container of rot-resistant redwood lined with plastic film, or have a sheet-metal shop make a tray to order.

Whatever kind of tray you use, it should be 2 or 3 inches deep so you will not need to replenish the water supply every day or two. The bottoms of the pots must be held above the water level, however, so they can drain properly and not draw up water that could rot the plants' roots. There are several ways to accomplish this. A square of hardware cloth—the large-mesh, stiff-wire screening available at hardware stores—can be cut to size and its edges bent down to form a wire platform for the pots. Or, you can use a plastic grid of the type used to diffuse light below fluorescent tubes, cut to fit and set in the bottom of the tray.

An even simpler solution is to line the bottom of the tray with an inch or two of stones; if they are a porous type like sandstone, pumice or scoria they will soak up water and increase the rate of evaporation from the multiple surfaces they expose. To prevent algae and insects from breeding in the water, add a tablespoon of an algicide-insecticide every month or so. Some orchid growers set their plants on low racks built of redwood slats, which have the added advantage of improving ventilation around the plants.

In addition to grouping plants and using humidifying trays, many orchid gardeners mist their plants daily. Misting deposits a thin film of tiny water droplets on leaves, temporarily raising the humidity around them; some growers occasionally add a small amount of liquid fertilizer to the misting water.

For misting, you can use almost any type of atomizer—a plastic squeeze bottle, a spray container with a top plunger, a pump sprayer. In any case be sure the device is clean, and never use any sprayer that has held a weed-killing chemical. The important thing is that the mister produces a fine foglike spray, not a drenching of large drops that will accumulate in crevices at the bases of leaves and remain there to invite disease. Misting is especially good for plants in hot weather, when the air evaporates moisture rapidly. A good rule is to increase the moisture on and around your plants whenever temperature and light intensity rise, and to decrease moisture as they drop. Misting should be done well before sundown—usually before 3 p.m.—so leaves have a chance to dry before dark. Most infections start with dampness at night.

To supply orchids with sufficient airborne moisture, many indoor gardeners move from misters and water trays to a mechanical humidifying device. This can be as simple as wet toweling hung on a frame so an electric fan can blow evaporated moisture from it toward the plants. One handyman elaborated on this idea with perforated tubing connected to the house plumbing to keep the toweling constantly moist with a slow, steady drip.

An easier but more costly solution is a room humidifier, which operates on the same general principle but combines fan and fabric in a compact unit. A reservoir holds eight or 10 gallons of water; some units can be connected to the house supply in such a way that the water will be shut off automatically when the tank is full. Adequate for many situations is the small cool-mist type of humidifier used in sickrooms; in most kinds a whirling disc disperses water droplets into the air. And many an amateur has unearthed an old croup kettle from the attic to moisturize his first plants.

Some humidifiers have a built-in humidistat, a device that turns the machine on automatically when the humidity drops below a specified level and turns it off when that level has been reached. A useful device—whether you are using a mechanical humidifier or just water-filled trays—is a hygrometer with a large, readable dial to measure the amount of moisture in the air; hang it on a wall close to your orchids and not down among the plants where it might get wet. To combine the accuracy of a hygrometer with the convenience of automatic control, you can buy a separate plug-in humidistat that you install between the humidifier and the wall outlet. It will switch the unit on or off to maintain the humidity your orchids require.

AUTOMATIC CONTROLS

To contain a humid miniclimate around more demanding species, some growers drape clear plastic film on a frame so the plant area is loosely enclosed on the top, back and sides; such a tent retains moisture but allows some air circulation through the front. Other growers display small species in terrariums with glass sides and open tops, fish tanks or special orchid cases. Extra humidity especially benefits orchids like phalaenopsises, paphiopedilums and miltonias. These also need less light than plants like cattleyas and thus can be grown successfully behind an additional layer of light-reducing glass.

Any such enclosure for orchids, however, can become too moist and muggy, encouraging rot and fungus disease, and will heat rapidly if exposed to direct sunlight. Be prepared to provide shade with mesh curtains when necessary. The best orchid cases have vent panels in the bottom and hinged tops that swing up to let the hot air escape. Hinged or sliding glass panels on the front, back or sides can be added to permit airing the case daily and to make it easier to care for the plants. When the sun changes position, curtains can be opened to give the plants maximum light again and vents can be closed to bring the humidity up.

A NEED FOR VENTILATION

Good air movement, another essential for orchids grown on a window sill or under lights, reduces the danger of disease and provides a good supply of the carbon dioxide that they need. An orchid room should never be stagnant or stuffy; on warm days open the windows, even if only for a short while. When it is impractical to introduce fresh outside air, run an electric fan constantly or at regular intervals, positioned and aimed to avoid drying out the plants. An old-fashioned slow-turning ceiling fan can be installed in a living room with high ceilings to provide good results. Small fans like those made for household appliances such as refrigerators have the additional advantage of being waterproof—an absolute necessity to avoid electric shock if the fan is exposed to misting or high humidity. Also, their blades should be caged with heavy wire for safety's sake. Favorites with many gardeners are the small muffin or whisper fans that are designed to cool electronic equipment. One orchid enthusiast uses four of these, mounted just above his plants and just below four banks of fluorescent lights, where they can scarcely be seen or heard.

Once you have established a good environment for your orchids, you can concentrate on such important particulars as containers and potting mixes, watering, fertilizing and other details of day-to-day care. Orchids can be grown in many ways: in clay or plastic pots containing different potting mixtures, in hanging baskets made of wire or slats, or mounted on chunks of wood or slabs of cork that recall the plants' tree habitats in the wild.

CHOOSING A CONTAINER
Most beginners start with ordinary clay or plastic flowerpots. If you buy a plant at a greenhouse or by mail, it will usually come in a plastic pot filled with a suitable potting mix that may serve many months. But as the plant outgrows that container, or the mix starts to disintegrate, or you decide to seek a container you like better, you have to choose another pot. Whatever material the new pot is made of, and whatever size it is, it must drain quickly. Any orchid, particularly one of the air-loving, tree-dwelling epiphytes, will grow poorly or die if water stands around its roots.

Plastic pots come in many sizes and colors and are inexpensive and easy to keep clean. Their lightness is an advantage for storage and ease of handling, though a tall plant in a plastic pot tends to tip. Pots made of clear rather than opaque plastic let you inspect the roots to see if they are showing signs of rot from too much water. Because plastic pots are smooth and nonporous, the orchid roots do not easily become attached to their surfaces; this makes a plant easier to remove without root damage when repotting is necessary. Since plastic pots are not porous, they hold moisture longer than unglazed clay pots; this suits them especially to those terrestrial orchids that need to be kept moist. But unless a plastic pot has several drainage holes, it should not be used for an epiphytic orchid. You can modify a plastic pot for this use by adding holes with a hot soldering iron and lining the bottom with such drainage material as coarse gravel, crumpled chicken wire or broken pieces of clay pots.

Clay flowerpots, sometimes hard to find in the desired size, are preferred by many orchid gardeners just because they are porous and absorb excess water, allowing epiphytes in particular to dry quickly and keeping the roots cool. Because they are heavier than plastic pots they are more stable, and the familiar terra-cotta color goes well with almost any flower. The short, wide type called azalea pots suit the shallow, spreading roots of most orchids. To ensure good drainage, enlarge the hole in the bottom by carefully chipping away its edges with a hammer and old screwdriver, and line the bottom with drainage material.

When you choose a container for an orchid, think small. The contents of a small pot dry out more quickly than those of a large one, reducing the danger of rotted roots. In addition, the masdevallias and most dendrobiums and oncidiums seem to flower better if slightly crowded. When you move a plant to a new container, choose one about 2 inches larger across the top than the old one, slightly more in the case of large plants or relatively fast-growing vertical types like the phalaenopsis and fast-spreading horizontal types like the oncidiums and coelogynes.

Most orchids will not grow if planted in garden soil or even in the sterile potting soil sold for other house plants. Over the years gardeners have tried all sorts of formulas, from activated charcoal to

THE BEST POT SIZES

SHIELDING THE BLADES OF A VENTILATING FAN

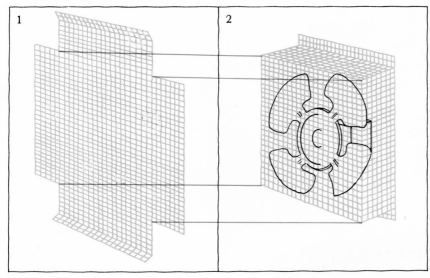

To provide good air circulation around orchids so that leaves will dry quickly after watering, a fan is essential, and the safest type is a waterproof refrigerator fan with a sealed-in motor, free from electrical hazard in the high humidity that orchids require. You can fashion a protective cover around the blades of such a fan from a sheet of 1/4-inch-mesh hardware cloth. For a wall-mounted fan, notch the corners of the mesh with wire cutters (1), allowing an extra inch on two sides to provide a lip for fastening the cover to the wall. Bend down all four sides (2) to fit around the fan. For a freestanding fan, make the sides deeper and lower the cover over the fan, like a cage.

plain road fill. One favorite has been osmunda, the dried roots of certain ferns. Many orchid growers still swear by it, though it is difficult to work with and has become scarce and expensive. Another old stand-by is tree-fern fiber made from shredded parts of tree-sized tropical ferns, but import restrictions have sharply limited the supply of this material.

PLANTING IN FIR BARK

The most popular and widely available potting material for orchids is the shredded bark of fir trees. It comes in various grades: particles ¼ inch or less for seedlings and thin-rooted plants like odontoglossums, medium grade for average-sized plants, and coarse chunks an inch or more in diameter for large, heavy-rooted plants like phalaenopsises and vandas that need an airy, open medium. Fir bark is quite easy to work with; it permits fast drainage and good air circulation, and it does not decompose and become mushy for two years or more except in very moist situations. It contains few nutrients, however, so plants growing in it must be given a high-nitrogen fertilizer at regular intervals.

To make fir bark easier to use and retain more moisture, some orchid gardeners mix 2 parts of bark with 1 part of coarse peat moss. More commonly used for the tree-dwelling epiphytes, however, is a potting mix of 7 parts medium-grade fir bark to 1 part each of coarse peat moss, redwood bark and perlite. Terrestrial orchids need special mixes tailored to the requirements of each, such as 2 parts coarse peat moss, 2 parts sandy loam and 1 part each of perlite and finely shredded fir bark for phaius orchids. In both cases, you can also buy various prepared mixes from commercial suppliers. With experience, some devotees work out homemade formulas, containing many kinds of supplements, from charcoal and bone meal to papaya juice and banana pulp.

WHEN TO REPOT

Whatever mix you choose, you will need to repot a plant when it begins to outgrow its container or when the potting material begins to decompose. When the growing tip of a plant's creeping rhizome reaches out over the rim of the container and roots that are visible on the surface seem crowded, repotting is in order. To be certain, you can check deeper roots by prying the plant out of its pot with an old screwdriver. Look for a mass of roots winding around like so much spaghetti. At the same time examine the potting mix itself. Chunks on the surface may still seem intact, but those at the bottom may have deteriorated into a packed mush that no longer drains quickly, and some of the roots may have turned brown or black. In either case, it is time to repot.

The best time to repot a healthy orchid is after it has flowered, gone through any resting period and is once more at the beginning of a growth cycle. At this time transplanting sets it back the least, old roots can be disturbed without danger and new roots will sprout into fresh potting mix. To recognize the right conditions for repotting, watch for tiny shoots of new top growth less than an inch high and new green root tips. These new roots should just be starting to swell; if they are longer they may break off when the plant is handled.

Choose a container large enough to allow about two years' growth; plants like cattleyas that creep across the surface generally grow one pseudobulb each year from each growing point, so you can estimate from existing pseudobulbs how much space you will need. If you are using old pots, clean and disinfect them to kill disease organisms. Soak and wash clay pots, rinse them thoroughly, let them dry, then place them in a 250° oven for an hour. Soak clean plastic pots for about 12 hours in a solution of water and chlorine bleach in proportions of about 10 to 1, then rinse and allow to dry overnight.

The potting process itself is not complicated. Place a thick layer of newspapers over your work surface and have a wastebasket at hand. As you finish one plant you can use the top two or three layers of paper to wrap up the old debris for disposal before beginning with the next plant. To make the bark mix easier to work with, fill a large dishpan with as much of it as you think you will need, wet it down, mix it, then let it stand until it is moist but not soggy. Use your fingers or a screwdriver to pry loose the roots that cling to the pot. Pry the first plant out of its container with the screwdriver; if it fails to come out easily, run a knife blade around the inside of the pot. Shake the plant gently and use your fingers to clean off as much of

THE POTTING PROCEDURE

A BREEZY ORCHID BENCH

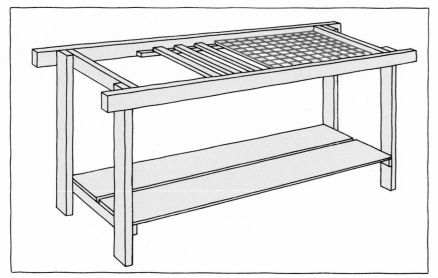

To build a plant bench that will provide good air circulation around orchid roots, construct a frame composed of two leg sections, each made from four 2-by-4s, cut to the length and width desired. Join the leg sections at the bottom with two horizontal 2-by-4s. Use rot-resistant redwood or cedar boards. Join leg sections at the top of the bench with two 2-by-4s, and attach two 1-by-1 cleats as ledges to the inside. Then nail 1-by-2-inch slats onto the cleats, spacing them 1 inch apart. For miniature orchids, cover a portion of the bench top with wire hardware cloth. Lengths of 1-inch board can be added below to make a storage shelf.

the old potting mix as you can. Clip off any dead roots with scissors or pruning shears; long roots should be trimmed back to a few inches so they will not be broken in repotting. Pull off dry, dead pseudobulb sheaths and remove old, shriveled back bulbs by cutting through the rhizome at the oldest end of the plant. Examine roots and crevices at the base of the leaves for evidence of scale insects, snails or slugs. Scrub off scale with an old toothbrush and insecticide. If you detect places chewed by slugs or snails, dust the roots with a pesticide formulated for this purpose.

FOR BETTER DRAINAGE Before you put a plant in its new pot, line the bottom with shards of broken pots, convex side up, a layer of coarse gravel, crumpled chicken wire or a square of hardware cloth. Any one of these will ensure drainage through the bottom holes while keeping bits of potting mix from washing out. Put in a couple of handfuls of fir-bark mix, then hold the plant in the pot so the juncture of the root system and the rhizome—the thickened stem—is about ½ inch below the rim, 1 inch in large pots. If the plant is the multistemmed sympodial type, as are most orchids, hold the back bulb on the oldest end of the rhizome so it touches the pot's rim, leaving room for new pseudobulbs to grow on the other end. If it is an upright monopodial orchid, simply center it in the pot like other house plants.

As you hold the plant with one hand, start filling in around the roots with more potting material. When the pot is about two-thirds full, settle the material by thumping the pot once or twice on the work surface. Keep adding potting mix, pressing it down around the roots with your fingers or thumbs. If you are potting a large orchid or several small ones, you can do a better job by tamping the mix into place with a potting stick made from a short scrap of wood. The stick should be blunt on one end for tamping, wedge-shaped on the other so it can be used as a lever. As you add mix, insert the wedge end so you can lever the material toward the center, working around the pot. Then use the blunt end to tamp the material down. Do not cover the rhizome (or the rosette of leaves that forms a crown on such orchids as the phalaenopsis) or you will invite disease later.

Since many newly potted orchids do not have enough roots to hold them upright and the pseudobulbs of sympodial types tend to sprawl, you will need to stake the plant until it anchors itself. For this purpose you can use a wire rhizome clip that attaches to the edge of the pot, or you can make your own stake from a length of stiff rustproof wire with its top bent into a hook to prevent accidental stabbing. Tie lengths of soft string or raffia fiber to the stake and loop them loosely like slings around the pseudobulbs to hold them in an upright position until the roots can support them.

Before moving on to the next plant, it is wise to take precautions against spreading diseases from one plant to another. Wrap up all old debris in a newspaper and dispose of it, then wash your hands with hot water and soap. Sterilize any tools you have used—knife, pruning shears, scissors—by holding their metal surfaces in the flame of a small alcohol lamp, a gas-stove burner or a propane torch until the tool is hot. Orchid growers often have a supply of disposable potting sticks or use metal sticks that are readily sterilized between uses. In addition to the containers themselves, any other material that is to be reused should be sterilized.

After you have finished potting, label each plant with a tag bearing its botanical name, the date repotted and any other pertinent notes, then set it out of bright light and water very lightly for

REPOTTING WITHOUT TRAUMA

1. *To repot a multistemmed orchid when it has outgrown its pot or the mix has become mushy, wait until new growth is just emerging. Water the day before. Flame-sterilize a screwdriver and use it to pry out the plant.*

2. *Shake and wash roots free of potting mix. Cut away dead roots with sterilized shears; trim back healthy roots by a third and eliminate the shriveled back bulb. Peel off dead outer skins of pseudobulbs. Use a soft toothbrush to scrub the pseudobulbs thoroughly with diluted insecticide. Coat cut surfaces with fungicide.*

3. *Choose a clean pot that allows for about two years' growth and cover the bottom with clean shards. Add a layer of fresh potting mix. Position the orchid with the oldest growth against the side of the pot. The plant's rhizome should be ½ inch below the rim of the pot. Fill in around the roots with potting mixture, tamping it down with your thumbs and a stick.*

4. *Hold the pseudobulbs upright with loops of string attached to a stake. Withhold water for a week or so to let roots become established.*

two weeks or more until the new roots get established. A light misting once or twice a day is all most newly potted plants can absorb. When new roots are growing healthily they will be ready for light watering, and when the plant reaches normal growth again you can give it the light, water and fertilizer that the species requires.

ROOM FOR ROAMING ROOTS

Some epiphytic orchids will grow more satisfactorily if they are not confined in pots but are placed in hanging baskets that give their roots ample air and freedom to roam or are mounted on logs or slabs that even more closely duplicate their ways of growing in the wild. Stanhopeas, gongoras, *Chysis aurea* and *Rodriguezia venusta,* for example, whose flower stalks are naturally pendant, are commonly suspended in round wire baskets or square wooden cages filled with a moisture-retaining material like long-fibered sphagnum moss. Such containers are available at major garden-supply centers, or you can make your own *(page 59).*

Plants like *Brassavola nodosa, Epidendrum tampense* and *Angraecum distichum* produce masses of clinging aerial roots that must dry quickly; they often grow best attached to slabs of tree-fern fiber, cork bark, oak logs, sassafras branches, even cedar shingles, hung on a wall with wire. To attach a plant to such a mounting, spread its roots on a shallow pad of moist sphagnum moss or osmunda fiber, place a little more moss on top to shield the roots and gently bind the plant to its mount by looping nylon fishing line or thin plastic-covered wire several times around both. A few species like the laelias, encyclias, *Broughtonia sanguinea* and *Brassavola digbyana* need little or no moss and can be tied directly to the log or slab. When roots have grown enough to anchor the plant firmly to its mount, remove the line or wire so it will not constrict the plant.

A WATER HAZARD

When and how to water and fertilize your orchids depends on how they are potted and mounted, the traits and growth cycles of particular species, and environmental conditions in your home at different times of the year. In general, however, more orchids go to an early grave from overwatering than from any other single cause.

The reasons become evident if you look closely at the plants themselves. The majority of orchids grown as house plants are epiphytes, adapted to drying out in treetop breezes between showers. Many have developed pseudobulbs that serve as storage tanks to tide them over, when necessary, with a reserve of water and nutrients. Pseudobulbs are not true bulbs but are swellings of above-ground stems that vary from slim pencil-like shapes to plump spheres that resemble smooth-skinned limes. If the epiphytic orchid is overwatered it cannot take up the excess moisture; if the moisture surrounds the roots for lack of drainage, they start dying from lack of air. This further limits the plant's capacity to absorb water. The pseudobulbs begin to shrivel, not because of insufficient water but because there is too much—the plant is dying in the midst of plenty.

The best rule for most orchids, then, is: if in doubt, do not water. Check the potting mix from time to time, not only by inspecting the surface, which may be deceptively dry and light-colored, but by poking a finger in. Some growers probe deeply with a thin wooden dowel or tongue depressor to see if the bottom is moist. If the material underneath is cool, damp and springy, do not water; if it is becoming dry and crisp, water the plant. The trick is to catch the mix just as it approaches dryness. If you let the bark mix become bone dry, it will be difficult to saturate again, requiring several waterings or a trip to a sink where you can immerse the entire pot. With experience, you will be able to tell when water is needed by the weight of the pot.

When you do water, do so thoroughly, watering twice if necessary until water comes out of the drainage holes. A heavy soaking will also wash out fertilizer salts before they build up to a point where they can damage tender roots. The best time for watering, like misting, is in the morning or early afternoon, so plants will take up moisture during daylight hours, leaving no excess remaining at night. Avoid watering on cloudy days. Tap water can be used unless it is unusually saline or alkaline—not a problem in most areas. But avoid using water that has been softened by the addition of sodium salts, as in many home water softeners; these salts are toxic to plants in any quantity and they displace other minerals like calcium and

DRENCHED BY DAYLIGHT

ARBOREAL PERCHES FOR INDOOR PLANTS

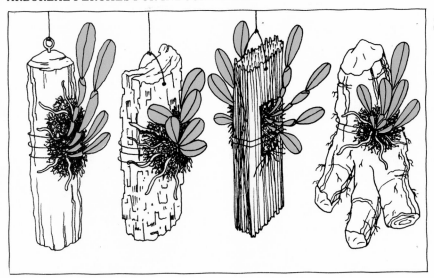

Tree-dwelling orchids can be given the open air and root space they need by mounting them on naturalistic supports, ranging from pieces of tree limbs and roots to chunks of cork, bark or blocks of tree fern fiber. For a tree fern support, cut a hole in the fiber large enough to accommodate the plant. For other supports, cover the roots with osmunda fiber or sphagnum moss to supply moisture, then tie the plant to the support with nylon fishing line or cotton string until the roots take hold. To hang plants, run a loop of wire through the support or, in tree limbs, attach eye screws. Supports for orchids that grow laterally should be hung laterally.

magnesium that make water "hard" but are beneficial to plants. If your water is highly chlorinated, let a supply stand in a shallow pan for a day or so to let the chlorine evaporate. Very cold water is apt to set a plant back, especially the phalaenopsis species; use water at room temperature.

In judging when to water, remember that small pots dry faster than large ones and clay pots more rapidly than plastic. Plants need less water when conditions are humid, more when the air is dry. They also use less water during winter, when temperatures are cooler and hours of sunlight shorter; more during the long, sunny days of summer when plants are growing vigorously and may be subjected to drying winds at an open window or on a terrace. Plants that rest between flowering seasons, like some dendrobiums and cattleyas, should be watered sparingly or not at all during that period; you can resume normal watering when they show signs of new growth. Orchids in moss-filled hanging baskets need more frequent watering than those in pots, and those mounted on slabs still more; such plants need periodic soaking and frequent misting in hot weather to keep their roots from drying completely. Small plants in hanging baskets or on mounts can be carted to a bathtub for a dunking; larger, more unwieldy hanging plants can be watered in place if pebble-filled humidifying trays are located to catch the drip.

THE RIGHT FERTILIZER   Many of the rules for watering orchids apply to fertilizing them as well. Plants in full summer sun need more fertilizer than those in low winter light; those in growth need more than those at rest. Most orchid growers use a fertilizer containing nitrogen, phosphorus and potassium, varying the proportions to suit particular needs. Plants potted in fir bark need a high percentage of nitrogen to make up for that used by bacteria and fungi in the bark's decomposition process; the best fertilizers for this use are soluble formulations labeled 30-10-10 or 30-10-20, both 30 per cent nitrogen compounds. (Because nitrogen promotes foliage growth, these are also used to give seedlings and small plants a boost toward flowering size.) The label may call for several teaspoons per gallon of water, applied every 10 days to two weeks during the growing season, but many experts prefer to use a fraction of this recommended strength—for example, half the strength suggested on the label at every third watering during growth and bright light, reduced to one-quarter strength while plants are resting or when days are short or skies overcast.

Orchids that are hung on slabs do not need extra nitrogen; they can be fertilized with a balanced orchid formula such as 20-20-20, 18-18-18 or 10-10-10.

As flower buds begin to form in their sheaths, you can give

plants one or two applications of a "blossom booster" formula such as 10-30-20 in place of regular feedings. Some special potting mixes made for orchids, especially those prepared for paphiopedilums, incorporate slow-release fertilizers; read the directions on the label before you add extra nutrients.

When fertilizing, as when watering, it is always safer to err on the conservative side. If you give a plant less fertilizer than recommended or miss a feeding, nothing serious will happen. If you overfertilize a plant, on the other hand, you may encourage an abundance of soft, weak green growth at the expense of vigorous flowers. Nor does it matter much if the kind of fertilizer is varied from time to time. Some growers are devotees of fish emulsion or other organic fertilizers and use them instead of inorganic chemical mixes, or substitute them as a change of diet. Whatever kind of fertilizer you choose, go easy with it and flush the plants with plain water every few weeks so salts left behind will not build up in concentrated form and injure sensitive plant tissue.

Given healthy growing conditions and judicious nourishment, orchids will generally have few problems, but even in a well-cared-for collection, plants will occasionally fail to flower, flower poorly or exhibit other ailments. The trouble will fall into one of three broad categories. If one of your plants seems sickly, first look for some detrimental factor in its environment. Yellowed leaves, for example, may be part of the normal aging process on the oldest parts of a plant. But on newer growth they may indicate that the plant is getting too much light or too little nitrogen, or is suffering from low

DIAGNOSING AILMENTS

ASSEMBLING AN AIRY BASKET

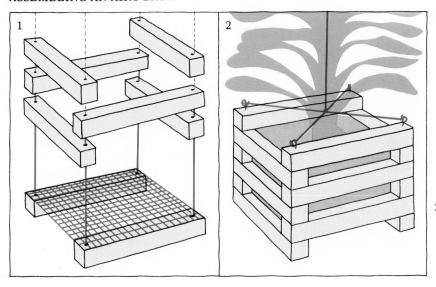

1. To make a slatted basket for a tree-dwelling orchid, arrange in a square alternating layers of 1-by-1-inch redwood slats with holes drilled equidistant from their ends. For the bottom, staple a square of 1/4-inch-mesh hardware cloth to the lower slats. Connect the slats by threading them on four lengths of 1/8-inch nonrusting wire, bending each wire against the bottom slat to anchor it and twisting it into a loop at the top.

2. Plant the orchid slightly off-center. Connect the four loops with two diagonal wires, and run a wire for hanging from the point where the two strands cross.

temperatures, or has been overwatered with a consequent loss of root function. Check these possibilities; simply moving the plant to a more shaded location or letting it dry out may bring it back to health.

Second, examine the plant for evidences of common pests like mites, scales, mealy bugs, slugs and snails. You may need a magnifying glass to see tiny pests. Once identified, each can be controlled by a pesticide *(page 148)*. Since all pesticides are poisons, follow the directions on the label scrupulously.

If neither an environmental condition nor a pest can be identified, look for symptoms of disease, which can be bacterial, fungal or viral. One of the commonest is a fungus disease called black rot, which develops when moisture collects in crevices in the top growth of a plant; black areas appear on new growth and spread downward into the rhizome. Most fungus diseases can be controlled by drying foliage, cutting away diseased tissue and treating the remaining healthy tissue with a fungicide.

DREADED VIRUSES

Virus diseases are a more serious problem, one that orchid growers properly regard with apprehension. Some viruses advertise their presence by stunting the growth of a plant or mottling its leaves. Plants afflicted with other viruses may show no outward signs of distress, but at the long-awaited flowering time the blossoms may be deformed or their color blotched or bleached. Still other plants can be silent carriers of a virus yet show no effects themselves. Since there is no cure for viral diseases, the most effective defense against them is good sanitation. Viral diseases spread from one orchid to another through the sap of infected plants, so experienced growers sterilize containers and tools after working on any one plant and follow a hands-off policy as they make their daily rounds. Resist the temptation to pinch, prune and otherwise fuss with orchids to keep them in shape; most orchids will not improve in appearance from such attention and you may unknowingly transmit a latent virus from one plant to another. When it becomes necessary to remove withered leaves or faded flowers from a plant, by all means do so, but flame-sterilize any cutting implement and wash your hands before going on to the next plant.

You may find it difficult to remember such precautions during the exciting period when your plants bloom. But you should follow the example of experienced growers and be content to sit back and enjoy the fruits of your labors; the process of flowering is breathtaking as buds gradually unfold and take on color and form. Wait until a prized specimen has reached its prime, then move it to a place of honor on a table or mantel. If the flowers are fully formed, neither they nor the plant will suffer from temporary reduction of light.

There may be occasions when you want to cut a few flowers for an arrangement or to give to a friend. Again, wait until the flowers have reached their peak, which is generally two days or more after they have opened. At that point the blooms will be at their richest color. Use a new razor blade or one that has been sterilized if it has come in contact with another plant. Remove each bloom with as much stalk as possible, cutting on a slant so more vascular tissue is exposed to take up water. Immerse the stalk immediately in a container partly filled with lukewarm water (the water should not touch the flowers) and place in a cool, shaded spot or in a refrigerator set no lower than 45°.

A long-lasting corsage can be made by stiffening the stalks with florist's wire and inserting them in a small water-filled vial made for this purpose or in wet cotton wrapped in clear plastic film. Then wrap them with floral tape. The corsage can be kept for repeated use by refrigeration; place it on a layer of shredded wax paper in a plastic food-storage bag. Kept in a cool, moist place, flowers from an orchid may last two weeks or more, ready for the next dinner party or perhaps the local orchid society's next meeting. And, of course, to all admiring inquiries you will be able to reply with a professional air: "Oh yes, isn't it lovely? It's a *Brassolaeliocattleya* Rosy Dawn 'Golden Princess,' variation *superba*. I grew it myself."

PRESERVING A CORSAGE

A STEPPED BENCH OF SHAPED MESH

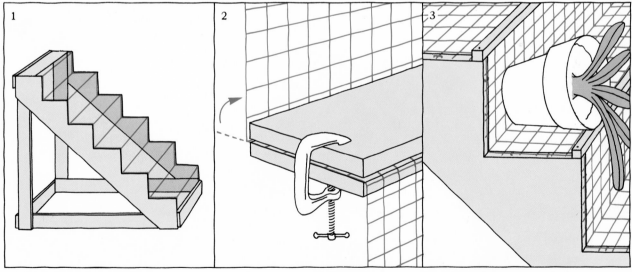

To make an airy stepped bench, join four 1-by-4s, each 3 feet long, to form a base. Add two 1-by-4 uprights, 3 feet high, and join them at the top with a 1-by-4 crosspiece. Add side pieces cut from 1-by-12 lumber.

Form steps from a 6-foot length of 36-inch hardware cloth with 1-by-1 or 1-by-2 mesh. Shape the mesh by clamping it between two 36-inch lengths of 1-by-6 lumber, then bending it in the direction of the step.

Staple the mesh steps to the frame. To help support the mesh and the tipped pots of orchids like phalaenopsis that are less likely to rot on their sides, nail 1½-inch square molding strips to the steps' edges.

A year-round spectacle, indoors and out

Orchids are surprisingly tough plants. With a little help from the gardener, many species will thrive throughout the house, their intricate and often fragrant blossoms providing a constant source of delight for owner and visitor alike. Far from requiring a room that is turned into a steamy, uninhabitable jungle, most orchids prefer conditions that are equally healthy for people: humidity of 40 per cent or higher, night temperatures between 55° and 60°, bright light and plenty of fresh air. These conditions can be achieved quite easily with the aid of a room humidifier, a few artificial lights, a small fan and a lowered thermostat.

Containers are generally more conspicuous when filled with orchids than with leafier house plants; if selected with discrimination, the containers themselves can add a decorative note to an indoor orchid display. Tree-dwelling orchids can hang in a slatted orchid basket made of teak, redwood or cedar or, for a natural look, they can be mounted on sawed-off tree branches, rafters or pieces of cork bark. Ground-dwelling orchids can be set in a formal plant bed, such as the one in the solarium at right, or lined up randomly in pots atop a redwood bench. The choices are legion—even an empty snail shell can be used to hold a miniature orchid.

Although orchids require containers with large drainage slots, water-stained rugs or floors need not be a problem when these plants are grown indoors. A watertight tray filled with gravel can be placed under the orchids to catch excess water; the damp gravel will provide added humidity for the plants. Larger orchid displays such as those in a bay window or attached greenhouse can be designed with brick or tile floors. Water can drip onto such surfaces without damage and can even be channeled into a hidden floor drain.

Orchids reward the indoor gardener with spectacular blossoms that outlast those of most other house plants. One popular lady's slipper, for example, holds its bloom for four to six weeks. And with combinations of species that flower at different seasons, an indoor orchid display can provide a year-round cycle of bewitching beauty.

The windows of this solarium automatically open when it becomes too warm for the orchids. Set into the ground are a cattleya, a spiky cymbidium and several phalaenopsises.

A sunny window display

A sunny window provides an ideal showcase for many orchids; even cattleyas, which require large amounts of light, can be brought into flower if given a southern or western exposure and placed close to the glass. Cheesecloth, a fine-mesh curtain or a redwood-slat screen can be hung to protect the plants when the midsummer sun reaches its apex. In mild weather, a window can be opened for fresh air.

Panels of glass span the top of this bay window full of orchids; in the far corner is a hidden fogger used to raise the humidity.

Orchids cascade in a window that has been extended to hold more plants; humidity is kept high with trays of moist gravel.

Summer in the open air

Orchids, which thrive on fresh air and rain, create an exotic atmosphere on any summer terrace. The plants can be hung from tree branches or from a wall as shown below, or they can be mounted on platforms of redwood laths that permit quick drainage. The best outdoor location for orchids is in a sheltered corner of the garden where they receive early morning sun and afternoon shade.

Lady's slippers decorate a backyard patio where they are hung on a wall to keep slugs and snails from reaching them. During afternoons when the sun is strong, the plants are moved to the shade. The red tree in the background is a flowering leptospermum.

Orchids are grown year round on this sheltered California patio where the temperature has never dropped below 42°.

French doors open from a formal dining room onto this latticed orchid room. A misting tube runs across the top of the lattice.

Rooms with an exotic view

When attached to a house, an orchid greenhouse can serve as more than just a plant laboratory. It can extend the living area or, placed beyond a wall of windows, it can create a view that beseeches a closer look. "Intermediate" species, which require night temperatures between 55° and 60° and day temperatures between 65° and 75°, make the most comfortable orchid companions for lived-in greenhouses.

A 10-foot-wide greenhouse runs along the side of a San Francisco townhouse, hiding the nearby house next door. The 3,000 orchids in this greenhouse, seen here from the library, receive light only through the roof, which is made of rigid plastic.

The orchids in this greenhouse, which doubles as a breakfast room, are arranged on shelves to provide a curtain of greenery.

Interspersed among the orchids are begonias and ferns. In summer, trees on the patio beyond shade and cool the plants.

Tree-dwelling orchids have been mounted on poles of bark and cork to create a dense, jungle-like effect in a greenhouse that

opens from a Victorian-style bedroom. The large dial at the top of the door monitors the humidity around the plants.

Toward a better collection 4

A persistent symptom of orchid fever is a restless, occasionally burning desire to acquire more plants. One victim, smiling ruefully, describes the feeling as one of "pure, unbridled greed." Says he: "I quit smoking to save money for orchids. I brown-bagged lunch to skimp for orchids. I even lost 35 pounds for orchids, and rewarded myself with one new plant for every five pounds I dropped." He also confesses to fudging the household accounts from time to time—"if there is a new orchid I absolutely must have."

You may not become quite so desperately addicted, but the chances are good that once you have grown a few orchids you will be back for more. Fortunately, there are several ways to improve a collection short of fasting or domestic embezzlement. Among them are swapping with other collectors, or specializing in one type, or substituting more unusual species for common ones you have outgrown. As you gain experience, you will probably progress from buying mature plants to trying smaller and less expensive ones as well as propagating new plants from those you already have. Finally, you may become sufficiently intrigued to go back to the beginning of the orchid's growth cycle, where you will find the ultimate excitement of doing your own pollination and raising plants from seed.

It is impossible to know all the present members of the vast orchid family, much less keep up with the new hybrids, so most growers specialize. Some raise only cymbidiums or paphiopedilums or oncidiums simply because they find them fascinating. Others build collections on a theme, perhaps classic types that starred in early orchid history, or those mentioned in the Nero Wolfe mysteries. Still others delight in owning different species with flowers that are all shades of a single color. For one devotee the familiar lavender corsage orchid started a "passionate purple" collection; he now has more than 75 plants with blooms ranging from palest violet to a purple so dark it is almost—but not quite—black.

Although the progeny of a single orchid seed pod, these three hybrid oncidium sisters show dissimilar characteristics. The blossoms of the plant at the top have inherited larger and more shapely petals.

As they become more experienced, some enthusiasts shift their interest from the showy, large-flowered modern hybrids to the less common species of orchids—known as botanicals. These include miniatures that accommodate nicely to limited space in terrariums and artificial-light gardens and mini-miniatures so small they must be admired through a magnifying glass. These rarer types, many of which are exquisite, are sometimes referred to as "queerie dearies" or "those dumb little weeds," but they almost always attract attention. "Don't let anyone tell you the botanicals do not have fantastic flowers," says one collector. "I put my queerie dearies on the coffee table when they are in bloom, and they never fail to fascinate my guests." Her small *Haraella odorata* proves the point. A tiny plant fastened to a piece of tree fern, it has flowers less than an inch across; at the center of each, within a frame of yellowish green and purple, an impudent little face smiles out.

MORE ORCHIDS THE EASY WAY

As a first step toward increasing their collections, most amateurs not only buy an occasional plant but also multiply their older ones. The process known as vegetative propagation is easy to do and costs nothing. It keeps older plants down to a manageable size and it provides extra specimens for use elsewhere, to give away or to trade for other plants. You will find that many orchid gardeners are happy to trade duplicates for species they lack. Some collectors hold horticultural garage sales, selling surplus plants at bargain prices. You may even work out a joint-ownership arrangement with a friend: two growers can share a treasured specimen; one keeps the plant until it has grown large enough to be divided, then the other is entitled to choose either the division or the original plant.

PSEUDOBULB DIVISION

Multiplying orchids by division is the simplest method of propagating new plants and the one that results soonest in specimens of flowering size. A plant must be well established before being subjected to the operation; most sympodial orchids need at least six healthy pseudobulbs so each division will have three to keep it going. (Each pseudobulb is a potential plant, but it may take several years to flower unless it is supported by other pseudobulbs.)

An orchid is best divided at its normal repotting time, when it has flowered and rested and is once more starting to produce new growth. If new roots are just beginning to show at the base of the front pseudobulb, it is easy enough to avoid injuring them. But if they are longer, it is better to wait until they are 4 or 5 inches long so they will be able to make new side roots if the old roots are broken. Water the plant thoroughly a day ahead of time to make it easier to remove from the pot. Use steady pressure on a long screwdriver to pry it out. If the plant proves stubborn, run a knife around the inside of the pot. Clean around the roots, then decide where you will make the cut through the rhizome to leave three or four pseudobulbs on each division. To make sure you will not spread any virus disease, flame-sterilize the blades of a sharp pair of garden shears, then sever the rhizome and pull the sections apart, gently disentangling the roots. Trim off dead roots and healthy ones that are very long, but be careful not to injure fragile new roots not yet capable of branching. Dust cut surfaces with a fungicide. The lead clump of bulbs is now ready for repotting, staking and labeling *(page 55)* and should produce flowers in the new growth cycle.

The older back bulbs have the potential for sprouting new leads, called back breaks, from their dormant eyes. These older pseudobulbs are less vigorous than those in front, however, and may

FOUR WAYS TO PROPAGATE

1. *Any orchid that sends up a series of pseudobulbs can be propagated by division. At the start of the growing season, using a sharp sterilized knife, cut the rhizome into sections with at least three pseudobulbs each. Dust the cuts with fungicide. Untangle the roots gently and repot the sections.*

2. *An orchid with long, canelike pseudobulbs can be propagated by cuttings. After it flowers, cut an old stem into sections, each containing several leaf nodes. Lay the cuttings on sphagnum moss and keep them shaded and moist until new plants grow, then repot.*

3. *Orchids that grow aerial roots from a stem can be propagated by removing and potting the plant's top. If aerial roots have not appeared, use a clean knife to cut halfway through the stem three or four leaves from the top. Dust the cut with rooting powder. When new roots are 1 to 2 inches long, cut off the top and pot it. The parent plant will still grow.*

4. *Some orchids can be propagated by planting the offsets, plantlets called keikis that form either on the flower stalks or at nodes along the stems. Just slice off the plantlet with its roots intact and pot it.*

take two years to bloom. Since back bulbs have few roots, you must encourage new ones before repotting. Stand the clump in a bed of damp sand and sphagnum moss, out of direct sunlight, and mist it once or twice a day. If the pseudobulbs are kept moist, new roots should form and a dormant eye begin to swell. At this point you can repot the clump, using stake and string to keep it upright.

A PIECE FROM THE TOP

Some kinds of orchids can be propagated by taking cuttings from the tops of mature specimens. Vertical-stemmed monopodial species such as vandas and tall-growing sympodial species such as the reed-stem epidendrums often grow so high that it is desirable to remove a top section simply to keep the plant within bounds. Such plants often sprout aerial roots from their stems. When this happens, sever the stem directly below a set of roots, leaving a generous number of leaves above and below the cut. Then plant the top section in fine bark or bark mixed with peat moss and sand. Wetting the aerial roots will make them more flexible so you can curl them into the pot with less danger of breaking them.

If such aerial roots are not evident, you can encourage their formation by making a small slanting cut, notch or slit in the stem just beneath a leaf, dusting the cut with rooting powder. When roots appear, sever the stem below them and plant the top cutting. Leave the bottom part in its pot unless it needs repotting anyway; it will sprout new growth and eventually will produce flowers again.

PROPAGATION BY PLANTLET

Epidendrums, dendrobiums, vandas and some phalaenopsises are even more obliging and will often produce small plantlets. Called keikis (pronounced kay-i-kees, which means "babies" in Hawaiian), these offshoots spring from stem joints and sprout their own aerial roots. When these roots are an inch or so long, you can sever a plantlet—a firm twist is usually sufficient—and plant it in a tiny pot filled with moistened fir bark. Hold the plant by its crown and funnel the bark in around it, firming gently to avoid breaking the fragile roots. Keep the plantlets out of bright light and mist them daily, or enclose them loosely, pots and all, in plastic bags to maintain moisture. Misting occasionally with a weak fertilizer solution, one quarter of normal strength, will help speed growth. When they are well established, give them the same conditions as mature plants, though they likely are several years away from blooming.

Plantlets can also be made to sprout from old canelike pseudo-bulbs of deciduous dendrobiums after the leaves have dropped and from old flower stalks of spray-type orchids like phalaenopsises after the blooms have faded. Cut the cane or stalk into sections a few inches long, each bearing one or more bumplike buds. Place the sections flat in a container on a bed of moist sphagnum moss and sand. Then set the container out of direct sun and mist daily. Within about two months, when buds have sprouted into plantlets with roots an inch or so long, cut them off and plant them in small pots.

However you propagate from your own plants, watch for other inexpensive ways of acquiring new orchids. Commercial growers frequently offer back-bulb divisions of fine hybrids, large plants that have been used for cut flowers and package deals of surplus stock.

One of the commonest ways to enlarge a collection without spending much money is to buy well-established young plants that are still far short of flowering age. The closer an orchid comes to blooming size, the more it will cost. If you know what you will eventually want and are willing to wait, buy it while it is young and save the grower the cost of raising it. Some commercial catalogues and plant lists indicate the approximate age of plants by their leaf length, others by their pot size—the top diameter in inches. Though some kinds of orchids grow more rapidly than others, an estimate of the time required to bring a plant to maturity can be made from standards established for the popular cattleyas. A cattleya sold in a 2-inch pot should flower in four years, while one in a 2½-inch pot will take three; a 3-inch pot indicates two years to go, a 4-inch pot one to one-and-a-half years, a 5-inch pot six months to a year. A 6-inch pot should contain a plant close to flowering size.

The quality of an orchid, too, affects its market value. In the late 1970s a mericlone offspring of an award-winning hybrid might cost $25 as a flowering plant but much less, perhaps $15, if it was two years away from blooming. Some newly honored plants, avidly sought by collectors and breeders, cost more. A mature specimen of the rare and beautiful *Angraecum comorense* 'Gwendolyn Copley' from the Comoro Islands of Malaya sold for $200 and up.

But many superb orchids are available at modest prices if you buy them when they are small. The surest bets are named hybrids of proven parentage; a high percentage will grow up to honor the family name. Other seedlings, usually from new crosses, may not even have names of their own but will be listed by the parental names, with the female seed-bearing parent first and an "×" indicating the cross—for example, *Blc*. Jane Helton 'Paul McKinley' × *Blc*. Lester MacDonald 'Kelly' AM/AOS. The breeder can provide only an educated guess as to how the flowers will turn out. The cross mentioned, for example, was made "with the hope of producing some fine green cattleyas." But a number of offspring, the grower noted, "will be yellow or chartreuse with a rose lip." So you take a chance. The seedlings you buy may someday win awards, but the odds are against it. Nonetheless, unnamed seedlings from reputable

NEW PLANTS FROM OLD BULBS

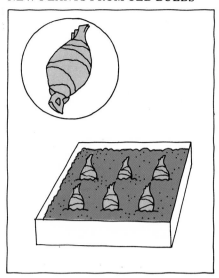

To propagate cymbidium orchids from old and inactive pseudobulbs—called back bulbs because each is farthest from the growing tip of its plant—sever the back bulbs with a flame-sterilized knife. Each bulb needs at least one bud, or eye (green on the inset), to initiate new growth. Insert several back bulbs upright in a flat filled with damp sphagnum moss and sand. Keep the flat in shade. When new roots start to sprout, plant each bulb in a 4-inch pot.

CHOOSING YOUNG PLANTS

breeders can be excellent buys, producing fine flowers, and gambling on the outcome can be half the fun.

Moving still closer to the beginning of the orchid's life cycle, you can buy bare-rooted seedlings, grown in large community flats and sold unpotted in dozen lots. You will have to plant them in individual pots, nurse them along and transplant them as they grow, but they too will reward you with flowers in due time. Also available, and even less expensive, are tiny seedlings sold in glass containers, 35 to 50 or more in a flask. Usually limited to the most popular hybrids and supplied to commercial greenhouses that need quantities of plants to grow and resell, flasks are a great bargain for anyone who can grow seedlings successfully and use many plants of one kind; the seedlings can cost as little as a quarter apiece. Some growers offer flasks containing as few as five or six seedlings.

BOTTLED SEEDLINGS

Despite a three- to five-year wait for flowers—and the special care that young plants need—many orchid fanciers are captivated by the delicate beauty of these "bottle babies" and cannot resist trying them. One amateur celebrated the birth of a daughter by buying a flask of seedlings, choosing a new phalaenopsis cross that promised white flowers striped with peppermint pink. "Frankly," he recalls, "I had no idea what we could do with 35 plants as they got bigger. But when they were ready for 3-inch pots, we had a party and used most of the little orchids as place favors. Then on our daughter's fourth birthday, in the year that the first flowers bloomed, we held a reunion. We delighted to see that some of the flowers were as pretty as she turned out to be."

If you try a flask of seedlings, they should arrive in reasonably

(continued on page 84)

The miller's daughter

Although the first hand-pollinated orchid hybrid bloomed in an English greenhouse in 1856 amid a flurry of publicity and enthusiasm, the difficulty of germinating seeds severely impeded hybridization during the 19th Century. By 1890, only 200 orchid hybrids had been registered.

But with the advent of modern germinating techniques, the number of registered hybrids exceeded 35,000 by the late 1970s, with scores of fascinating new crosses being made each year by amateur gardeners as well as professional hybridizers. Many of these new orchid plants permit an intriguing study of genetics, for their family trees have been recorded with remarkable precision.

On the following pages is the saga of the Miller's Daughter, a 1971 award-winning Paphiopedilum hybrid with ancestry that goes back to the 1880s. Apparent in this plant's blossoms are traces of its earliest forebears (opposite)—the faint red speckles of Paph. niveum (upper right), for example, and the rounded shape of Paph. bellatulum (upper left).

These six Paphiopedilum species were crossed to produce some of the 38 hybrids in the Miller's Daughter's family tree.

80

Ancestors

PAPH. BELLATULUM

PAPH. NIVEUM

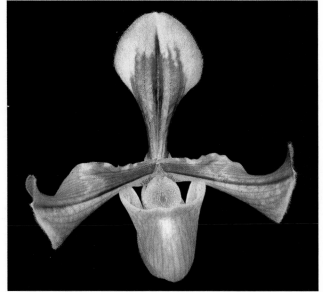

PAPH. VILLOSUM

PAPH. DRURYI

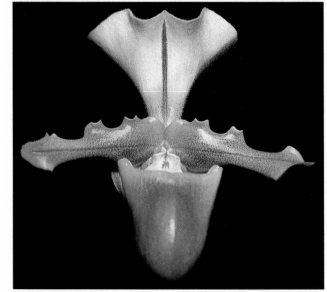

PAPH. SPICERIANUM

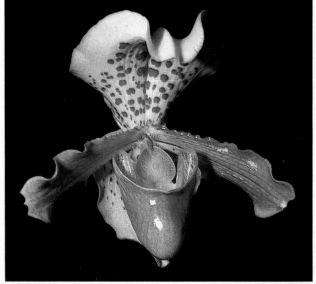

PAPH. INSIGNE

Grandparents

Parents

PAPH. BRADFORD

PAPH. CHILTON

PAPH. CHANTAL

PAPH. F. C. PUDDLE

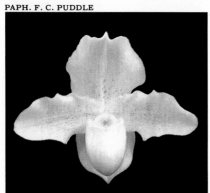

PAPH. DUSTY MILLER

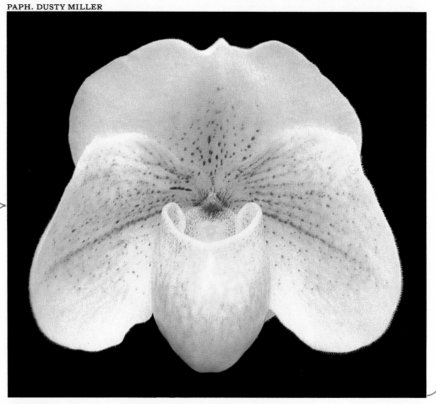

PAPH. CHARDMOORE

The Miller's Daughter comes from a long line of award-winning orchids, including the perfectly shaped Dusty Miller above. Perhaps the most famous member of the clan is F. C. Puddle, known for its ability to produce white offspring.

Offspring

With its satiny white petals, rounded shape, strong stalk and bird's-egg-shaped lip, this orchid is a triumph of some 90 years of hybridizing. But far from being the final descendant, the Miller's Daughter itself is being used as a hybrid parent.

good condition, even if some have been jarred out of the agar growing medium. If you are not able to shake them out of the flask, pour in lukewarm water, then pour the water and seedlings out together. If some remain stuck or are too large to slip out easily, wrap the flask in layers of newspaper and break the glass. Rinse the seedlings in lukewarm water, gently pulling tangled roots apart. Then shift them to a weak fungicide-bactericide bath; this will help protect them from damping off, a fungus disease that can kill seedlings quickly. Make a planting bed by filling a wide, shallow pot or tray with drainage material topped with fine bark; or a seedling mix such as 3 parts bark to 1 part sand; or equal parts of bark, sand and finely screened peat moss. Sterilize the growing medium and container by baking them in a 300° oven for an hour. When the medium is cool, dampen it with the fungicide solution.

To plant the seedlings, make small holes in the mix no more than an inch apart; you can use any pointed object like a screwdriver, but be sure to flame-sterilize the tip. Settle each seedling's roots into place and press the mix gently around it. Put the pot or tray in a shaded place where the temperature will not drop below 60°. Mist daily to keep the humidity high or cover loosely with a tent of clear plastic film propped up on sticks. Give the seedlings a weak solution of fertilizer (about ¼ teaspoon in a gallon of water) once or twice a week. After a few weeks you can move the seedlings into bright indirect light, or place them under fluorescent tubes kept on 14 to 16 hours a day. In eight months to a year they should be large enough to be lifted out of their bed and replanted in small pots.

CREATING A NEW ORCHID
Working with tiny seedlings may give you confidence to take the ultimate step: starting new orchids from scratch. Only a handful of advanced amateurs attempt the meristemming method: it involves removing minuscule pieces of tissue from the tips of young shoots under a dissecting microscope, agitating the pieces of tissue in vials on rotary shakers and later redissecting the growing tissue under sterile laboratory conditions—a process that requires not only equipment but patience and skill. An older method, raising orchids from seed, is less demanding and within the grasp of many amateurs.

The easiest step in growing orchids from seed is the first one: pollinating the flower. What in nature requires elaborate cooperation between insect and flower can be done instantly by a human hand. A large-flowered cattleya is good for a first try because its reproductive parts are easy to see. Wait until a bloom is fully opened, then, using clean tweezers or a toothpick, poke upward on the anther cap at the top of the column while you hold a piece of paper below to catch the little pollen bundles, called pollinia. If the whole anther cap falls, the pollinia must be eased out of their tiny chambers. The pollinia can then be placed on the stigma of the same flower, of another flower on the same plant or of a flower on another plant that is genetically compatible. To make this easier, touch the tweezers or toothpick to the sticky coating of the stigma, then to one of the loose pollinia. Press the pollen bundles into the fluid in the cavity of the stigma, one on each side, and pollination is finished.

Within a day or two the pollinated flower will wilt. When it does, cut off the wilted petals and sepals to minimize the danger of infection, leaving the column intact. In a week or so, if you look closely, you will see the tip of the column beginning to swell and the ovary at its base starting to enlarge. This happens as pollen grains send out long, hairlike tubes carrying sperm cells to the ovules below. Within two or three months, fertilization will occur. In about six months the seed pod will swell to the size of a small lemon and in about nine months, it will begin to yellow, and cracks will appear in its sides. Before any seed can spill, cut off the pod and store it in an open glass jar in a dry place until it is completely split. Then shake the seed onto a piece of paper, fold the paper to form a small envelope, and record the hybrid name and date on the outside. Place the package in a clean, tightly lidded jar with a couple of tablespoons of calcium chloride to absorb moisture and refrigerate it.

HARVEST TIME ARRIVES

OUT OF THE FLASK AND INTO THE FLAT

Orchid seeds started professionally come in small flasks. To transplant the delicate seedlings, pour a little tepid water into the flask and swirl it gently to separate the agar—a jelly-like growing medium—from the roots.

Pour the seedlings from the flask into a shallow dish of water, freeing them with a bent wire if necessary. Wash each seedling until all traces of agar are removed from the roots; then rinse with a fungicide solution.

Sort the seedlings by size. Plant each group in a separate flat in fine fir bark, setting them into small holes ½ inch apart. Gently press the bark around the roots. Move plants to individual pots after a year.

The next step, germinating the seed, is more complicated. It requires a near-sterile environment, laboratory equipment, and a great deal of care. But it is simple and inexpensive to send your seed to a commercial flasking service. Professionals will examine the seed for viability, culture it in agar in sterile flasks and send you the flasked seedlings six months to a year later when they are flourishing and ready to be transplanted. If you are willing to wait up to two years, the professionals will transplant for you. This can be further simplified if you leave the seed pod on the plant for a shorter period, from one to six months depending on the species, then cut it off still unripe, wrap it in sterile cotton and send it in for a green-pod culture.

THE ETERNAL DREAM

Beyond the excitement of propagating a favorite orchid from seed lies the ultimate dream: the alluring possibility that someday, by crossing the right plants, you may create a sensational new orchid, even though the odds are against you. Hybridizing is a complex science, and thousands of hybrids already exist.

But to anyone with orchid fever, the beautiful can always be more beautiful, the fragrant more fragrant, the bizarre more bizarre; flowers can be more reliably abundant, or longer lasting, or occur dazzlingly at more frequent intervals. The combinations possible are nearly infinite; there is always a chance that in a new mating something unexpected will unfold. And, as has often happened in the

POLLINATING IN PURSUIT OF A HYBRID

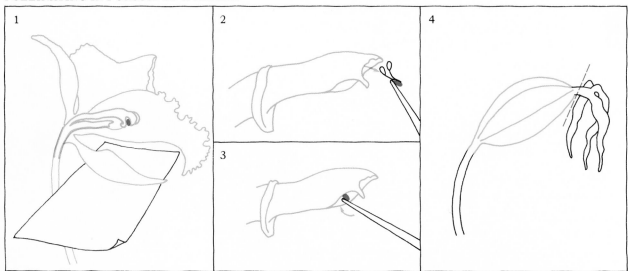

When crossing two orchids, the smaller flower should be host and the larger one the pollen donor. Begin after both have been in bloom for several days. Keep paper under the donor flower to catch pollen pellets.

With a clean toothpick, remove the smaller flower's anther at the column's tip. Lift the donor's anther cap and, with another toothpick, remove pollen pellets (2). Press them onto the sticky stigma of the smaller flower (3).

When the host flower wilts, trim off its sepals and petals. The ovary will enlarge, ripening in nine to 12 months. Harvest the seed pod while it is green or after it has yellowed for a professional to germinate.

past, there is always the possibility that this will be accomplished not by a professional but by an imaginative and persistent amateur.

Still, it is well to heed the experience of those who have gone before. You may be tempted to pick two of your favorite plants and place the pollen from one on the stigma of the other just to see what happens. But do not expect the impossible. In the first place, only genetically related orchids can be crossed successfully; a cattleya can be mated with a laelia, for example, but not with a paphiopedilum. Moreover, if the cross takes at all, you may find you have waited several years only, in the words of an amateur who tried it, to "wind up with dogs." Handsome, healthy parents do not necessarily have handsome, healthy offspring; their genes may produce throwbacks to unwanted characteristics. This is particularly true in crosses of hybrids, which are less predictable than crosses of species and produce a wide variety of progeny, including oddballs and runts.

In orchid breeding, the merit of a parent must be proven with many crosses over a long period of time. John Dominy performed the first cross-pollination in 1852; 20 years later another hybrid was produced—by someone else. Almost 20 years after that, by 1890, only 200 crosses had been made.

By 1895, however, the number began to multiply so rapidly that an English horticultural firm, Frederick Sanders and Sons, started a registry of hybrids. This remarkably detailed work was carried on by the Sanders family until it was assumed in 1961 by the Royal Horticultural Society, which has since registered all new hybrids and issued periodic bulletins to keep the list up to date.

A WINNING GENEALOGY

By consulting *Sanders' List of Orchid Hybrids*—available at many botanical libraries, orchid societies and commercial growers— you can trace the ancestry of any named hybrid back to its origin or look up any hybrid to see what it has already been crossed with. Certain plants perform their parental roles better than others and more consistently pass on desirable traits to their young. Their names appear over and over in orchid catalogues; superb stud plants like *Phalaenopsis* Cast Iron Monarch or *Paphiopedilum* F. C. Puddle are famous among orchid breeders.

Proven parents enormously increase the odds that any hybridizer will be able to create a new orchid that is notable—as well as the odds, of course, that any given cross he contemplates has already been tried. Nevertheless, there are certain sought-after hybrids that no one, at this writing, has yet perfected: an absolutely clear red cattleya, for example, or a pure white paphiopedilum. And for the true romantic, there is still that mysterious and elusive black orchid, which thus far exists only in the world of Nero Wolfe.

An illustrated encyclopedia of orchids 5

Although orchids are exotic, a surprising number will live and bloom under ordinary household conditions. In this encyclopedia there are orchids from tropical forests that require a warm, moist atmosphere and some from fog-shrouded mountains that require cool, damp surroundings. But the great majority listed will adapt to the intermediate temperatures and moderate humidity that can be provided in a home. To help you identify orchids by their needs, each entry specifies the temperatures, light and humidity suited to that plant. If precise greenhouse controls are called for, that fact is noted.

Also noted is the plant's habit of growth, which has as much bearing as habitat on how it is handled. Terrestrial orchids develop their root systems in the earth. Others are epiphytic, clinging to trees and rocks and putting out aerial roots to collect nutrients and moisture. It is possible to grow tree-dwelling orchids in soilless potting mixtures composed mainly of fir bark, and even to suspend them in baskets or mount them on slabs of cork bark or tree fern. Earth-growing orchids, however, must be potted in a soil-like mix. These different mediums demand different fertilizers, whose composition is also given in each entry. Thus, a tree-growing orchid mounted on a slab needs a balanced formula of equal parts of nitrogen, phosphorus and potassium compounds, whereas the same orchid grown in a fir-bark mix will require a high-nitrogen formula.

A total of 82 orchid genera is included in the encyclopedia, but a number of listings contain several species and varieties or hybrids. The genus name is given first and is capitalized; when abbreviated, the form is that used by the International Orchid Commission. Species names are italicized but not capitalized. The names of natural hybrids include the names of the parent plants joined by a multiplication sign; man-made hybrids eliminate the × but can be recognized by the fact that the name is in roman type.

The cluster of orchids includes some that are pictured individually on the pages that follow and others that are only described. The latter are red Masdevallia coccinea (bottom center); Phalaenopsis Diane Rigg 'Pink Mist' (left center); ribbon-petaled Brassavola nodosa (upper left); veined blue Vanda Rothschildiana (center); brown-spotted Brassia lanceana (upper right) and, below it, Laelia pumila with the long bicolor lip.

Aerangis rhodosticta

Aeranthes grandiflora

A

AERANGIS
Aergs. citrata; Aergs. rhodosticta

The waxen, star-shaped flowers of aerangis orchids are cream or yellow, and each is characterized by a spur that is often longer than the blossom itself. Aerangis is a tree-dwelling plant, single-stemmed and usually small. *Aergs. citrata* blooms in late winter and spring. From a 4-inch stem, the graceful flower spray arches downward 8 to 15 inches, bearing numerous pale yellow ¾- to 1-inch blossoms that have 1-inch spurs. Six to 10 fleshy evergreen leaves grow 3 to 6 inches long. *Aergs. rhodosticta* has very short stems and fleshy, pendant leaves up to 6 inches long. It has a spectacular hanging flower stalk that grows 15 inches long, bearing six to 25 creamy white 1-inch blossoms with bright red columns. The flowers are long-lasting and are produced from autumn to spring.

HOW TO GROW. Aerangis grows best in night temperatures of 60° to 65° and day temperatures of 70° to 80°. It requires indirect or filtered sunlight most of the year, with direct sunlight in winter, or 1,500 to 3,000 foot-candles of artificial light for 14 to 16 hours a day. Attach plants to slabs of cork bark or tree fern, or pot them in a mixture of 7 parts fir bark to 1 part redwood bark, 1 part perlite and 1 part coarse peat moss. Repot when plants become crowded or the potting mixture begins to deteriorate and drain poorly. After roots are established, keep the mixture constantly moist and provide 50 to 60 per cent humidity with good ventilation. At every third watering of potted plants, use a high-nitrogen orchid fertilizer such as 30-10-10; for plants hung on slabs use a balanced fertilizer such as 18-18-18 at every third watering. Dilute fertilizer to half the strength recommended on the label. Propagate by separating and planting offsets after they have grown and developed roots.

AERANTHES
Aerth. grandiflora

The generic name of this spidery, pale green orchid means "air flower," because it appears to float in the air. Aeranthes has a single upright stem; leathery, glossy new leaves form at its top, while flower stalks and aerial roots sprout from joints along the stem's lower length. Fragrant, long-lasting blooms are distinguished by the broad bases and long slender tips of their sepals and petals. Of the cultivated species, *Aerth. grandiflora* produces leaves up to 10 inches long. One or two waxy flowers, which are 4 to 6 inches across, grow on a wiry, arching stalk 6 to 9 inches long. The sepals and shorter petals taper to form a five-pointed star; the broad, pale lip makes a fleshy tongue. *Aerth. grandiflora* blossoms any time from summer to winter.

HOW TO GROW. *Aerth. grandiflora* grows best in a moist, tropical atmosphere. Keep the air temperature between 60° and 65° at night and 70° and 80° during the day. Place the plant where it will receive abundant but diffused sunlight, or provide 1,500 to 3,000 foot-candles of artificial light for 14 to 16 hours a day. Maintain a high humidity of 50 to 70 per cent. Keep *Aerth. grandiflora* moist, even in winter, but provide quick drainage to avoid root rot.

For best results, grow in osmunda-filled baskets or on slabs of cork bark or tree fern. If grown in pots, use a mixture of 7 parts fir bark, 1 part redwood bark, 1 part perlite and 1 part coarse peat moss. Fertilize every third watering. For baskets and slabs use a balanced formula such as 18-18-18; for pot-grown plants use a high-nitrogen fertilizer such as 30-10-10. Dilute either formula to half the strength recommended on the label. Repot plants in fresh potting mixture every two years. When the stem grows leggy and begins to lose its lower leaves, propagate by division, choosing a time at the beginning of the growth period.

AERIDES
Aer. japonicum; Aer. odoratum

The tree-dwelling aerides produce long clusters of small, fragrant, long-lasting blossoms. *Aer. japonicum* is a pretty, small species. On its single short stem grow three or four short, leathery leaves. Early in summer, an arching stalk bears up to 12 flowers that last for several weeks. Each white or greenish-white blossom, 1 to 1½ inches long, consists of oval sepals and petals; the lateral sepals are barred at the bases with purple, and the lip is white with purple markings. *Aer. odoratum* is more frequently cultivated. Its central stalk can grow 5 feet tall, forming a dense mass of branches. The base of the stem is sheathed by glossy strap-shaped leaves 8 to 10 inches long and 2 inches broad. In summer and early autumn more than 20 waxy 1- to 1¾-inch blossoms weigh down the flower stalks, which may grow up to 2 feet long. The fragrant white flower is sometimes flushed and spotted with magenta to purple, while the lip is marked with a broad purple ridge. The base of the lip is a horn-shaped spur, and the column is shaped like a miniature bird's head.

HOW TO GROW. Grow aerides in bright sunlight or provide 3,000 foot-candles of light 14 to 16 hours a day. Keep *Aer. japonicum* at 55° to 60° at night and 65° to 75° during the day with a humidity of about 50 per cent. *Aer. odoratum* grows best in a greenhouse with temperatures kept at 60° to 65° at night and 70° to 80° during the day, especially during the growing season. Maintain high humidity—about 70 per cent—by setting the plant on a moisture tray, misting daily, and using a humidifier. Ventilate well to avoid fungus disease. Water both species generously during the season of growth, providing good drainage to prevent root rot. Reduce watering and humidity during the winter.

Pot the orchids in a mixture of 7 parts shredded fir bark, 1 part redwood bark, 1 part perlite and 1 part coarse peat moss. Pots should be roomy in order to accommodate the plants' fast root growth. Baskets filled with osmunda or tree-fern chunks as a growing medium are a good alternative. Fertilize aerides every third watering, using a high-nitrogen fertilizer such as 30-10-10 for potted plants and a balanced formula such as 18-18-18 for basket-grown plants. In each case dilute the fertilizer to half the strength recommended on the label. Repot aerides only when the potting mixture begins to decompose, after 3 or 4 years, since the roots are brittle and easily broken.

Propagate either species when the stem grows leggy and begins to lose its lower leaves. At the beginning of the growth period when green root tips begin to lengthen noticeably, cut off the upper section so as to leave roots on either side of the severance point. Then coax the aerial roots of the upper section into a new pot and surround them with potting mixture. The base of the plant can also produce offsets.

ANGRAECUM
Angcm. distichum, also called *Mystacidium distichum; Angcm. sesquipedale* (star-of-Bethlehem orchid, Christmas star orchid, comet orchid, rocket orchid)

More than 200 species of diverse size, structure and growing habit make up the genus *Angraecum*. Tree-dwelling, the angraecums produce single upright stems and most species bear white or pale green star-shaped flowers with drooping

Aerides odoratum

STAR-OF-BETHLEHEM ORCHID
Angraecum sesquipedale

91

spurs. *Angcm. distichum* is a dwarf species with stems 3 to 5 inches tall. A well-grown plant blooms profusely during the fall, bearing as many as 100 narcissus-fragrant white ¼-inch flowers, which last about two weeks. Blooming may continue throughout the year. Fleshy bright green ¼-inch leaves overlap like shingles along the stems. The star-of-Bethlehem orchid, *Angcm. sesquipedale,* blooms in winter, often during the Christmas season, bearing two to four fragrant and long-lasting flowers per stalk. Star-shaped and ivory-colored, they measure up to 7 inches across and have green-tinged spurs almost 1 foot long hanging from each blossom. The 2-to-3-foot stem bears dark, arching leaves, often white-powdered, about 1 foot long and up to 2 inches wide.

HOW TO GROW. Adaptable to a window sill, most angraecums grow best in indirect sunlight or in 1,000 to 2,000 foot-candles of artificial light provided 14 to 16 hours a day. Optimum night temperatures range from 55° to 60° and day temperatures from 65° to 75°. Angraecums may be grown in baskets with osmunda or tree-fern chunks, on slabs of cork bark or tree fern or in pots in a mixture of 7 parts fir bark, 1 part redwood bark, 1 part perlite and 1 part coarse peat moss. The mixture should be kept damp at all times, but with good drainage, and the pot should be set on a humidifying tray to maintain 60 per cent humidity.

Fertilize angraecums every third watering, using a high-nitrogen formula such as 30-10-10 for potted plants and an 18-18-18 formula for plants grown in baskets or on slabs. In each case dilute the fertilizer to half the strength recommended on the label. To propagate, sever and repot rooted offsets. Or when a healthy plant has developed aerial roots at least 8 inches long, divide it, leaving several roots on each side of the cut. Pot the detached part and continue to care for the mother plant, which will rejuvenate and flower again in about three years.

ANGRAECUM ARCUATA See *Cyrtorchis*
ANGRAECUM FALCATUM See *Neofinetia*

ANGULOA

Ang. clowesii; Ang. rueckeri (both called tulip orchid or cradle orchid)

A cuplike formation of sepals gives anguloas the common name tulip orchid; the other name is derived from a hinged lip that rocks in the lightest breeze. Long, broad deciduous leaves grow from pseudobulbs; a flower stalk sprouts from each pseudobulb. Late in the spring the 8- to 12-inch-long sheathed stalks of *Ang. clowesii* bear solitary waxy flowers with lemon- to golden-yellow sepals and petals that almost conceal small downy white lips. The cup measures up to 3 inches deep and 2 to 3 inches in diameter. Two to four wrinkled leaves 18 to 24 inches long sprout from the top of each pseudobulb. *Ang. rueckeri* is similar in appearance to *Ang. clowesii* but its leaves are smaller and its flowers larger. Olive green to yellow on the outside, these fragrant blossoms vary from pure white to blood-red inside. *Ang. rueckeri* blooms from spring into summer.

HOW TO GROW. Give tulip orchids a cool, shaded environment. If they are grown under artificial light, provide 1,500 foot-candles or less for 14 to 16 hours daily. Maintain a cool temperature range of 50° to 55° at night and 60° to 70° during the daytime. Keep the humidity at about 50 per cent. Water the plants generously during the growing season, but suspend watering for several weeks after they have flowered, until root growth begins. This period of dormancy is essential to promote blooming.

TULIP ORCHID
Anguloa clowesii

Pot anguloas in a well-drained mixture of 2 parts coarse peat moss, 2 parts sandy loam and 1 part each perlite and fine fir bark, or pot in a commercial cymbidium mix. During the active growing period, fertilize every third watering with a balanced fertilizer such as 18-18-18 diluted to half the strength recommended on the label. Propagate new plants by dividing pseudobulb clumps when repotting, leaving three or four pseudobulbs on each division.

ANOECTOCHILUS DISCOLOR See *Haemaria*

ANSELLIA

Aslla. africana (leopard orchid)

The leopard orchid, *Aslla. africana,* is named for the bold brown markings that spot and bar its yellow blossoms; it is easy to bring into flower and is an attractive plant even when it is not in bloom. Amid a dense mass of upright aerial roots, it sends up pseudobulbs that grow 2 to 3 feet in height. Four to seven leathery leaves, up to 12 inches long and 1¼ inches wide, grow along the sides of each canelike pseudobulb. From spring through summer the leaf joints sprout long, branching flower stalks that droop under the weight of many blossoms. The flowers, which are 1 to 2 inches long, last up to one month.

HOW TO GROW. This tropical orchid requires bright direct sunlight or 2,500 to 3,000 foot-candles of artificial light for 14 to 16 hours daily. During the growing season, maintain temperatures of 60° to 65° at night and 70° to 80° in daytime. During this growth period, drench the plants, then let the potting mix become moderately dry before the next watering. Maintain high humidity—50 to 70 per cent—by standing the pot on a moisture tray, misting daily and using a room humidifier. Guard against fungus disease by providing good air circulation around the plant. As pseudobulbs mature, decrease moisture and humidity somewhat to induce as many flowers as possible. Plant in a mix of 7 parts fir bark, 1 part redwood bark, 1 part perlite and 1 part coarse peat moss. Fertilize every third watering with a high-nitrogen fertilizer such as 30-10-10 diluted to one half the strength recommended on the label. Propagate from offsets that form at stem joints or by dividing pseudobulb clumps when repotting, leaving three or four pseudobulbs per division.

ARACHNIS

Arach. flos-aeris (scorpion orchid)

Sickle-shaped petals, inward-curving lateral sepals, and a pouchlike spur at the base of the lip mark this popular tree-dwelling orchid. In the wild, the scorpion orchid's stout central stem wraps around trees, sometimes climbing to a height of 15 feet and bearing 4- to 7-inch leaves and flower stalks 4 to 5 feet long; blossoms appear almost year round. In cultivation, eight to 15 musk-scented blossoms appear on each flower stalk during the fall. The glossy pale yellow blooms, up to 4 inches long and 3½ inches across, have purple to brown spots and bars.

HOW TO GROW. The scorpion orchid, *Arach. flos-aeris,* requires abundant direct sunlight to induce bloom. Maintain a warm temperature range of 60° to 65° at night and a daytime range of 70° to 85°. Maintain high humidity of 50 to 70 per cent, which can be achieved by setting the plant on a moisture tray, misting daily and using a room humidifier. The scorpion orchid's needs may best be met by cultivation in a greenhouse. Good ventilation is needed to prevent fungus growth, since this orchid needs to be watered abundantly the year round. Grow the plant in a pot that allows ample

LEOPARD ORCHID
Ansellia africana

SCORPION ORCHID
Arachnis flos-aeris

Ascocenda Meda Arnold

Ascocentrum ampullaceum

room for root expansion in a medium of 7 parts fir bark, 1 part redwood bark, 1 part perlite and 1 part coarse peat moss. Feed with every third watering, using a nitrogen-rich fertilizer such as 30-10-10 diluted to half the strength recommended on the label. Repot the plant every two years to renew the potting mixture.

When the scorpion orchid begins to lose its lower leaves, choose a time at the beginning of the growth period to divide the plant; leave several roots on either side of the cut. Moisten the roots of the upper section and wind them into a new pot, then surround them with fresh potting mixture. The base of the plant may also produce new growth if it is covered with a layer of sphagnum moss.

ASCOCENDA
Ascda. Meda Arnold; *Ascda.* Tan Chai Beng; *Ascda.* Yip Sum Wah

Ascocenda orchids are a popular cross between the genera *Ascocentrum* and *Vanda,* combining the lower height and the vivid flower colors of ascocentrum with the larger size of the vanda blossom. Clusters of 1- to 3-inch blossoms, with flat petals and sepals and small cup-shaped lips, appear on flower stalks that sprout from the lower nodes of the central stem, which is 8 to 15 inches long.

Ascda. Meda Arnold produces flowers ranging in color from orange to red to mauve, sometimes pure and sometimes mottled. *Ascda.* Tan Chai Beng yields blue to purple blossoms. Flower color in *Ascda.* Yip Sum Wah, one of the best known ascocendas, is pink, orange or red, sometimes mottled. Ideal for orchid gardening on a small scale, ascocendas will often begin blooming in 4- or 5-inch pots, with one or more flowerings during spring and summer, each producing blossoms that may last as long as a month.

HOW TO GROW. Although ascocendas adapt to a variety of conditions, they bloom best when given abundant light and warmth. Give them direct sunlight or 2,500 to 3,000 foot-candles of artificial light for 14 to 16 hours a day. Keep the temperature between 60° and 65° at night and 70° to 80° during the day. Provide high humidity—50 to 70 per cent—by setting the plant on a moisture tray, misting frequently and using a room humidifier. Keep the growing medium evenly moist and well drained. Ensure good air circulation around the container.

Plant ascocendas in such containers as teak or redwood baskets using osmunda or tree-fern chunks, or plant in pots using a mixture of 7 parts fir bark, 1 part redwood bark, 1 part perlite and 1 part coarse peat moss. A commercial potting mix formulated for vandas may also be used. Fertilize every third watering, using a nitrogen-rich formula such as 30-10-10 for potted plants and an 18-18-18 formula for basket-grown plants. In each case dilute the fertilizer to half the strength recommended on the label.

Repot ascocendas when the planting mix begins to decompose, after 3 or 4 years. Propagate new plants at the beginning of the growth period; divide the stem so that some aerial roots are left on each side of the cut; moisten the roots of the new plant and wind them into a pot or basket. Surround the roots with well-packed growing medium. The base of the old plant may also produce new growth.

ASCOCENTRUM
Asctm. ampullaceum; Asctm. miniatum; Asctm. Sagarik Gold

Myriad blossoms in brilliant shades of red, yellow and orange give excitement to ascocentrums, which are all compact tree-dwelling orchids. During the spring and early summer, *Asctm. ampullaceum* produces a stem up to 10 inches tall bearing one or more erect 6-inch sprays of long-lasting deep rose flowers ½ to ¾ inch across. Dense, leathery leaves are 5 to 6 inches long and ¾ inch wide. *Asctm. miniatum,* a dwarf species, bears 20 to 40 bright yellow-orange to orange-red flowers on an upright stalk in spring and early summer. Fleshy leaves 3 to 8 inches long hide the stem, which is usually less than 4 inches tall. *Asctm.* Sagarik Gold has a slightly longer stem and flowers of a deeper tone than *Asctm. miniatum.* It is named for the Thai hybridizer who crossed that species with *Asctm. curvifolium.*

HOW TO GROW. Ascocentrums, with their need for bright light and warmth, grow best in a greenhouse where they will get direct sunlight; or give them 2,500 to 3,000 foot-candles of artificial light for 14 to 16 hours a day. Night temperatures from 60° to 65° and day temperatures from 70° to 85° are ideal. Maintain humidity of at least 50 per cent. Ascocentrums may be planted in baskets using osmunda or tree-fern chunks or in pots using a mixture of 7 parts fir bark, 1 part redwood bark, 1 part perlite and 1 part coarse peat moss. A commercial vanda potting mixture may also be used. Water often enough to keep the growing medium from drying out. Fertilize every third watering, using a nitrogen-rich formula such as 30-10-10 for potted plants and an 18-18-18 formula for basket-grown plants. In each case dilute the fertilizer to half the strength recommended on the label. Repot when the growing medium begins to break down and no longer drains well. Propagate new plants by severing offsets, called keikis, after they have grown several roots.

ASCOCENTRUM HENDERSONIANUM See *Saccolabium*

ASPASIA
Asp. epidendroides

The dark, evergreen foliage of the tree-dwelling *Asp. epidendroides* makes it valued as a year-round house plant; it is easy to grow and produces long-lived flowers. Its pseudobulbs are 2 inches broad and almost 6 inches tall; two leathery leaves almost 1 foot long issue from the top of each. In spring and summer, one or two flower stalks rise from the base of each pseudobulb and bear 1½-inch-long blossoms, from two to 12 on a stalk; the flowers last for five to seven weeks. Colors vary from white to green, with lavender to brown markings. The lip is generally white with lavender or purple markings and has a yellow center.

HOW TO GROW. *Asp. epidendroides* requires intermediate temperatures of 55° to 60° at night and 65° to 75° by day when it is actively growing; in winter, temperatures should be 50° to 60° at night and 60° to 70° in the daytime. Maintain high humidity of 50 to 70 per cent. This orchid's light requirements are unusually low; it can be grown on a window sill or under 1,500 or fewer foot-candles of artificial light for 14 to 16 hours a day.

Mount *Asp. epidendroides* on a hanging slab of cork bark or tree fern or pot it in a mixture of 7 parts fir bark, 1 part redwood bark, 1 part perlite and 1 part coarse peat moss. During the growing season, keep the medium moist but not soggy, then give the plant a month's rest without letting the pot dry out entirely. With every third watering, fertilize the plant using a high-nitrogen formula such as 30-10-10 for potted plants and a balanced formula such as 18-18-18 for slab-mounted plants. In each case dilute the fertilizer to one half the strength recommended on the label. Repot aspasias when new roots are starting if the bark mixture has begun to

Aspasia epidendroides

Bifrenaria harrisoniae

Brassavola digbyana

deteriorate and fails to drain well. Propagate new plants at the same time by dividing the plant into clumps, each containing three or four pseudobulbs.

B

BEE ORCHID, YELLOW See *Oncidium*

BIFRENARIA
Bif. harrisoniae

In tropical forests bifrenarias grow on trees and moss-covered rocks, often amassing huge clumps of angular, glossy pseudobulbs that send up leathery leaves and large handsome flowers. *Bif. harrisoniae* usually produces two flower stalks from the newest pseudobulbs, each bearing one or two 3-inch creamy-white blossoms with hairy purple or maroon lips whose crests are bright yellow. The long-lasting sweet-smelling flowers bloom in spring or early summer. Evergreen leaves up to 1 foot long and 5 inches broad that have a lacquered look come from the clusters of 2- to 3-inch-tall egg-shaped pseudobulbs.

HOW TO GROW. Provide *Bif. harrisoniae* with daytime temperatures of 65° to 75° and temperatures of 55° to 60° at night while the plant is in active growth through the summer. During this period, give the plant three or four hours of exposure to bright sunlight daily or 1,500 to 3,000 foot-candles of artificial light for 14 to 16 hours daily. Water frequently to keep the potting mixture evenly moist, and maintain at least 50 per cent humidity.

When new pseudobulbs mature, rest *Bif. harrisoniae* in a cooler, shadier spot for 3 to 5 weeks to promote flowering. Mist just enough to prevent the pseudobulbs from shriveling. Plant in pots using a mixture of 7 parts fir bark, 1 part redwood bark, 1 part perlite and 1 part coarse peat moss. Fertilize every third watering only in the growing season with a high-nitrogen fertilizer, such as 30-10-10, diluted to half the strength recommended on the label. Repot during the resting period only when necessary to relieve crowding or to renew the potting mix. Propagate by division after flowering, leaving four or five pseudobulbs in each clump.

BIRD'S-HEAD ORCHID See *Ornithocephalus*
BLACK ORCHID See *Coelogyne*
BLUE ORCHID See *Vanda*
BRAIDED ORCHID See *Lockhartia*

BRASSAVOLA
B. cordata; B. digbyana, also called *Rhyncholaelia digbyana; B. glauca,* also called *Rhyncholaelia glauca; B. nodosa* (lady-of-the-night orchid)

Tree-dwelling brassavolas typically have slender pseudobulbs with a fleshy single leaf at the top of each, and a blossom that has narrow, tapered sepals and petals and a broad heart-shaped lip. The flowers may be borne singly or in clusters of up to seven on one stalk. Flowering time varies, depending on the species.

B. cordata produces 3- to 5-inch pseudobulbs and 16-inch leaves. From summer through autumn, three to six fragrant pale green flowers appear. Each is about 1½ inches across, with a large white lip enclosing the column like a claw. The unmistakable feature of *B. digbyana* is its unusually broad, frilly lip. In spring or summer a solitary bloom appears, which is prized for its 7-inch spread, its waxy luster and its nocturnal lemony fragrance. The sepals and petals are pale yellowish-green; the 3- to 4-inch-wide lip is white with a splash of yellowish-green at the throat and a golden tinge at the lower edge. The plant sometimes grows to 18 inches tall.

The leaves and pseudobulbs of *B. glauca* are pale green and often are covered with a white powder. In autumn or spring solitary fragrant blossoms 3 to 4 inches across appear. The pale green sepals and petals form a star behind a white lip with waxy edges. Lady-of-the-night orchid, *B. nodosa,* is known for its sweet nocturnal scent. The orchid's spidery 2- to 3½-inch flowers have white lips and white or greenish sepals and petals; they grow in clusters of one to six blossoms on each stalk. This orchid may flower only in late summer or winter, but under ideal conditions it blossoms year round, producing as many as 50 flowers.

HOW TO GROW. Brassavolas grow best with night temperatures of 55° to 60° and day temperatures of 65° to 75° and with humidity from 40 to 60 per cent in winter and 40 to 70 per cent in summer. During their period of active growth, the plants need three to five hours of sunlight a day at a south window or 14 to 16 hours under 2,000 to 3,000 foot-candles of artificial light. You can grow brassavolas on hanging slabs of bark or you can pot them in a mixture of 7 parts fir bark, 1 part redwood bark, 1 part perlite and 1 part coarse peat moss. Place the pots above a humidifying tray, but water sparingly until the plants are well rooted. Then let them dry between thorough waterings until the growing medium is barely moist. For two weeks after flowering, rest the plants by watering them only enough to prevent the growing medium from drying completely.

Fertilize brassavolas every third watering, using a high-nitrogen fertilizer such as 30-10-10 for potted plants and an 18-18-18 formula for slab-mounted plants. In each case dilute the fertilizer to half the strength recommended on the label. Repot brassavolas when the potting medium starts to deteriorate and fails to drain well or when the plant's creeping rhizome grows over the edge of the pot, about every two or three years. Propagate by dividing the plants into clumps with three or four pseudobulbs in each.

BRASSIA

Brs. caudata (cricket orchid); *Brs. lanceana; Brs. maculata* (all called spider orchids)

Long, thin sepals that look like spider legs characterize the brassia orchids. These tree-dwelling plants have 3- to 6-inch pseudobulbs, each bearing one to three leaves and one or two flower spikes.

Brs. caudata blooms in the fall, sending up two arching 15- to 18-inch flower stalks bearing three to 12 flowers 5 to 8 inches long. The sepals and petals are colored yellow to green and are marked with brown; the broad, ruffled yellow or yellow-green lip tapers to a point and has brown dots near its base. Leathery evergreen leaves grow up to 12 inches long and 2½ inches wide. The very fragrant flowers of *Brs. lanceana,* up to 5 inches long, have light greenish-yellow sepals and petals blotched with brown and a wavy cream-colored lip, often spotted with brown. The 1½-foot flower stalks bear seven to 12 flowers in summer and fall. The flowers of *Brs. maculata* also grow 5 to 8 inches long; each has a wavy cream-white lip mottled with brown or purple. The fragrant blossoms, which appear once or twice from autumn through spring, may last for six weeks.

HOW TO GROW. Easily brought into flower, spider orchids grow well on a window sill. Under artificial light they need 1,500 to 2,500 foot-candles for 14 to 16 hours daily to bloom. Provide temperatures of 55° to 60° at night and 65° to 75° in the daytime. Water abundantly during their period

SPIDER ORCHID
Brassia caudata

Brassocattleya Daffodil

of active growth and maintain high humidity—50 to 70 per cent. Provide good air circulation. When new pseudobulbs mature, let the plants rest for about two weeks, withholding fertilizer, reducing water and lowering the temperature. Pot spider orchids in 7 parts fir bark, 1 part redwood bark, 1 part perlite and 1 part coarse peat moss, or mount them firmly on cork-bark slabs. Fertilize every third watering during periods of active growth, using a high-nitrogen fertilizer such as 30-10-10 for potted plants and an 18-18-18 formula for plants that are mounted on slabs. In each case dilute the fertilizer to half the strength recommended on the label. Repot whenever the plant grows over the edges of the pot or when the bark mixture begins to deteriorate. Propagate new plants by division, with three or four pseudobulbs in each clump.

BRASSOCATTLEYA
Bc. Daffodil

This hybrid genus, the result of a cross between a *Brassavola* and a *Cattleya,* retains the waxy texture, flatness and compact shape of the flowers of its brassavola parent. These it combines with the broader sepals and petals and the flower color of the cattleya. Each flower stalk of the plant produces three or four rich yellow blossoms 2 to 2½ inches long, appearing from winter through spring.

HOW TO GROW. Like a cattleya, *Bc.* Daffodil grows best in night temperatures of 55° to 60° and day temperatures of 65° to 75°. Humidity should range from 40 to 60 per cent in the winter and up to 70 per cent in the summer, always accompanied by good air circulation. Bright indirect sunlight is necessary for good growth; alternatively, *Bc.* Daffodil requires 1,500 to 2,500 foot-candles of artificial light for 14 to 16 hours a day.

Plant the orchid in a pot using a mixture of 7 parts fir bark, 1 part redwood bark, 1 part perlite and 1 part coarse peat moss, or use a commercial potting mix for cattleyas. Water lightly for the first few weeks to encourage rooting, then increase watering as new growth develops. Between waterings, let the potting mix become almost dry. With every third watering, use a high-nitrogen fertilizer such as 30-10-10 diluted to half the strength recommended on the label. Dilute this strength by half again during rest periods after flowering or during intervals of dark weather, and do not fertilize at all when the plant is dormant. Repot every two or three years when new root growth is beginning if the potting medium begins to deteriorate or the creeping rhizome begins to grow over the edge of the pot. Propagate new plants when repotting by dividing the plant into clumps, with each containing three or four pseudobulbs.

BRASSOLAELIOCATTLEYA
Blc. Ermine 'Lines'; *Blc.* Fortune; *Blc.* Malworth 'Orchidglade'; *Blc.* Norman's Bay

Brassolaeliocattleyas are hybrids crossing three genera—*Brassavola, Laelia* and *Cattleya.* They are noted for their large, richly colored flowers whose lips are usually full and darker than the petals and sepals; the lips are often ruffled around the edges. Most blossoms are yellow or lavender, and many are more than 7 inches across; they last about two weeks. All are tree-dwelling, or epiphytic, plants, growing from pseudobulbs, and most produce only one leaf from each of the pseudobulbs.

Blc. Ermine 'Lines' has a clear yellow flower with sepals that are much narrower than the petals; its lip is elongated, slightly ruffled around the edge and tubular at the base. In winter, three to six flowers 4½ inches wide blossom on

Brassolaeliocattleya Malworth 'Orchidglade'

each stalk. The plant ranges from 15 to 24 inches in height.

Blc. Fortune bears bright yellow flowers 6½ inches across, with rose-colored lips. It blooms in the summer and fall, producing two to four blossoms per stalk. The plant grows up to 2 feet tall.

Blc. Malworth 'Orchidglade' is a yellow orchid 6 inches across, with flat sepals and petals; its peach-colored lip is spade-shaped, with rose-colored frilled edges. This orchid normally flowers between fall and winter, producing two blossoms per stalk, but it will sometimes bloom twice a year; the flowers last about six weeks. The plant grows about 30 inches high. *Blc.* Norman's Bay bears a lavender flower, with a slightly darker lip, gold-veined and somewhat ruffled. The blossoms grow two to four on a stalk, are 6 to 8 inches across and may bloom any time from fall to spring. The plant stands about 30 inches tall.

HOW TO GROW. Brassolaeliocattleyas require intermediate temperatures of 55° to 60° at night and 65° to 75° during the day. In winter, maintain humidity between 40 and 60 per cent, in summer between 40 and 70 per cent. Provide good air circulation around the plants. They need bright but diffused sunlight or 1,500 to 2,500 foot-candles of artificial light for 14 to 16 hours a day.

To grow brassolaeliocattleyas, pot them in a commercial orchid potting mixture for cattleyas or in a mixture of 7 parts fir bark, 1 part redwood bark, 1 part coarse peat moss and 1 part perlite. Water the plants only when the mixture is almost completely dry. Fertilize every third watering with a high-nitrogen fertilizer, such as 30-10-10, diluted to half the strength recommended on the label. Repot brassolaeliocattleyas when the growing medium begins to deteriorate or the creeping rhizomes grow over the edges of the pots. Propagate new plants at the same time, dividing the plants into clumps of three or four pseudobulbs.

BROUGHTONIA
Bro. sanguinea

The tree-dwelling *Bro. sanguinea* is less than a foot tall and grows in tight clusters of 2-inch pseudobulbs, often flattened against each other, with a pair of rigid 4-inch leaves at the top of each. Each slender 15-inch flower stalk bears six to 12 stunning red 1- to 2-inch blossoms. The sepals of the flower are narrower than the petals, and the darkly veined lip is very full and rounded, becoming tubular at the base, where it is sometimes marked with a splash of yellow. Typically, the plant blooms between autumn and spring, but under ideal conditions flowering may continue throughout the year, and the flowers are long lasting. Broughtonia, related to the cattleyas, can be crossed with them.

HOW TO GROW. *Bro. sanguinea* grows best in warm temperatures that range from 60° to 65° at night to 70° to 85° during the day and needs a year-round humidity of 40 to 60 per cent. In warm climates, such as southern Florida, this orchid grows well outside in full sun, but when grown indoors, it does best in an east or west exposure. Give the plant full sun from fall to spring, when it is in bloom. When lighting is artificial, provide 2,000 to 3,000 foot-candles of light for 14 to 16 hours a day. *Bro. sanguinea* flowers most readily if grown on a hanging slab of cork bark or tree-fern fiber. A basket with osmunda or tree-fern chunks is also suitable. Broughtonia can be potted in a mixture of 7 parts fir bark to 1 part redwood bark, 1 part coarse peat moss and 1 part perlite. But the plant is particularly susceptible to root rot and must have very good drainage. Be especially careful not to overwater broughtonias when they are dormant. Wa-

Broughtonia sanguinea

ter regularly, but only enough to keep the growing medium moist, never soggy. Fertilize these orchids at every third watering, using a balanced fertilizer such as 18-18-18 for slab-mounted or basket-grown plants and a high-nitrogen fertilizer such as 30-10-10 for plants grown in pots. In each case dilute the fertilizer to half the strength recommended on the label. Broughtonia should be disturbed as little as possible; repot only when the rhizome grows over the edge of the pot or when the growing medium has begun to deteriorate. Choose a time when new root growth is starting for both repotting and propagation, dividing the plant into clumps of three or four pseudobulbs.

BULBOPHYLLUM

Bulb. lobbii; Bulb. longissimum, also called *Cirrhopetalum longissimum; Bulb. medusae* (medusa's head orchid); *Bulb. ornatissimum,* also called *Cirrhopetalum ornatissimum*

In terms of numbers, these tropical orchids surpass all others: the genus contains approximately 2,000 species, all of them tree dwelling and most of them with a common habit of growth. They spread laterally from rhizomes, which send up pseudobulbs, each producing one or two fleshy leaves. The flowers are often more curious than beautiful and frequently possess a strong scent, which may be pleasant or fetid, depending on the species. They come in an almost limitless variety of colors.

Bulb. lobbii grows about a foot tall, and each flower stalk produces a solitary 3- to 4-inch waxy, fragrant blossom, pale yellow to copper-colored, spotted and stained with purple. It blooms in late spring to summer and lasts about two weeks. *Bulb. longissimum* has two to five vividly colored flowers that open fanlike at the top of a 6- to 8-inch stalk. Their petals and sepals are pink streaked with purple and their small lips are yellow-green. But the flower's oddest feature is its sepals; the two at the bottom end in trailing 4- to 6-inch tails. The plant blooms in winter. *Bulb. medusae* bears dense heads of yellow flowers, most of whose parts are tiny, less than ½ inch long. But the two lower sepals are exceptions; they trail and divide into thin 5-inch-long tails. The flowers appear in the fall and winter. *Bulb. ornatissimum* has yellow or brownish flowers streaked with red or purple that bloom in tight clusters of three to five at the top of each stalk. Their lower sepals too are elongated, extending about 3 inches below the 4-inch flowers. *Bulb. ornatissimum* blooms in autumn and early winter.

HOW TO GROW. Most of these bulbophyllums grow best when they are given warm night temperatures of 60° to 65° and day temperatures of 70° to 85°, but *Bulb. lobbii* should have cool night temperatures of 50° to 55° and day temperatures of 60° to 70°. All of them need filtered sunlight or semishade or artificial light equivalent to 1,500 to 2,500 foot-candles for 14 to 16 hours a day. Maintain the humidity between 60 and 70 per cent.

Grow bulbophyllums on hanging slabs of cork bark or tree fern, in pots, or in shallow baskets that are filled with osmunda or tree-fern chunks and are large enough to accommodate the spreading rhizomes. In pots use a mixture of 7 parts fir bark, 1 part redwood bark, 1 part perlite and 1 part coarse peat moss. Keep the mixture constantly moist for *Bulb. lobbii, Bulb. longissimum* and *Bulb. medusae,* but allow it to become almost dry for *Bulb. ornatissimum* when that plant moves into its period of dormancy. At every third watering fertilize plants growing in pots with a high-nitrogen fertilizer such as 30-10-10 diluted to half the strength recommended on the label; give slab-mounted or basket-grown

MEDUSA'S-HEAD ORCHID
Bulbophyllum medusae

plants a balanced formula such as 18-18-18, also diluted to half the recommended strength. Repot only when the growing medium shows signs of decomposing. Propagate by dividing the plant into sections containing four pseudobulbs each.

BUTTERCUP, COLOMBIA See *Oncidium*
BUTTERFLY ORCHID See *Oncidium*

C

CALANTHE
Cal. vestita

In winter the graceful blossoms of *Cal. vestita* are favorites of corsage wearers and indoor gardeners alike. The orchid bears sprays of six to 12 flowers, each 1½ to 3 inches across, on stalks as long as 2½ feet. Blossoms are white, red, pink or purple, and may have orange or yellow markings. Petals and sepals of almost identical size and shape spread and overlap; the very wide lip is cleft into four distinct rounded lobes and has a tubular base that ends in a forward-curving spur that is 1 inch long. Another remarkable feature of this earth-dwelling orchid is its large, angular pseudobulb with a nipped-in waist. The pseudobulb produces three or four broad, wrinkled leaves that fall before the flower stalk appears from its base or when the flowers appear.

HOW TO GROW. Calanthes grow best when they are given night temperatures of 55° to 60° and day temperatures of 65° to 70° with 40 to 60 per cent humidity. The plants require curtain-filtered sunlight or 1,500 or fewer foot-candles of artificial light for 14 to 16 hours daily. Pot in a mixture of 2 parts coarse peat moss, 2 parts sandy loam and 1 part each perlite and fine fir bark. Water sparingly until new growth starts, then keep the potting mix moist. Do not mist the leaves until they have fully opened. At every other watering during active growth, fertilize the plant with a balanced fertilizer such as 18-18-18 diluted to one half the strength recommended on the label. Reduce the frequency of watering again when the leaves yellow.

After the plants have flowered, withhold water and fertilizer, and either lay the pot on its side in a cool place until spring or unpot the pseudobulbs, dust them with fungicide and store them at 60° in a dry place. (Sometimes a plant does not become dormant, with new growth appearing before the flowers fade; if this happens, resume frequent waterings.) Repot pseudobulbs as soon as new growth appears. Propagate new plants by separating pseudobulbs. Replant singly or in clumps of three or four pseudobulbs.

CATASETUM
Ctsm. fimbriatum

Noted for shooting pollen at visiting insects, the catasetums are among the most fascinating of all orchids. A single plant may carry both male and female flowers, bearing them simultaneously or at different times but usually on different stalks. The male and female flowers differ markedly from each other in size, shape and color, the male flowers tending to be more contorted, the female flowers simpler. In general, the male flowers predominate, especially in cultivation. The spicy-smelling blooms, pale yellow or pale green with brown spots, are 1½ to 2½ inches across and grow in clusters of seven to 15 flowers on each arching 18-inch stalk. Each flower has a mechanism on its lip that triggers the release of pollen when touched by a wandering insect or inadvertent gardener. The plant typically blooms in the summer or fall, after its 10-inch leaves have fallen.

Calanthe vestita

Catasetum fimbriatum

Cattleya aurantiaca

Cattleya Bob Betts

HOW TO GROW. *Ctsm. fibriatum* will grow best in intermediate night temperatures of 55° to 60° and day temperatures of 65° to 75°. It requires a humidity of 50 to 70 per cent during the growing season, but this should be lowered while plants are dormant. Give them bright indirect sun until the leaves fall, then full sun while they are in bloom. Under artificial light they need 1,500 to 2,500 foot-candles for 14 to 16 hours a day. The plants may be summered outdoors. Grow them on hanging slabs of tree fern, in baskets filled with osmunda or tree-fern chunks, or in pots. Use a commercial orchid potting mix, or combine 7 parts fir bark with 1 part redwood bark, 1 part coarse peat moss and 1 part perlite. Water regularly while plants are actively growing; after leaves drop off, water only occasionally, just enough to keep the pseudobulbs from shriveling.

Fertilize potted plants every third watering during the growing season with a high-nitrogen fertilizer such as 30-10-10; for slab- or basket-grown plants use a balanced formula such as 18-18-18. In every instance dilute the fertilizer to half the strength that is recommended on the label. Repot each year in late spring, just as new root growth begins. Propagate new plants when repotting by separating pseudobulbs. Replant singly or in clumps of three or four.

CATTLEYA

C. aurantiaca; C. Bob Betts; *C. bowringiana; C. citrina,* also called *Encyclia citrina; C. gaskelliana; C. intermedia; C.* Louise Georgianna; *C. luteola; C. mossiae* (Easter orchid); *C. percivaliana; C. skinneri* (flower of San Sebastian); *C. trianaei* (Christmas orchid)

Cattleyas are prized because they are easy to grow and produce many spectacular flowers in exotic shapes and colors, which last as long as six weeks on the plants. In the wild, cattleyas grow on rocks and trees. They range in size from 6 inches to over 3 feet tall. Cattleyas are divided into two groups: one, termed unifoliate, produces a single leaf from each pseudobulb; the other, termed bifoliate, produces two leaves, and sometimes three. The pseudobulbs of the single-leaved species are seldom more than 1 foot tall, but the flowers are large and full. Double-leaved cattleyas produce smaller flowers in greater numbers; the pseudobulbs may reach a height of 3 feet. *C. aurantiaca,* a bifoliate, is a small plant with fleshy, light yellow-green leaves; it sends forth short flower stalks with many reddish-orange 1½-inch flowers in early spring.

C. Bob Betts is a hybrid derived by crossing *C.* Bow Bells and *C. mossiae* 'Wageneri.' Its rounded 7-inch white flower has a prominent yellow throat; the blooms appear in various seasons. Pseudobulbs of *C. bowringiana,* a bifoliate, grow up to 3 feet tall; its 7-inch flower stalk bears some five to 20 rosy magenta flowers, 2½ inches across, in late fall and winter. *C. citrina,* a pendulous, bifoliate species, grows downward from 2-inch egg-shaped pseudobulbs. The leaves are gray-green; the flowers are bright yellow with frilly lips that have white borders. They do not open fully, giving the 3- to 3½-inch-long blossom a tubular appearance. The blooming season is fall to spring. *C. gaskelliana,* a unifoliate, has variable characteristics, but generally its club-shaped pseudobulbs bear two to five fragrant 6-inch flowers in summer. They are in various shades of purple, and there is also a white variety. Because the species is so easy to cultivate, French growers named it *Cattleya chou,* or cattleya cabbage.

C. intermedia, a bifoliate, produces pseudobulbs up to 18 inches tall. It flowers in summer, bearing 3- to 5-inch blossoms with sepals and petals of pale rose or lavender, and a lip marked with magenta. There is also a pure white variety. *C. Louise Georgianna* is a cross between *C. intermedia* and *C. Souvenir de Louis Sander*. Its open, 5-inch star-shaped flower is pure white.

The 2- to 3-inch pseudobulb of *C. luteola,* a unifoliate, produces a short flower stalk bearing two to six 2-inch waxy yellow flowers that are fragrant and long lasting. The lip may be yellow or white streaked with purple or red. It blooms in the early winter, and sometimes it flowers more than once a year. The Easter orchid, *C. mossiae,* a unifoliate, blooms in spring and is widely used in corsages for Easter and Mother's Day. As large as 8 inches across, the blossom has lavender sepals and petals, a ruffled lip and a yellow throat. Purple markings extend into the throat from the lip.

C. percivaliana, a unifoliate, produces flowers 4 to 5 inches across. Petals and sepals vary from light to deep rose-purple; the lip's midlobe is purple with darker purple streaks on the yellow-orange throat. The flowers bloom in winter and have a musty odor. *C. skinneri,* the national flower of Costa Rica, is a bifoliate. It bears five to 10 odorless flowers about 3 inches across in spring and early summer. The sepals and petals are rose to purple with a white throat. The Christmas orchid, *C. trianaei,* the national flower of Colombia, is a unifoliate. It blooms in winter, bearing 6- to 7-inch flowers that have narrow, curling sepals and broad petals ranging in color from pure white to deep amethyst. The lip is crimson-magenta with a yellow-orange throat.

HOW TO GROW. Cattleyas grow best in bright curtain-filtered light, or in 1,500 to 3,000 foot-candles of artificial light for 14 to 16 hours a day. *C. percivaliana* needs direct sunlight. Maintain night temperatures of 55° to 60° and day temperatures of 65° to 75° with humidity of 50 to 60 per cent. *C. citrina* needs slightly cooler temperatures.

Pot cattleya orchids, except for *C. citrina,* in a mixture of 7 parts fir bark to 1 part redwood bark, 1 part perlite and 1 part coarse peat moss, or use a commercial potting mix especially formulated for cattleyas. *C. citrina,* because of its pendulous habit, is best grown on slabs of tree fern or cork bark. Water sparingly for two or three weeks after potting to encourage rooting. When growth starts, water frequently, but allow the mixture to become nearly dry between waterings. Fertilize pot-grown plants at every third watering during active growth with a high-nitrogen formula, such as 30-10-10, diluted to one half the strength recommended on the label. For slab-mounted plants, use a balanced fertilizer such as 18-18-18 diluted to half the recommended strength. When the new pseudobulbs have matured, let the plant rest for two weeks or so by reducing water and withholding fertilizer. Repot cattleyas just as new roots are forming if they are starting to grow over the edge of their pots or if the growing medium has begun to deteriorate and does not drain well. Propagate new plants by division, keeping three or four pseudobulbs in each clump.

CAULARTHRON BICORNUTUM See *Diacrium*
CHAIN ORCHID See *Dendrochilum*
CHRISTMAS ORCHID See *Cattleya*
CHRISTMAS STAR ORCHID See *Angraecum*

CHYSIS
Chy. aurea

This tree-dwelling orchid is distinguished by unusually long pendulous club-shaped fleshy pseudobulbs. From these grow several 12- to 15-inch thin leaves, which appear simultaneously with the flowers. Normally in summer, the plant

Cattleya citrina

FLOWER OF SAN SEBASTIAN
Cattleya skinneri

Chysis aurea

BLACK ORCHID
Coelogyne pandurata

bears clusters of five to 10 fragrant waxy 2-inch flowers, which last for two to three weeks. The broad yellow petals and sepals may be paler at the bases; the white or yellow cup-shaped lip of the blossom is marked with red, maroon or brown and is ornamented on the middle lobe by velvety ridges that look like teeth.

HOW TO GROW. *Chy. aurea* grows best in temperatures from 55° to 60° at night and 65° to 75° during the day and in 40 to 60 per cent humidity. The plants can be grown in filtered sunlight in an east or west window or in a greenhouse under 1,500 to 2,500 foot-candles of artificial light for 14 to 16 hours a day. Plant in a basket containing osmunda or tree-fern chunks or in a pot with a mixture of 7 parts fir bark to 1 part redwood bark, 1 part perlite and 1 part coarse peat moss. Mist daily and water generously, especially while the plant is actively growing, but let the mix dry almost completely before each watering.

At every third watering, fertilize basket-grown plants with a balanced formula such as 18-18-18; use a high-nitrogen formula such as 30-10-10 for pot-grown plants. Dilute fertilizer to half the strength recommended on the label. At the end of the growth period, when new pseudobulbs have matured, let the plant rest in cooler temperatures, water less frequently and do not fertilize. When new growth appears, raise temperatures, increase watering and resume fertilizing. Repot when the potting mixture begins to deteriorate and when new roots appear on young growth. Propagate at the same time by dividing the plant into clumps, each containing three or four pseudobulbs.

CIRRHOPETALUM See *Bulbophyllum*
CLAMSHELL ORCHID See *Epidendrum*
COCKLESHELL ORCHID See *Epidendrum*

COELOGYNE

Coel. cristata; Coel. graminifolia; Coel. massangeana; Coel. pandurata (black orchid)

The fragrant tree-dwelling coelogyne bears its flowers in clusters on arching-to-pendulous stems. Its pseudobulbs rise from rhizomes and each pseudobulb produces one to four narrow pleated evergreen leaves 3½ inches to 2 feet long. *Coel. cristata* has plump bright green pseudobulbs and pure white flowers, 3 to 4 inches wide, with raised streaks of yellow on the lips. The flowers bloom from winter to early spring, in clusters of five to 15 blooms, which, if kept cool, may last up to six weeks. *Coel. graminifolia* usually blooms in the summer, producing 3- to 6-inch-long sprays of two to four flowers, each 2 inches across. The blossoms are white streaked with brown and with yellow-orange. From spring to fall the 15-inch-tall flower stalks of *Coel. massangeana* bear clusters of up to 20 very fragrant 2-inch blossoms. The petals and sepals are pale yellow; the lip is brown and veined with white. *Coel. pandurata* bears 1½- to 2½-foot-long sprays of 5 to 15 greenish-yellow flowers, 3 to 4 inches wide. The lip is marked with parallel ridges of velvety black, source of its common name, the black orchid. Its long blooming season may run from winter to late summer or fall.

HOW TO GROW. These orchids do best when they are given bright but indirect or curtain-filtered sunlight or 1,500 to 2,500 foot-candles of artificial light 14 to 16 hours daily. *Coel. cristata* thrives in cool temperatures of 50° to 55° at night and day temperatures of 60° to 70°; *Coel. graminifolia, Coel. massangeana* and *Coel. pandurata* require intermediate temperatures of 55° to 60° at night and 65° to 75° during the day. All four species need 60 to 75 per cent humidity.

Because of their pendulous blossoms, coelogyne orchids are most suited to slabs of cork bark or tree fern, or to orchid baskets, which should be filled with osmunda or tree-fern chunks. If they are potted, use a growing mixture of 7 parts fir bark to 1 part redwood bark, 1 part perlite and 1 part coarse peat moss.

Water plants frequently during the growing season, which varies with each species, but allow the potting mixture to become almost dry between waterings. Withhold water after flowering, providing only enough to keep the pseudobulbs from shriveling. Fertilize plants during the growing season at every third watering, using a balanced fertilizer such as 18-18-18 for plants grown on slabs or in baskets and a high-nitrogen formula such as 30-10-10 for potted plants. Dilute either formula to half the strength recommended on the label. Repot only when the potting mixture starts to deteriorate or the plant outgrows its pot. Work fresh potting mix around the pseudobulbs as new growth starts. Propagate new plants while repotting by dividing plants into clumps of at least three pseudobulbs each.

COLOMBIA BUTTERCUP See *Oncidium*
COMET ORCHID See *Angraecum*

COMPARETTIA
Comp. coccinea

Though not large—they measure only 1 inch across—the flowers of this tree-dwelling jungle plant have an unusual structure. The petals and upper sepal form a hood; the lower sepals unite to form a spur that sheaths the two spurs of the lip, in effect creating a lip with three spurs. The lip itself is broad and heart-shaped. The flowers appear in sprays of three to eight blooms along 10-inch flower spikes from late summer to midwinter, growing from the base of a small pseudobulb. The blossoms are red-orange shaded with yellow. Simultaneously each pseudobulb produces a solitary leaf about 4 inches long.

HOW TO GROW. *Comp. coccinea* grows best in intermediate temperatures of 55° to 60° at night and 65° to 75° in the daytime. Give it bright indirect or curtain-filtered sunlight or 1,500 to 2,500 foot-candles of artificial light for 14 to 16 hours a day. Maintain 50 to 70 per cent humidity. Pot comparettia in a mixture of 7 parts fir bark, 1 part redwood bark, 1 part perlite and 1 part coarse peat moss, or attach it to a slab of tree fern or cork bark. Keep the growing medium constantly moist. At every third watering, fertilize with a nitrogen-rich formula such as 30-10-10 for plants grown in a potting mixture, or with a balanced formula such as 18-18-18 for slab-mounted plants; dilute either fertilizer to half the strength recommended on the label. Replace the top layer of potting mix in early spring every year. Repot plants when rhizomes begin to creep over the edges of the container or when the potting mixture begins to deteriorate. Propagate new plants when repotting by dividing the rhizomes, leaving at least three pseudobulbs per division.

CORAL ORCHID See *Rodriguezia*
COW-HORN ORCHID See *Schomburgkia*
CRADLE ORCHID See *Anguloa*
CRICKET ORCHID See *Brassia*
CUCUMBER ORCHID See *Dendrobium*

CYCNOCHES
Cyc. chlorochilon (swan orchid)

The tree-dwelling cycnoches, or swan orchid, is character-

Comparettia coccinea

SWAN ORCHID
Cycnoches chlorochilon

Cymbidium finlaysonianum

Cymbidium Jungfrau

ized by the slender curving column that issues from the center of its lip, which suggests the arching neck of a swan, and by its sepals and petals, which fold backward and upward to suggest a swan's body and its lifted wings. This plant has a cylindrical pseudobulb 8 to 12 inches long, sheathed near the top with five to eight leaves up to 2 feet long; the leaves die and fall as the flowers begin to develop. Flower stalks 6 to 12 inches long emerge from the base of the upper leaves, mostly in the summer; each stalk bears two to 10 flowers 4 to 6 inches across. The sepals and petals are yellow-green and the lip is white, marked with dark green at the base. The flowers are waxy and have a spicy fragrance that is particularly pungent in the morning; the blossoms last for about three weeks.

HOW TO GROW. Cycnoches grows best in at least four hours of direct sunlight a day but should be shielded from midday sun in the summer. To grow it under lights, provide 2,000 to 3,000 foot-candles for 14 to 16 hours a day. Warm night temperatures of 55° to 60° suit these orchids, and day temperatures should be between 65° and 75°. Provide them with 50 to 75 per cent humidity.

Grow the plants in small pots or hanging baskets, using a mixture of 7 parts fir bark, 1 part redwood bark, 1 part perlite and 1 part coarse peat moss. Keep the medium evenly moist when plants are actively growing. After new pseudobulbs have matured, usually in winter, water only enough to keep the pseudobulbs from shriveling. Fertilize during active growth with a high-nitrogen fertilizer such as 30-10-10 diluted to half the strength recommended on the label. Repot as often as once a year, or whenever the plant and its rhizomes grow over the edge of the container. Propagate when new growth begins in early spring, separating pseudobulbs into single bulbs or into clumps of up to four.

CYMBIDIUM

Cym. devonianum; Cym. finlaysonianum; Cym. Geraint; Cym. Hawtescens; Cym. Jungfrau; Cym. Mary Pinchess; Cym. Peter Pan 'Greensleeves'; Cym. pumilum

For color range and quantity of long-lasting flowers, few orchids can compete with the cymbidium. Depending on the species or cross, its flowers bloom in white, pink, maroon, bronze, mahogany, yellow and green, and as many as 30 blossoms, 2 to 5 inches across, are produced on each flower stalk. The petals and sepals of the flowers are roughly equal in size, and the lip, with its erect side lobes and pendulous bottom lobe, looks like the hull of a boat.

Most cymbidium orchids bloom in the spring. When they are grown in cool temperatures, the blossoms will last up to 12 weeks; as cut flowers they last from 4 to 6 weeks. Some cymbidiums are earth dwelling; others are tree dwelling. But all of them grow from rhizomes, producing pseudobulbs that vary in thickness from a slight swelling of the stem to definite spheres. Their foliage, which is narrow and grasslike, lasts for several years.

Cym. devonianum produces two to five leaves up to 14 inches long and a pendulous flower stalk 14 inches long. Its flowers, which are 1 to 1½ inches wide, are light olive-green streaked or spotted with purple, and the lips are red to purple with darker edges. *Cym. finlaysonianum* has leaves 2 to 3 feet long and hanging flower stalks 3½ feet long. Its blossoms are yellow-brown speckled on the lip with red-brown; some petals and sepals have reddish-brown stripes down the middle. *Cym.* Geraint is a miniature hybrid, growing only 15 inches tall; it produces eight to 12 lime-green flowers 2 to 3 inches across on 15- to 20-inch stalks.

The hybrids *Cym.* Hawtescens and *Cym.* Jungfrau are both large plants, taking up as much as 4 square feet of space, with flowers up to 5 inches across. The flowers of Hawtescens are a bright yellow, while Jungfrau's are white. *Cym.* Mary Pinchess and *Cym.* Peter Pan 'Greensleeves,' both miniature hybrids, grow 12 to 15 inches tall and have flowers 2 to 3 inches wide. Those of Mary Pinchess are yellow; those of Peter Pan 'Greensleeves' are green with a red lip. *Cym. pumilum,* a dwarf species with leaves 6 to 12 inches long and flower stalks only 4 to 5 inches long, has 1-inch-wide blossoms of reddish-brown edged with yellow, and a white lip spotted with reddish-brown.

HOW TO GROW. Cymbidiums need cool nights and warm sunny days to produce blooms and grow well. Most species and hybrids require night temperatures of 50° to 55° and day temperatures of 60° to 75°, but the miniature hybrids will grow and bloom in warmer night temperatures—55° to 60°. The most important time for cool temperatures is in the fall when the flower spikes are being formed. Provide 50 to 60 per cent humidity.

Cymbidiums grow best with at least four hours of direct sunlight a day but should be protected from hot midday sun to keep their leaves from scorching. The larger species and hybrids are difficult to grow under lights because of their size, but it is possible to grow the miniatures successfully in over 3,000 foot-candles of artificial light for 14 to 16 hours daily. In addition, because of their size and cultural requirements, the larger plants are best grown in a greenhouse or on a cool sun porch; in summer they can be placed outdoors.

Grow cymbidiums in pots, using a mixture of 5 parts medium-grade fir bark, 3 parts redwood bark and 2 parts coarse peat moss, or use a commercial cymbidium mix. Keep the potting mixture constantly moist when the plants are actively growing; when the pseudobulbs have matured, water less frequently for several weeks. Feed at every third watering with a high-nitrogen fertilizer such as 30-10-10 diluted to half the strength recommended on the label. Repot after flowering when the mix begins to deteriorate. Propagate new plants at the same time by dividing into clumps of three or four pseudobulbs.

CYPRIPEDIUM

Cyp. acaule (pink lady's slipper, pink moccasin flower); *Cyp. calceolus* (yellow lady's slipper); *Cyp. reginae* (showy lady's slipper)

These familiar wild orchids, native to the temperate zones of North America, Europe and Asia, number about 50 species of mostly earth-dwelling plants. Besides their odd pouch-shaped lip, they are distinguished by two fertile stamens instead of one, as in most other orchids.

The pink lady's slipper, *Cyp. acaule,* has 2- to 8-inch-long leaves, dark green on top, silvery beneath. Its 2-inch-long flowers bloom singly in late spring and summer on stalks 8 to 15 inches long. Sepals and petals vary from yellowish-green to greenish-brown and are streaked with brown or purple. The velvety lip varies in color from crimson-pink to pure white and is veined with rose.

The yellow lady's slipper, *Cyp. calceolus,* has erect 2-foot stems sheathed in leaves 2 to 8 inches long. It bears one to three flowers, 3 to 5 inches across, in spring and summer. Sepals and petals vary in color from yellow tinged with green to purplish-brown, and the lip may be light to deep yellow, usually veined or spotted inside with purple.

The showy lady's slipper, *Cyp. reginae,* has a tall stem 1½ to 3 feet high, which is enfolded by broad fuzzy leaves as

YELLOW LADY'S SLIPPER
Cypripedium calceolus

Cyrtorchis arcuata

Dendrobium aggregatum

large as 8 inches long and 5 inches wide. In early summer the plants produce one to three fragrant 3-inch white flowers with rose or purple stripes across the inflated lip.

HOW TO GROW. Though the cultural requirements of the cypripediums seem easily met in nature, they are difficult plants to cultivate. Plants purchased from nurseries may have a better survival chance since they are more likely to have adapted to garden conditions—and besides, in most areas the collection of the wild plants is forbidden. All cypripediums require shade and a moist, acid soil, although the degree of moisture and acidity needed by each may differ. *Cyp. acaule* does best in a very acid soil, augmented if necessary with such acid materials as pine needles or leaf mold. *Cyp. calceolus* requires a mildly acid soil ranging from slightly moist to boggy, and does best in partial shade. *Cyp. reginae* needs an acidic, very moist soil ranging from boggy to downright swampy.

Plant cypripediums in the fall, setting the rhizomes of *Cyp. acaule* and *Cyp. calceolus* 1 to 1½ inches deep and the shallow-growing roots of *Cyp. reginae* only ½ inch deep. Space the plants 1 to 2 feet apart and water them thoroughly, then mulch them lightly with dead leaves or pine needles. Water the plants abundantly while in active growth; reduce moisture after shoots have flowered and begun to wither. Do not move the plants. They will increase by forming new rhizomes, and the flowers will improve as the clumps age.

CYRTORCHIS
Cyrtcs. arcuata, also called *Angraecum arcuata*

A small star-shaped white flower formed by petals, sepals and lip of uniform size distinguish this tree-dwelling orchid. Stiff 4- to 6-inch evergreen leaves alternate along the single stem, and the flower stalks grow horizontally from the bases of the leaves. In the winter and spring each stalk bears at least eight flowers, each 1½ inches across. The blossom is waxy, fragrant, and besides being star-shaped, has a distinctive curved green spur 3 inches long that issues from under the lip.

HOW TO GROW. Cyrtorchis grows best in warm night temperatures of 60° to 65° and day temperatures of 70° to 80°. Give it at least four hours of direct sunlight a day except in summer, when it should be shielded at midday. Under artificial lights, this orchid needs 1,500 to 3,000 foot-candles for 14 to 16 hours a day. Maintain 50 to 60 per cent humidity. Cyrtorchis grows well on slabs of cork bark or tree fern. It can also be grown in pots in a mixture of 7 parts fir bark, 1 part redwood bark, 1 part perlite and 1 part coarse peat moss. Keep the potting mix evenly moist when the plants are actively growing. Fertilize at every third watering; for slab-mounted plants use a balanced formula such as 18-18-18; feed pot-grown plants with a high-nitrogen fertilizer such as 30-10-10. Dilute either formula to half the strength recommended on the label. When plants become dormant, allow the potting mixture to dry slightly between waterings and discontinue feeding. Repot cyrtorchis just as new growth starts, whenever the growing medium deteriorates or when the plants outgrow their containers. Propagate by separating the new plants that grow at the base of the older plant.

D

DANCING-LADY ORCHID See *Oncidium*

DENDROBIUM
Den. aggregatum; Den. bigibbum; Den. cucumerinum (cu-

cumber or gherkin orchid); *Den.* Gatton Sunray; *Den. kingianum; Den. loddigesii; Den. nobile; Den. pulchellum; Den.* × *superbiens*

The second largest genus of orchids, with over 1,600 species, dendrobiums range in size from less than 1 inch to 9 feet tall. Most are tree-dwelling plants and all grow from creeping roots, or rhizomes, but some dendrobiums have pseudobulbs while others have slender, jointed stems resembling canes. Some species are evergreen, others deciduous, and their flowering habits also vary widely. On some species the blossoms appear in pendulous sprays at the tops of the plants; on others they appear at the leaf nodes, where the leaves join the stem, and may occur as either single blossoms or clusters. All flowers, however, are characterized by the "chin" that is formed at the foot of the column by the fusion of the two side sepals. Most dendrobium blossoms last for two or three weeks.

Den. aggregatum produces a 2-inch pseudobulb with a single evergreen 3-inch leaf. In spring, pendulous flower spikes bear 5 to 15 flowers, each about 1½ inches in diameter. The blossoms are golden yellow with a slightly deeper color on the lip. *Den. bigibbum* has 1- to 1½-foot-tall canelike stems with 4-inch evergreen leaves. Each spring, arching flower stalks appear from the upper nodes of both old and new canes. The stalks are up to 12 inches long and produce sprays of two to 12 flowers. The 2-inch magenta blossom has a notched lip with a white crest.

Den. cucumerinum, which is sometimes called the cucumber orchid, gets its name from its swollen leaves, 1 inch long, which are covered with little bumps. An evergreen plant, it blooms in the spring, producing short sprays of somewhat ill-smelling flowers on 1-inch stalks that rise directly from the rhizome. The flowers are very small, only ½ inch across, and are greenish-white with wavy red lips. The hybrid *Den.* Gatton Sunray, which is a cross between *Den. pulchellum* var. *luteum* and *Den.* Illustre, is a cane-type orchid that bears fragrant 4-inch flowers, yellow except for the center of the lip, which is dark brown. Clusters of eight to 12 flowers bloom in the summer.

Den. kingianum has tapering pseudobulbs 6 to 12 inches high with three to six 4-inch leaves crowded near the top of each. In early spring, flower stalks 4 to 8 inches long rise from among the evergreen leaves. Each stalk bears two to nine small flowers, each 1 inch across. They are fragrant and waxy, and they range in color from white to mauve with purple markings.

Den. loddigesii, a cane-type orchid, has slender branching stems that develop aerial roots from the point where the stems branch or from any node. The stems are 4 to 8 inches long and bear deciduous leaves, up to 3 inches long. The fragrant flowers, 1½ inches across, bloom singly from nodes in late winter to spring; they are rose-purple with large fringed lips and yellow-orange centers.

Den. nobile is the most widely grown and hybridized orchid of this genus. Its canelike stems, which grow up to 2 feet tall, produce deciduous 3- to 4-inch leaves, most of which drop in the fall. The flowers that follow, in winter through early summer, bloom on leafless, 2-year-old stems. They appear at the nodes in clusters of two or three, and each flower is 3 inches wide. Both the sepals and petals are white with purple tips; the lip, mostly white, has a rose-colored tip and a magenta throat.

The canelike stems of *Den. pulchellum* are 3 to 5 feet long with 6-inch evergreen leaves. Pendulous stalks of five to 12 musk-scented flowers emerge from the upper nodes of the

Dendrobium bigibbum

Dendrobium Gatton Sunray

stem in spring. Each blossom is 3 to 5 inches across and is yellow with rose-pink veins; the lip is fringed and has dark purple spots on its throat. *Den.* × *superbiens* is a natural hybrid between *Den. discolor* and *Den. bigibbum* var. *phalaenopsis.* It has 3- to 5-foot canes, 1½- to 4½-inch evergreen leaves, and from its upper leaf nodes an arching flower stalk, up to 3 feet long, emerges in the fall. The stalk bears up to 20 red-purple blossoms, each 3 inches across; the flowers have pale edges and darker, very wavy lips.

HOW TO GROW. Dendrobiums grow best in bright filtered sunlight. Many are difficult to grow under lights because of their large size. Some of the smaller species may nevertheless bloom if a range of 1,500 to 3,000 foot-candles is provided for 14 to 16 hours a day. *Den. aggregatum, Den. cucumerinum, Den. kingianum, Den. loddigesii* and *Den. nobile* require intermediate night temperatures from 55° to 60° and day temperatures of 65° to 75° when actively growing, and a lower night temperature of 50° to initiate flowering. Warm-growing *Den. bigibbum, Den. pulchellum, Den.* × *superbiens,* and *Den.* Gatton Sunray require warmer night temperatures of 60° to 65° and day temperatures of 70° to 85°. Provide 50 to 70 per cent humidity.

Pot dendrobium orchids in a mixture of 7 parts fir bark, 1 part redwood bark, 1 part perlite and 1 part coarse peat moss; stake tall-growing canelike varieties. Smaller plants may alternatively be attached to slabs of tree fern or cork bark. Keep evergreen species evenly moist all year round, but reduce the amount of moisture when the plants are not growing. Keep deciduous species constantly moist during the growing season, but allow the potting medium to become almost dry when the plants are at rest, watering them only when the stems start to shrivel. Or, in lieu of watering, plants can be misted during this interval. Fertilize potted plants at every third watering during their period of active growth with a high-nitrogen formula such as 30-10-10 diluted to half the strength recommended on the label; for slab-mounted plants use a balanced formula such as 18-18-18 also diluted to half strength.

Repot dendrobium orchids when their growing medium starts to deteriorate and drain poorly, preferably just as new roots and leaves are beginning to develop. Propagate additional plants at the same time by dividing the older plants into clumps of three to four canes or pseudobulbs each. When starting new evergreen plants, include a few of the old stems with the new growth because the blossoms appear on the preceding year's growth.

DENDROCHILUM

D. filiforme, also called *Platyclinis filiformis* (chain orchid, necklace orchid)

Double ranks of tiny blossoms numbering up to 100 line the pendant stalks of the chain orchid, *D. filiforme.* No larger than ¼ inch across, each fragrant flower has white-to-yellow oval sepals and petals, a three-lobed yellow lip and a toothed column. The tree-dwelling, or epiphytic, plant produces clustered egg-shaped pseudobulbs 1 inch long, each topped with a single 6-inch evergreen leaf; and a flower stalk, 8 to 10 inches long, emerges from the base of the leaf to bloom during the early spring and summer.

HOW TO GROW. The chain orchid, *D. filiforme,* grows best in intermediate night temperatures of 55° to 60° and day temperatures of 65° to 75°. Give it at least four hours a day of direct sunlight, but shield it from the midday sun in summer; otherwise, provide 1,500 to 2,500 foot-candles of artificial light for 14 to 16 hours a day. Maintain 50 to 60

CHAIN ORCHID
Dendrochilum filiforme

per cent humidity. Plants will grow well mounted on slabs of cork bark or tree fern, or they can be potted in a mixture of 7 parts fir bark, 1 part redwood bark, 1 part perlite and 1 part coarse peat moss. When the plants are actively growing, keep the growing mixture evenly moist; allow it to dry slightly between waterings in winter when the plants are dormant. Fertilize at every third watering during active growth. With potting mix, use a nitrogen-rich formula such as 30-10-10; for plants on slabs, use a balanced formula such as 18-18-18; dilute either type to half the strength recommended on the label. Repot in spring just as new growth begins, whenever the potting medium starts to deteriorate. Propagate new plants by dividing when repotting, leaving four pseudobulbs in each division.

DIACRIUM

Diacm. bicornutum, also called *Caularthron bicornutum* (virgin orchid)

Widely acclaimed for the grace and beauty of its pure white flowers, 2 to 3 inches wide, the virgin orchid, *Diacm. bicornutum,* discourages amateur orchid-hunters. In the wild, along the Caribbean seacoast, its hollow pseudobulbs are often inhabited by biting fire ants. The tree-dwelling, or epiphytic, plant produces three to five 8-inch-long leaves at the top of a 9-inch pseudobulb and an erect flower spike up to 12 inches long, which bears five to 20 sweet-smelling flowers. The lip of each flower is delicately freckled with purple or crimson and has a yellow crest. Diacrium blossoms from late spring to summer. It hybridizes readily with cattleya, epidendrum and laelia orchids.

HOW TO GROW. The virgin orchid, *Diacm. bicornutum,* grows best when it is given warm temperatures of 60° to 65° during the night and 70° to 85° in the daytime. It requires at least eight hours of bright sunlight a day except when the plant is producing new growth; during that period it needs to be protected from bright light. Under artificial lights the virgin orchid should receive 2,000 to 2,500 foot-candles of light for 14 to 16 hours a day. Maintain a humidity level of 50 to 60 per cent.

Grow the virgin orchid, *Diacm. bicornutum,* in a mixture of 7 parts fir bark, 1 part redwood bark, 1 part perlite and 1 part coarse peat moss. When the plants are actively growing, keep the potting mix evenly moist, and at every third watering fertilize them with a high-nitrogen fertilizer such as 30-10-10; dilute the formula to half the strength recommended on the label. When flowering has ceased, discontinue fertilizer, and water the plants just enough to keep the pseudobulbs from shriveling. Diacrium orchids flower most abundantly when the plants are not disturbed, so repot them only when the growing medium begins to deteriorate. If repotting is necessary, do it when the new growth begins, using the occasion to propagate new plants by separating the pseudobulbs into clumps of four.

DINEMA See *Epidendrum*

DORITAENOPSIS

Dtps. Jerry Vande Weghe; *Dtps.* Memoria Clarence Schubert

Doritaenopsis is a hybrid of *Doritis* and *Phalaenopsis* orchids. Tree-dwelling and single-stemmed, these hybrids have two or three pairs of glossy, dark green leaves, 6 to 12 inches long, growing on short, thick stems; usually the leaves are shaded with purple. Upright, slightly arching flower stalks emerge from between the lower leaves and grow 2 to 3 feet

VIRGIN ORCHID
Diacrium bicornutum

Doritaenopsis Jerry Vande Weghe

111

Doritis pulcherrima

SPICE ORCHID
Epidendrum atropurpureum

long. Each spike usually produces 10 to 20 flat flowers, 2 to 3 inches across. *Dtps.* Jerry Vande Weghe, a cross between *Dtps.* Red Coral and *Phal.* Therese Frackowiak, has white or dark pink flowers with a red lip. *Dtps.* Memoria Clarence Schubert, a cross between *Dor.* pulcherrima var. *buyssoniana* and *Phal.* Zada, produces dark rosy-purple blossoms. Both plants begin to flower in summer and may continue to bloom for several months.

HOW TO GROW. Doritaenopsis orchids grow best when they are given intermediate night temperatures of 55° to 60° and day temperatures of 65° to 75°. Provide indirect or curtain-filtered sunlight or 1,000 to 1,500 foot-candles of artificial light for 14 to 16 hours daily. Maintain 40 to 60 per cent humidity. Grow doritaenopsis in a mixture of 7 parts fir bark, 1 part redwood bark, 1 part perlite and 1 part coarse peat moss. During their period of active growth, keep the plants evenly moist; afterward, allow the potting mix to dry slightly between waterings. Fertilize these orchids during growth at every third watering with a high-nitrogen fertilizer such as 30-10-10 diluted to half the strength recommended on the label. Repot the plants when the lower leaves die and fall off, exposing 1 to 1½ inches of the stem, choosing a time when new leaves are just starting to grow. Propagate new plants from the offsets that are produced at the base of the stem, when the offsets form roots.

DORITIS
Dor. pulcherrima

This plant—believed to be the only species of the *Doritis* genus—bears as many as 20 blossoms on each branch of its 2- to 3-foot flower stalk. Occurring in shades of rose-purple, with lip colors of orange, red or purple, the flowers are about 1 inch wide. New buds open gradually during the fall and winter, and the flowering period continues from two to five months. A tree-dweller, *Dor. pulcherrima* produces thick, alternating leaves 5 to 8 inches long. Doritis orchids have been crossed with *Phalaenopsis* to create hybrids that are known as *Doritaenopsis*.

HOW TO GROW. These orchids bloom best in semishade or in 1,500 foot-candles of artificial light for 14 to 16 hours daily. They need less light during the summer when new leaves and roots are developing. Night temperatures of 60° to 65° and day temperatures of 70° to 80° are ideal. Provide high humidity of 60 to 70 per cent; give plants good ventilation but keep them out of drafts. Once the flowers have faded, another flower stalk may grow if the first stalk is cut just above its top node. Pot in small containers, using a mixture of 7 parts fir bark, 1 part redwood bark, 1 part perlite and 1 part coarse peat moss. Keep the mixture evenly moist and fertilize every third watering with a high-nitrogen formula such as 30-10-10 diluted to half the strength recommended on the label. Repot when a plant is overcrowded. To propagate new plants, divide clumps that develop at the base of the parent plant.

E

EASTER ORCHID See *Cattleya*
EL TORO ORCHID See *Stanhopea*
ENCYCLIA ATROPURPUREA See *Epidendrum*
ENCYCLIA CITRINA See *Cattleya*
ENCYCLIA MARIAE See *Epidendrum*
ENCYCLIA STAMFORDIANA See *Epidendrum*
ENCYCLIA TAMPENSIS See *Epidendrum*
ENCYCLIA VITELLINA See *Epidendrum*

EPIDENDRUM

Epi. atropurpureum, also called *Encyclia atropurpurea* (spice orchid); *Epi. ciliare*; *Epi. cochleatum* (clamshell orchid, cockleshell orchid); *Epi. ibaguense*, also called *Epi. radicans* (fiery reed orchid); *Epi. mariae*, also called *Encyclia mariae*; *Epi. nocturnum*; *Epi. polybulbon*, also called *Dinema polybulbon*; *Epi. pseudepidendrum*; *Epi. stamfordianum*, also called *Encyclia stamfordiana*; *Epi. tampense*, also called *Encyclia tampensis*; *Epi. vitellinium*, also called *Encyclia vitellina*

The epidendrum orchids are known for their bright, fragrant, long-lasting flowers, which, in many species, bloom abundantly most of the year. There are more than 1,000 species. Most of them are tree-dwelling plants that fall into two groups: those with pseudobulbs bearing one to three leathery leaves, and those with thin, reedlike stems, no pseudobulbs and several fleshy leaves. Both types bear waxy flowers, singly or in clusters, at the ends of erect flower stalks that grow up to 3 feet tall.

The spice orchid, *Epi. atropurpureum*, has pear-shaped pseudobulbs 2 to 4 inches high and leaves 12 to 15 inches long. In late spring and early summer it bears clusters of five to 10 fragrant blossoms at the ends of 18-inch stalks. Each 2- to 3-inch-wide flower has brown curving petals and sepals, sometimes with green tips, and a large white lip heavily streaked with purple. *Epi. ciliare* bears one or two leaves 6 to 10 inches long on its 4- to 7-inch pseudobulb. Its 3- to 7-inch-wide flowers bloom abundantly during the winter in clusters of three to seven; each blossom has greenish-yellow sepals and petals and a fringed, three-lobed white lip.

The pseudobulbs of the clamshell orchid, *Epi. cochleatum*, are slender and cone shaped, grow 5 to 8 inches tall, and each produces a pair of glossy 6- to 12-inch leaves. At any season of the year this species may begin its five- to seven-month blooming season, producing a succession of scented flowers in clusters of three to 10 on an arching stalk. Spidery yellowish-green petals and sepals, 2½ to 3½ inches long, hang below a shell-shaped green-and-purple-striped lip.

Epi. ibaguense, the fiery reed orchid, has a vinelike stem 2 to 3 feet long and produces short leaves and long aerial roots. Throughout the year its flower stalks bloom in rounded clusters of 1- to 1½-inch blossoms, brilliantly colored from yellow to red. *Epi. mariae* has small pseudobulbs and short leaves. In summer its 6- to 8-inch flower stalk is capped by one to four 3-inch flowers; the yellow-green sepals and petals surround a broad, frilly white lip with green veins. *Epi. nocturnum* produces canelike pseudobulbs, 1 to 2½ feet long with 6- to 8-inch leaves. Its spidery, pale yellow or green flower, 3 to 4 inches long, resembles that of *Epi. ciliare* and is most fragrant at night.

Epi. polybulbon forms a flat carpet of miniature pseudobulbs, each with two leaves 1 to 2 inches long. During the winter and spring, every pseudobulb produces a single ½- to 1-inch red-tinged yellow-green flower with a spreading white lip. *Epi. pseudepidendrum* has canelike stems 2 to 3 feet tall and dark leathery leaves. On its striking 3-inch-long flower, green sepals and petals sweep back from a waxy orange-red lip; this orchid blooms in clusters of three to five and will bloom more than once from the same flower stalk. *Epi. stamfordianum* has flower spikes arching from the base of each 10-inch pseudobulb. Its fragrant 1½-inch blossom has yellow sepals and petals spotted with red and a yellow and white lip with a fringed mid-lobe. Clusters of these fragrant blossoms appear from winter into spring.

Epi. tampense has small pseudobulbs and leaves 6 to 15

Epidendrum ciliare

FIERY REED ORCHID
Epidendrum ibaguense

Epidendrum pseudepidendrum

inches long. Throughout most of the year it bears clusters of 1-inch yellow-green flowers tinged with brown; the lip is white marked with purple. *Epi. vitellinum* produces two slender 6- to 9-inch leaves from 2-inch pseudobulbs and an 18-inch flower stalk that bears at least 10 or more orange-red blossoms in early fall.

HOW TO GROW. Epidendrums bloom best in bright indirect sunlight or 1,500 to 3,000 foot-candles of artificial light for 14 to 16 hours a day. They need temperatures of 55° to 60° at night and 65° to 70° in daytime. Provide a relative humidity of 50 to 75 per cent, and ventilate the plants well without exposing them to drafts.

Pot epidendrum orchids in a mixture of 7 parts fir bark to 1 part redwood bark, 1 part perlite and 1 part peat moss or mount them on slabs of cork bark or tree fern. After potting, water them lightly so the potting mix is just damp to the touch and mist the plants often until new roots are established. During periods of active growth, allow the medium to become almost dry between waterings. Fertilize pot-grown plants every third watering with a high-nitrogen formula such as 30-10-10 diluted to half the strength recommended on the label. For slab-mounted plants use a balanced formula such as 18-18-18, also diluted to half the recommended label strength. After plants have flowered, reduce watering and discontinue fertilizing. Repot every year or two when the plants start to creep over the edges of their pots, or when the potting mix begins to deteriorate and drains poorly. Propagate pseudobulb species by division into clumps of three or four pseudobulbs each; propagate reed-stem epidendrum orchids from stem cuttings.

ERIA
E. javanica

These tree-dwelling orchids rarely appear in the collections of orchid hobbyists. *E. javanica* has egg-shaped 3-inch pseudobulbs about 2 inches apart along a rhizome, or creeping stem. From the pseudobulbs grow flower stalks 12 to 15 inches tall, bearing as many as 30 starry white or cream-colored flowers that may be veined with purple; each is up to 1½ inches wide. Two broad fleshy leaves grow up to 18 inches long from each pseudobulb. They flower mostly in spring and summer, and sometimes more than once a year.

HOW TO GROW. *E. javanica* grows best in indirect or filtered sunlight or under 1,500 foot-candles of artificial light provided for 14 to 16 hours a day. Night temperatures of 60° to 65° and day temperatures of 70° to 80° are ideal. Provide humidity of 60 to 70 per cent, with good air circulation.

Pot plants in a mixture of 7 parts fir bark to 1 part redwood bark, 1 part perlite and 1 part coarse peat moss. During the growth period, keep the mix moist and fertilize every third watering with a high-nitrogen fertilizer such as 30-10-10, diluted to half the strength recommended on the label. After flowering, let the plant rest for about two weeks; resume watering and fertilizing when new growth appears. Repot only when necessary, when the creeping stem grows over the edge of the pot or the growing medium starts to deteriorate and drains poorly. Propagate by division, allotting three or four pseudobulbs to a pot.

EUANTHE SANDERIANA See *Vanda*

F

FIERY REED ORCHID See *Epidendrum*
FIRE ORCHID See *Renanthera*

Eria javanica

FLOWER OF SAN SEBASTIAN See *Cattleya*
FOXTAIL ORCHID See *Rhynchostylis*
FU MANCHU ORCHID See *Phragmipedium*

G

GHERKIN ORCHID See *Dendrobium*
GOBLIN ORCHID See *Mormodes*
GOLDEN SHOWER ORCHID See *Oncidium*

GONGORA

G. armeniaca; G. galeata (both called Punch-and-Judy orchid)

Tree-growing gongoras have erect aerial roots and long, drooping flower stalks that hang below the plant base, some arching and some dangling like chains. Each stalk bears as many as 30 fragrant blossoms up to 2 inches wide. The inverted position and intricate structure of the flower forces nectar-gathering bees to slide down the column, thus picking up pollen at its tip before flying on to another flower. Both species have small pseudobulbs 1 to 2 inches tall with broad, pleated leaves at their apexes. *G. armeniaca* has paired leaves about 9 inches long. Its waxy, apricot-scented flowers with sacklike lips all face inward on a flower stalk that grows 2 to 3 feet long. *G. galeata* grows like *G. armeniaca* but is smaller. Its intensely fragrant brownish-yellow flowers have proportionately broader sepals and petals. Both species flower in summer and early autumn and keep their blossoms for only 1 to 2 weeks.

HOW TO GROW. Gongora orchids grow best in filtered or indirect sunlight or under 1,500 foot-candles of artificial light for 14 to 16 hours daily. Night temperatures of 55° to 60° and day temperatures of 65° to 70° are best. Maintain a humidity of 50 per cent.

If flowers start to drop, move the plant to a cooler position in deeper shade. Plant in baskets filled with osmunda or tree-fern chunks or on slabs of cork bark or tree fern. Or pot in a mixture of 7 parts fir bark to 1 part redwood bark, 1 part perlite and 1 part coarse peat moss. Make sure the plant sits slightly above the edge of the basket or pot so that the stalks can project over the side. During periods of active growth, keep the potting mix evenly moist, and fertilize at every third watering. Use a high-nitrogen formula such as 30-10-10 for pot-grown plants and a balanced fertilizer such as 18-18-18 for plants in baskets or on slabs. Dilute either formula to half the strength recommended on the label. Rest the plant in winter until new growth appears. Repot when a plant becomes crowded or when the potting mix begins to deteriorate and drain poorly. Propagate new plants from pseudobulbs, three or four to a group.

H

HAEMARIA

Haem. discolor, also called *Ludisia discolor* and *Anoectochilus discolor* (jewel orchid)

Beautiful gemlike leaves rather than flowers usually attract collectors to jewel orchids, but *Haem. discolor* bears attractive flowers as well. A tropical earth-dwelling plant, it grows in humus-filled soil and blooms in fall and winter. At the center of each ½- to ¾-inch waxy white flower, the yellow column and the slightly anchor-shaped lip twist in opposite directions. The fragrant blossoms cluster on stalks that grow up to 12 inches tall. Many growers pinch off the flower stalks to encourage growth of the attractive leaves,

PUNCH-AND-JUDY ORCHID
Gongora armeniaca

JEWEL ORCHID
Haemaria discolor

Hexisea bidentata

VIOLET ORCHID
Ionopsis utricularioides

which have glistening green surfaces with veins that are red or gold and reddish-purple undersides. About 3 inches long, the leaves grow in whorls on a 6-inch stem.

HOW TO GROW. Difficult to grow, a jewel orchid needs warmth, low light and high humidity. The light of a northern exposure is sufficient, or if grown under artificial light, give it 1,000 to 1,500 foot-candles for 14 to 16 hours daily. The temperatures should be kept between 60° and 65° at night and 70° to 80° during the day, with 70 to 80 per cent humidity. To maintain these conditions, grow a jewel orchid within a glass enclosure such as a bell jar, a terrarium or a special orchid case. Open the enclosure regularly to admit air without creating a draft. Plant in a mixture of 2 parts coarse peat moss, 2 parts sandy loam and 1 part each perlite and fine fir bark. Use a small pot or, for several well-rooted plants, a shallow pan. Keep the mix evenly moist but not soggy; water standing around the roots will quickly rot this delicate plant. During active growth periods fertilize at every third watering, using a balanced formula such as 18-18-18 diluted to half the strength recommended on the label. Repot when the plants become crowded or when the potting mix starts to deteriorate, preventing fast drainage. Propagate new plants by dividing the creeping rhizome.

HEXISEA
H. bidentata

The jointed stem that characterizes tree-dwelling hexisea is formed of pseudobulbs growing one on top of another. A pair of slender 3- to 4-inch leaves grows from the apex of each bulb. From the short stalk, tight clusters of bright cup-shaped flowers, ½ to ¾ inch wide, blossom in spring and summer, or in some cases at irregular intervals throughout the year. Although there are no registered hexisea hybrids, growers have made successful crosses with cattleyas, laelias and epidendrums.

HOW TO GROW. Intermediate temperatures suit hexisea orchids; they need a range from 55° to 60° at night and from 65° to 75° during the day. They grow well when they are given bright diffused sunlight, such as that provided by a lightly curtained southwest window, or where they receive 1,500 to 2,000 foot-candles of artificial light for 14 to 16 hours a day. Keep the humidity between 40 and 60 per cent and provide good ventilation around the plants. Pot hexiseas in a mixture of 7 parts fir bark to 1 part redwood bark, 1 part perlite and 1 part course peat moss, or fasten to a slab of cork bark or tree fern. Allow the growing medium to become slightly dry between waterings. Fertilize every third watering, using a high-nitrogen formula such as 30-10-10 for pot-grown plants or a balanced formula such as 18-18-18 for plants mounted on slabs; dilute either formula to half the strength recommended on the label. Since this species may bloom for much of the year, it does not require a rest period after flowering. Repot hexiseas when the bark mixture begins to deteriorate or when the pot becomes overcrowded. Propagate by dividing a plant, keeping a cluster of four or five pseudobulbs in each division.

I

IONOPSIS
Inps. satyrioides; Inps. utricularioides (both called violet orchid)

These tree-dwelling miniature orchids grow naturally in humid tropical forests. They bear branching sprays of tiny blossoms whose size and shape as well as their color make them look like showers of delicate violets. *Inps. satyrioides* produces ⅓-inch white blossoms and has no pseudobulbs. *Inps. utricularioides* has ½-inch flowers in colors that vary greatly from one plant to another; some are pure white, others pink or lilac with purplish veins, still others a rich purple. Its thick 5-inch leaves rise from the base of a very small pseudobulb. The blossoms of both species have broad, flat lips that are about twice the length of the sepals. They bloom in winter and early spring. They are fragile plants, and they have a life expectancy of only five or six years.

HOW TO GROW. Although ionopsis should be kept damp, it is singularly intolerant of staleness in the potting mix, deteriorating rapidly in anything but a fresh mix. It grows best on a slab of cork bark or tree fern or in a small basket filled with osmunda or tree-fern chunks. Or place in a small pot in a mixture of 7 parts fir bark, 1 part redwood bark, 1 part perlite and 1 part coarse peat moss. During active growth, let the medium become slightly dry between thorough waterings. At every third watering, fertilize with a balanced formula such as 18-18-18 if grown on a slab or in a basket. For pot-grown plants use a high-nitrogen fertilizer such as 30-10-10. Dilute either formula to half the strength recommended on the label.

After the orchids have flowered, reduce watering and discontinue fertilizing until new growth starts. Ionopsis needs bright indirect or curtain-filtered sunlight or 1,500 to 2,500 foot-candles of artificial light for 14 to 16 hours a day. Night temperatures of 55° to 60° and day temperatures of 65° to 75° are best for them. Keep humidity high, between 50 and 70 per cent. Repot only when the growing medium begins to deteriorate, disturbing the roots as little as possible. Propagate new plants by stem division.

ISOCHILUS
I. linearis

A dainty tree-dwelling plant that grows 2 feet tall, with wiry stems and grasslike leaves that are 2½ inches long and only ⅛ inch wide, *I. linearis* blooms intermittently throughout the year. Its small flowers, which are less than ½ inch long, range in color from nearly white to vivid magenta with darker lips; they grow in clusters of five to 15 on a stalk. The flowers never open very wide, always remaining somewhat tubular in appearance. Like others of its genus, this orchid is easy to grow; it develops rapidly into an attractive plant soon after propagation.

HOW TO GROW. This orchid does best when it is grown in partial shade or indirect or curtain-filtered sun. If it is grown under artificial light, isochilus should be given 1,500 or less foot-candles of light for 14 to 16 hours a day. Night temperatures should range from 55° to 60°, day temperatures from 65° to 75°. Humidity should average between 60 and 70 per cent. Isochilus will grow equally well in pots, in baskets filled with osmunda or tree-fern chunks or on slabs of tree fern or cork bark. Pot the plants in a mixture of 7 parts fir bark, 1 part redwood bark, 1 part perlite and 1 part coarse peat moss. Keep the mixture evenly moist at all times, but do not let it become soggy. Fertilize pot-grown plants every third watering with a high-nitrogen formula such as 30-10-10, diluted to half the strength recommended on the label; fertilize plants grown on slabs or in baskets with a balanced formula such as 18-18-18, also at half the recommended strength. Repot only when orchids become overcrowded or potting mixture begins to deteriorate and drains poorly. Plants may be propagated by dividing clumps, but they bloom more frequently if they are left undisturbed.

Isochilus linearis

Laelia anceps

Laelia cinnabarina

JEWEL ORCHID See *Haemaria*

L

LADY-OF-THE-NIGHT ORCHID See *Brassavola*
LADY'S-SLIPPER ORCHID See *Cypripedium, Paphiopedilum* and *Phragmipedium*

LAELIA

L. anceps; L. autumnalis; L. cinnabarina; L. crispa; L. lundii, also called *L. regnellii; L. pumila*

Of all orchids these tree dwellers are most similar in appearance to cattleyas and are often crossed with that genus. The vivid yellows, fiery red-oranges and rich violet tones of laelia species are used to produce brilliantly colored hybrids. Laelias have an unusually long blooming period, some sprays producing flowers for more than two months. *L. anceps* is one of the best-known species of laelia orchid. Its pseudobulbs grow 3 to 5 inches tall with a single leaf 6 to 8 inches long. Flowers 1½ to 4 inches wide blossom in winter in clusters at the tips of tall, arching stalks that grow up to 3 feet long. The blossoms are lavender with yellow and deep purple lips. *L. autumnalis* closely resembles *L. anceps* except that it has two or three leaves sprouting from its pseudobulbs. Blossoms 3 to 4 inches wide are borne in loose sprays in fall or early winter and cap stalks 2 feet long. Each pink and purple flower has a distinctive lip with two white outer lobes dotted with purple and one yellow inner lobe. The pseudobulbs of this species are ground up and used in some parts of Mexico to make festival candies in the shapes of animals and fruits.

L. cinnabarina, found on rocks as well as in trees, grows from a large, tapering pseudobulb 5 to 12 inches tall and produces a single 6- to 11-inch leaf. It blossoms in spring or summer on 1- to 2-foot stalks of five to 15 flowers each. The flower is bright red-orange, 2 to 3 inches wide, and the lip has a frilly middle lobe. *L. crispa,* a summer-flowering species, also has large pseudobulbs, up to 11 inches high, and a single 9- to 12-inch leaf. The plant bears clusters of five or six fragrant white flowers 4 to 6 inches wide with yellow and purple lips. *L. lundii* is tiny, seldom more than 4 or 5 inches tall. Its 1½- to 2-inch pseudobulb bears two 3-inch leaves, and its flowers bloom singly or in pairs in midwinter, often before the narrow leaves begin to emerge. The blossoms are 1 to 1½ inches wide, white with purple-pink shading; the lips are ruffled, and veined in red. *L. pumila,* another miniature, has pseudobulbs 2 to 4 inches long, each with a single leaf about the same length, and reaches a maximum height of 8 to 9 inches. In the fall it produces 3- to 4-inch rose-to-lavender flowers with bicolor lips, red-purple on the outer lobes with a white throat.

HOW TO GROW. These plants prefer night temperatures between 55° and 60° and day temperatures between 65° and 75°. Provide four to eight hours of sunlight a day, but the light should be filtered when the sun's rays are strongest. If grown under artificial lights, the plants need 1,500 to 2,500 foot-candles of light for 14 to 16 hours a day. Humidity should range between 40 and 60 per cent. Plant these orchids in a mixture of 7 parts fir bark to 1 part redwood bark, 1 part perlite and 1 part coarse peat moss, or fasten them to a slab of tree fern or cork bark.

During the growing season, allow the potting medium to become moderately dry to the touch between thorough waterings. After flowering, until the start of new growth, water only when the pseudobulbs are in danger of shriveling. During active growth, fertilize potted plants every third watering with a high-nitrogen formula such as 30-10-10, diluted to half the strength recommended on the label. For plants that are slab mounted, use a balanced fertilizer such as 18-18-18, also diluted to half the recommended strength. Do not fertilize laelias during the rest period after flowering. Repot every two to four years if plants become overcrowded or when the potting mixture begins to deteriorate and drain poorly. Propagate new plants when new growth appears by dividing pseudobulbs into clusters of three or four.

LAELIA See also *Schomburgkia*

LAELIOCATTLEYA

Lc. Cassandra; *Lc.* Derna; *Lc.* Jay Markell; *Lc.* South Esk 'Judy Doig'

Brilliant clusters of 3- to 6-inch flowers characterize these popular hybrids of *Laelia* and *Cattleya*. Over 2,000 varieties are available, with flower colors that range from greenish-yellow and orange to pink and purple. Their vivid colors are derived from the laelias and their general structure and growth habit is inherited from the cattleyas. *Lc.* Cassandra, which blossoms in winter, has flowers in colors ranging from pink to purple, each with two yellow eyelike spots on the lip. *Lc.* Derna, blooming mostly in winter, produces a yellow flower with a red lip. The white flower of *Lc.* Jay Markell, which blooms in winter, has a deep red tube and a ruffled reddish-purple lip that is marked with two bright yellow eyes. *Lc.* South Esk 'Judy Doig' produces purple blossoms in the late fall and winter.

HOW TO GROW. Laeliocattleyas bloom best when they are given bright indirect or curtain-filtered sunlight or 1,500 to 2,500 foot-candles of artificial light for 14 to 16 hours a day. Night temperatures of 55° to 60° and day temperatures of 65° to 75° are best. Provide 40 to 60 per cent humidity. Pot laeliocattleyas in a mixture of 7 parts fir bark to 1 part redwood bark, 1 part perlite and 1 part coarse peat moss. During the active growing season, allow the potting mixture to become slightly dry between thorough waterings; after flowering, water the plants only enough to keep the pseudobulbs from shriveling.

Fertilize during the growing season at every third watering, using a high-nitrogen orchid formula such as 30-10-10, diluted to half the strength recommended on the label. Propagate when new growth appears, dividing plants into clusters of three or four pseudobulbs.

LEOPARD ORCHID See *Ansellia*

LEPTOTES

Lpt. bicolor

This fragrant tree-dwelling miniature with disproportionately large flowers sends up slender pseudobulbs only 1 inch high; each pseudobulb bears a solitary, almost cylindrical leaf 3 to 5 inches tall. The plant also produces seed pods that, like the beans of the vanilla orchid, are dried and used to flavor candies and iced desserts in Brazil. From its short flower stalk, seldom more than 1 to 2 inches long, spring two to four white 2-inch flowers with slender sepals and petals that curve around purple-flushed lips. Because of its dwarf size and striking blooms, *Lpt. bicolor* is excellent for windowsill gardens. It normally blooms from winter to spring.

HOW TO GROW. Leptotes orchids need bright indirect or curtain-filtered sunlight or 1,500 to 2,000 foot-candles of

Laelia lundii

Laeliocattleya Jay Markell

Leptotes bicolor

artificial light for 14 to 16 hours daily. Night temperatures of 55° to 60° and day temperatures of 65° to 75° are ideal. Provide 40 to 60 per cent humidity. Grow leptotes on slabs of tree fern or cork bark, or pot plants in a mixture of 7 parts fir bark to 1 part redwood bark, 1 part perlite and 1 part coarse peat moss. During the growing season, allow the medium to dry slightly between thorough waterings. At every third watering, fertilize with a high-nitrogen formula such as 30-10-10 for plants potted in bark mixture, or with a balanced formula such as 18-18-18 for plants mounted on slabs; dilute either to half the strength recommended on the label.

After the plants have flowered, water them only enough to keep the pseudobulbs from shriveling, and do not fertilize again until new roots appear. Leptotes may stop flowering if it is disturbed. When the potting mixture needs changing, do not repot, but simply remove old mixture from around the base of the plant and add fresh growing mixture. Propagation by division also disrupts these plants, and they are better left alone.

LILY-OF-THE-VALLEY ORCHID See *Odontoglossum*

LOCKHARTIA
L. acuta, also called *L. pallida; L. lunifera; L. oerstedii* (all called braided orchid)

Distinguished by their overlapping leaves that climb, one over another, on stems growing up to 2 feet long, these tree-dwelling orchids are ornamental plants even when not in flower. But their blossoms are attractive too, the flowering period lasting from six weeks to three months. The flowers are small and delicate, mostly yellow with red-spotted lips, and dangle on thin stalks from the bases of the upper leaves. *L. acuta* has six to 12 blossoms per stalk, each blossom less than ½ inch wide; it blooms during the summer. *L. lunifera* produces one to three flowers on each stalk from summer to fall; the flowers are ½ to ¾ inch wide. *L. oerstedii* bears two to four flowers at a time on each stalk throughout the year; the flowers are 1 inch wide.

HOW TO GROW. Braided orchids need night temperatures between 55° and 60° and day temperatures between 65° and 75°. Give them diffused or filtered sunlight or 1,500 to 2,000 foot-candles of artificial light for 14 to 16 hours a day. Provide humidity of 50 to 60 per cent. Though they are naturally tree-growing, braided orchids under cultivation do best planted in pots containing a mixture of 7 parts fir bark, 1 part redwood bark, 1 part perlite and 1 part coarse peat moss. Because lockhartias do not have water-storing pseudobulbs, they need to be kept evenly moist but not soggy throughout the year. Feed them during active growth at every third watering with a high-nitrogen fertilizer such as 30-10-10 diluted to half the recommended strength.

Repot lockhartia when the plant begins to climb out of the pot or when the potting mixture begins to deteriorate and drains poorly. Choose a time when the plant is beginning to show new growth at the end of its period of dormancy. Propagate new plants by cutting and rooting sections of the stems or by dividing stem clusters. Such division will inhibit flowering for a time, but so will excessively large clusters.

LUDISIA DISCOLOR See *Haemaria*

LYCASTE
Lyc. aromatica; Lyc. virginalis, also called *Lyc. skinneri*

As many as 10 flower spikes at a time, each bearing a single waxy blossom, may grow from a single pesudobulb of

BRAIDED ORCHID
Lockhartia acuta

this deciduous, tree-dwelling orchid. A plant may continue to flower over several months. Lycaste orchid's sepals bend back from a tulip-like cup formed in the center by the petals and lip; the petals are often darker in color than the sepals. The spring-blooming *Lyc. aromatica* produces 2- to 3-inch blossoms with deep yellow petals, lighter yellow sepals, and lips spotted with orange. The flower stalks are about 6 inches high, and the whole plant is shaded by immense leaves 4 inches wide and up to 18 inches long.

Lyc. virginalis blooms in fall and winter, producing flowers 4 to 6 inches across on 6- to 12-inch stalks. Each blossom is white or pink tinged with rose; the petals are often flushed with a darker tone than the sepals and the lip has purple markings. A variety, *Lyc. virginalis* var. *alba,* called white nun orchid, has a flower that is completely white except for a faint yellow crest on the lip.

HOW TO GROW. Lycaste orchids grow best when they are given filtered sunlight or 1,500 foot-candles of artificial light for 14 to 16 hours daily. They need night temperatures of 50° to 55°, day temperatures of 60° to 70° and humidity between 40 and 60 per cent. Plant them in a mixture of 7 parts fir bark and 1 part redwood bark, 1 part perlite and 1 part coarse peat moss. During active growth keep the mixture evenly moist but not soggy, and fertilize at every third watering with a high-nitrogen fertilizer such as 30-10-10 diluted to half the strength recommended on the label. Discontinue fertilizing when the plant is at rest and allow the medium to remain almost dry until new growth begins. Repot when the medium begins to deteriorate and drains poorly. Propagate new plants as new growth starts, separating pseudobulbs into clusters of three or four.

M

MANDARIN ORCHID See *Phragmipedium*
MEDUSA'S HEAD ORCHID See *Bulbophyllum*

MASDEVALLIA

Masd. bicolor; Masd. chimaera; Masd. coccinea; Masd. erythrochaete; Masd. infracta; Masd. tovarensis

Masdevallias are mostly tree-dwelling plants with fascinating sepals. Far bigger than the rest of the flower, these sepals join to form a tube which often encloses the tiny petals and lip, then separate, spread outward and taper into long tails. The plant's small, thick leaves rise in tufted clumps from an inconspicuous rhizome, and its flower stalks develop at the plant base, each usually carrying one flower at a time. *Masd. bicolor,* with orange-yellow tails and an erect purple lip, usually blooms in winter, though flowers may appear off and on throughout the year. A small species, its flowers are 1 to 1½ inches long and its leaves are only 2 to 2½ inches tall. *Masd. chimaera* has a fluted white lip and hairy yellow sepals with red-brown spots. The sepals spread out to form a triangle 8 to 9 inches long, then taper into 3- to 4-inch tails. It blooms from late fall to summer.

Masd. coccinea bears a single 2- to 3-inch waxy crimson flower with joined lower sepals that split into two blunt tails. Leaves are 6 to 9 inches long; the bloom appears in late spring and summer. *Masd. erythrochaete* flowers in the late summer and fall, bearing downy flowers up to 4 inches long that are creamy yellow with red-purple spots; the red-purple tails are 2 inches long. *Masd. infracta* has a yellowish-white slender upper sepal that becomes pale violet where it joins the other, broader sepals; all three sepals have yellowish-white 1½- to 2-inch tails. It flowers in late spring and sum-

Lycaste virginalis

Masdevallia tovarensis

Maxillaria picta

mer. *Masd. tovarensis* blooms in fall and winter, producing two to five pure white, long-lasting flowers on each stalk. The upper sepal is slender; the side sepals are broad and end in short tails that often cross each other below the flower; the entire blossom is 2 inches long.

HOW TO GROW. Masdevallias are best grown in a cool greenhouse. *Masd. bicolor, Masd. coccinea, Masd. chimaera, Masd. erythrochaete* and *Masd. tovarensis* should have night temperatures of 50° to 55° and day temperatures of 60° to 70°; but *Masd. infracta* requires slightly warmer night temperatures of 55° to 60° and day temperatures of 65° to 75°. Give all the masdevallias bright indirect light or curtain-filtered sunlight or 1,500 to 2,500 foot-candles of artificial light spread over a 14 to 16 hour day. Keep the humidity between 50 to 70 per cent.

Plant masdevallias in slatted baskets in osmunda or tree-fern chunks or in pots using a mixture of 7 parts fir bark, 1 part redwood bark, 1 part perlite and 1 part coarse peat moss. Keep the potting mixture evenly moist but never soggy throughout the year. Fertilize potted plants at every third watering with high-nitrogen fertilizer such as 30-10-10, basket plants with a balanced fertilizer such as 18-18-18; either formula should be diluted to half the strength suggested on the label. Repot when the potting mixture begins to deteriorate and drain poorly, when new growth starts. Propagate new plants by dividing clumps.

MAXILLARIA
Max. crassifolia; Max. picta; Max. sanderiana

These tree-dwelling orchids vary widely in their habits of growth: some of them are creeping miniatures, other species are large specimens with flower stalks that grow several feet tall. Many bear striking flowers that are notable for their size, scent or color. And in all species the flower has a distinctive shape, a jawlike lip from which the genus derives its Latin name. *Max. crassifolia* has narrow fleshy leaves, 8 to 15 inches long and 1 to 2 inches wide; they fan out from the tops of tiny pseudobulbs that are less than 2 inches tall. Its ¾-inch-long yellow blossoms are occasionally streaked with purple on the lips. The flowers bloom singly in late summer, or sporadically throughout the year, on stalks that grow 1 to 3 inches long.

The profusely blooming *Max. picta* has clustered pseudobulbs, producing a bushy effect. It has straplike leaves 9 to 15 inches long, and its fragrant flowers, tawny yellow inside and white outside, with purple or red spots, are 2½ inches wide. Blossoms are borne singly on 3- to 4-inch stalks from late winter through early spring. *Max. sanderiana* blooms from summer to fall, producing spectacular 5- to 6-inch-wide white flowers with blood-red markings. The blossoms are produced singly on 3- to 6-inch flower stalks. The solitary leaf is 7 to 12 inches long.

HOW TO GROW. Maxillarias require night temperatures of 55° to 60° and day temperatures of 65° to 75°—except for *Max. sanderiana,* which needs cooler night temperatures (50° to 55°). All species do best when they are given bright indirect sunlight or grown under 1,500 to 3,000 foot-candles of artificial light for 14 to 16 hours daily. Keep the humidity level at 40 to 60 per cent.

Grow maxillaria orchids on slabs of cork bark or tree fern, in baskets filled with osmunda or tree-fern chunks, or pot them in a combination of 7 parts fir bark, 1 part redwood bark, 1 part coarse peat moss and 1 part perlite. During active growth, keep *Max. crassifolia* and *Max. sanderiana* evenly moist but not soggy; allow *Max. picta* to become

PANSY ORCHID
Miltonia roezlii

moderately dry between thorough waterings. Fertilize all species every third watering with a high-nitrogen formula such as 30-10-10 if grown in pots, or a balanced formula such as 18-18-18 if grown on slabs or in baskets. Dilute either formula to half the strength recommended on the label. After the plants have flowered, do not feed, and reduce watering, but do not allow the plants to become completely dry. When new growth appears, resume regular watering and fertilizing. Repot maxillarias just as new growth appears, when plants are overcrowded or when the potting mix begins to deteriorate and drain poorly. Propagate new plants by dividing the pseudobulbs into clumps of three or four.

MILTONIA
Milt. × bluntii; Milt. candida; Milt. cuneata; Milt. roezlii; Milt. spectabilis (all called pansy orchids)

Like their garden namesakes, the tree-dwelling miltonias often have flat open faces and dark butterfly masks. They bloom in loose sprays at the ends of slender flower stalks 6 to 18 inches long, which rise from the bases of the youngest pseudobulbs. Each pseudobulb produces one to three narrow yellowish-green leaves. They flower abundantly and the blossoms last up to a month, or even longer on hybrids. *Milt. × bluntii*, a natural hybrid, blooms in summer and fall, each flower stalk producing one to five white-tinged yellow blossoms, each about 3 inches long, with purple-brown markings at the center and a white lip with a purple base. *Milt. candida* blooms in fall, bearing clusters of three to six 2½-inch brown flowers edged with yellow; its ruffly white lip is blotched with purple. *Milt. cuneata* has brown flowers 2½ to 3 inches wide with yellow tips and square white lips; the individual petals and sepals are slender. The flowers appear in clusters of three to eight in the spring.

Milt. roezlii blooms in the fall and occasionally again in the spring, producing two to five fragrant white flowers 3 to 4 inches long. The blossom has red-purple masklike markings; the lip is flat, two-lobed and has a yellow base. *Milt. spectabilis* is especially valued for its profusion of blossoms, as many as 50 at a time opening simultaneously during the summer and fall. The 2½-inch-wide flowers have creamy white petals and sepals tinged with purple; the wavy lips are rose-purple with deep purple veins. Miltonia species have been bred for a wide range of beautiful hybrids and many have been crossed with such other genera as *Brassia, Cochlioda, Odontoglossum* and *Oncidium*.

HOW TO GROW. Miltonias grow best with intermediate night temperatures of 55° to 60° and day temperatures of 65° to 75° except for *Milt. roezlii*, which needs a day temperature not exceeding 70°. These miltonias need bright indirect or curtain-filtered sunlight or 2,000 to 2,500 foot-candles of artificial light for 14 to 16 hours daily. *Milt. roezlii* requires less light, or 1,000 to 1,500 foot-candles of artificial light. Provide humidity of 40 to 60 per cent.

Pot miltonias in a mixture of 7 parts fir bark, 1 part redwood bark, 1 part perlite and 1 part coarse peat moss. Keep the growing medium moist at all times, watering thoroughly during the hot summer months, but do not let the potting mixture become soggy. At every third watering during the active growing season, fertilize the plants with a nitrogen-rich fertilizer such as 30-10-10 diluted to half the strength recommended on the label. Repot miltonias about every two years when they become overcrowded or when their growing medium begins to deteriorate and drains poorly. Repot just before new growth starts. Propagate at the same time, dividing the clusters of pseudobulbs into groups of three or four.

PANSY ORCHID
Miltonia spectabilis

GOBLIN ORCHID
Mormodes igneum

Mystacidium capense

MOCCASIN FLOWER, PINK See *Cypripedium*

MORMODES
Morm. igneum; Morm. variabilis (both called goblin orchid)

The foliage of this tropical tree-dwelling orchid is fanlike, 12 to 14 inches tall, and is deciduous. The flowers appear after the leaves turn yellow and fall. They rise above the bare pseudobulb on erect flower stalks 2 to 3 feet high and are unusually lurid, with twisted and contorted shapes that give them a goblin-like appearance. They bloom in late winter or spring, bearing flowers that last for about three weeks. *Morm. igneum* bears lightly spotted 1- to 2-inch blossoms of various colors—yellow, olive green, red or golden brown; their fleshy orange lips fold down at the sides, giving them the look of hoods. *Morm. variabilis* has 1½- to 2-inch deep-pink flowers with lighter pink lips that curl under at the front and back.

HOW TO GROW. Mormodes orchids do best when they are given bright indirect sunlight or 1,500 to 2,500 foot-candles of artificial light for 14 to 16 hours daily; if they are given direct sunlight, as in a window with a western exposure, plants must be shaded during the brightest part of the day. A night temperature of 60° and day temperatures of 65° to 75° are ideal, although the plants will tolerate winter night temperatures as low as 55°. Humidity should be maintained at 50 to 60 per cent; do not mist the plants, for their pseudobulbs rot easily.

Pot mormodes in a mixture of 7 parts fir bark to 1 part redwood bark, 1 part coarse peat moss and 1 part perlite; or grow on slabs of cork bark or tree fern. After potting, water the plants sparingly until the roots are established, then keep the growing medium evenly moist, but do not let it become soggy. Fertilize every third watering with a high-nitrogen formula such as 30-10-10 if the orchids are grown in pots, or a balanced formula such as 18-18-18 if grown on slabs. Dilute either formula to half the strength recommended on the label. When the leaves start to wither, water only enough to prevent the pseudobulbs from shriveling and discontinue fertilizing. Once the flower spikes appear, resume normal watering and feeding. If new leaves do not form when the flowers have faded, reduce water again until signs of growth appear. Repot every two to three years in the spring. Propagate new plants by dividing the pseudobulbs either singly or in clumps of two or three.

MOTH ORCHID See *Phalaenopsis*

MYSTACIDIUM
M. capense

This tree-dwelling miniature has a short, stout stem with narrow leathery leaves 2 to 3 inches long. In spring and summer it sends out arching flower stalks from which grow as many as 20 perfumed waxy white flowers, each 1 inch wide. The slender sepals and petals and a somewhat wider lip are all pointed, and the spur, a characteristic of this orchid, is almost 2 inches long.

HOW TO GROW. Mystacidium orchids need bright indirect or filtered sunlight or 1,500 to 2,500 foot-candles of artificial light for 14 to 16 hours a day. Warm night temperatures of 60° to 65° and day temperatures between 70° and 85° are best for this plant, although it tolerates slightly cooler temperatures. Provide a humidity of 50 to 60 per cent. Pot in a mixture of 7 parts fir bark, 1 part redwood bark, 1 part perlite and 1 part coarse peat moss. After potting, water very little until the roots are established. Then, during the active growing season, water generously, keeping the bark mixture evenly moist. With every third watering feed plants with a high-nitrogen fertilizer such as 30-10-10 diluted to half the strength recommended on the label.

After the plant has flowered, discontinue fertilizing and allow the growing medium to become somewhat dry but not completely so. Resume regular watering and fertilizing once leaf growth begins. Repot only when the growing medium becomes deteriorated and drains poorly. Propagate by severing the stem when there is enough root growth along it for each division to have at least four roots of its own.

MYSTACIDIUM DISTICHUM See *Angraecum*

N

NECKLACE ORCHID See *Dendrochilum*

NEOFINETIA

Neof. falcata, also called *Angraecum falcatum* (samurai orchid)

This tiny tropical tree-growing orchid has a stem only 2 to 2½ inches tall with alternating pairs of 3-inch leathery leaves. During summer and autumn, 3- to 4-inch flower stalks bear clusters of three to seven waxy white flowers 1 to 1¼ inches in diameter; each blossom has slender sepals and petals, a triangular lip and a curving 1½-inch-long spur. The flowers are especially fragrant at night.

HOW TO GROW. Neofinetia grows best when it is given bright indirect or filtered sunlight or from 1,500 to 2,500 foot-candles of artificial light for 14 to 16 hours a day. It requires intermediate night temperatures between 55° and 60° and day temperatures between 65° and 75°. Maintain humidity at 40 to 50 per cent.

Plant these orchids in a mixture of 7 parts fir bark, 1 part redwood bark, 1 part perlite and 1 part coarse peat moss. After potting, water the plants very little until roots are established. During active growth, keep the mixture evenly moist and fertilize the plants at every third watering with a high-nitrogen fertilizer such as 30-10-10 diluted to half the strength recommended on the label. After flowering, reduce the amount of water without allowing the potting mixture to become completely dry; do not fertilize. Resume regular watering and fertilizing as soon as leaf growth begins. Train aerial roots into the pot by moistening and bending them into the growing mixture. Repot only when the medium begins to decompose. Propagate by dividing offshoots when the offshoots have developed enough to show their own roots.

NOTYLIA

N. barkeri; N. xyphophorous

These miniature, mainly tree-dwelling orchids are prized for their long, dangling chains of tiny flowers with triangular lips. *N. barkeri,* the larger of these two species, bears ½-inch white blossoms on flower stalks 8 to 12 inches long during the spring. The 1-inch-high pseudobulb produces a single leathery 6-inch leaf. *N. xyphophorous* produces pale purple flowers less than ½ inch wide on 1- to 2-inch stalks during the late summer. The pseudobulb is either short or nonexistent and the leaves, which are only 1 inch long, are prickly, like cactus, and open into a fan.

HOW TO GROW. Notylias require a high humidity of 70 to 75 per cent, especially in summer, and therefore they are best suited to greenhouse cultivation. They need dim indirect or filtered sunlight; if they are grown under artificial

SAMURAI ORCHID
Neofinetia falcata

Notylia barkeri

TIGER ORCHID
Odontoglossum grande

COLOMBIA BUTTERCUP
Oncidium cheirophorum

light they should receive 1,000 to 1,500 foot-candles of light for 14 to 16 hours a day. They require intermediate night temperatures between 55° and 60° and day temperatures between 65° and 75°.

Mount them on slabs of tree fern or cork bark, or pot them in a mixture of 7 parts of fir bark, 1 part redwood bark, 1 part perlite and 1 part coarse peat moss. Keep the growing medium evenly moist throughout the year, and at every third watering fertilize potted plants with a high-nitrogen fertilizer such as 30-10-10; give a balanced 18-18-18 formula to plants that are mounted on slabs. Dilute either formula to half the strength recommended on the label. These plants tend to flower more profusely when they are grown singly in small pots, but this means that they need to be repotted annually instead of every two or three years. Propagate additional plants at the start of new growth by dividing plants into clumps of three or four pseudobulbs.

NUN ORCHID, WHITE See *Lycaste*
NUN'S ORCHID See *Phaius*

O

ODONTOGLOSSUM

Odm. grande (tiger orchid); *Odm. pulchellum* (lily-of-the-valley orchid)

Odontoglossums are evergreen orchids with smooth, bright green pseudobulbs, each with two leaves emerging from the apex. The flowers are white or blends of yellow, brown, bright red or purple, and grow on elegantly arching stems. Ruffled sepals and petals and toothlike projections on the lips are characteristics of most of these flowers. Both the tiger orchid, *Odm. grande,* and the lily-of-the-valley orchid, *Odm. pulchellum,* are as hardy as they are beautiful, and can be easily grown by beginners.

The striped tiger orchid, *Odm. grande,* grows up to 20 inches tall, producing three to seven flowers, each 6 inches in diameter. Waxy long slender sepals are yellow barred with brown; petals are brown with yellow on the ends. The rounded lip is white, or white tinged with yellow, with brown specklings. It blooms from fall through spring.

Lily-of-the-valley orchid, *Odm. pulchellum,* is named for both its appearance and its fragrance. It grows up to 10 inches tall; the 1- to 2-inch waxy white flowers are borne in slender sprays. These graceful flowers are long-lived and bloom in the winter and spring.

HOW TO GROW. Both of these species require filtered or indirect sunlight; the thin leaves can be scorched by direct sunlight. If grown under artificial light, *Odm. grande* needs 2,000 to 3,500 foot-candles for 14 to 16 hours a day, *Odm. pulchellum* 1,500 to 2,000 foot-candles. Intermediate temperatures are needed, ranging from 55° to 60° at night and between 65° and 70° in the daytime. Pot in a mixture of 7 parts fir bark to 1 part redwood bark, 1 part perlite and 1 part peat moss. Feed with a high-nitrogen fertilizer such as 30-10-10 during the active growing period at every third watering, diluting the fertilizer to half the strength recommended on the label. Keep the potting mix moist but not soggy at all times and maintain humidity at 40 to 60 per cent. To propagate, divide and repot annually in the spring, placing at least three pseudobulbs in each pot.

ONCIDIUM

Onc. ampliatum (turtle orchid, yellow bee orchid); *Onc. cheirophorum* (Colombia buttercup); *Onc. jonesianum; Onc.*

lanceanum; Onc. papilio (butterfly orchid); *Onc. pulchellum; Onc. pusillum; Onc. sphacelatum* (golden shower orchid); *Onc. splendidum* (dancing-lady orchid); *Onc. stramineum*

Most oncidiums produce showers of up to 100 bright, sunny blossoms on long, arching flower stalks. These are known as "dancing ladies" for their flickering forms. In the wild, several hundred species range from tropical river valleys to mountain peaks. Primarily tree dwellers, they sometimes spread to create large treetop colonies. The flowers vary greatly except for one feature: the base of the lip always runs perpendicular to the short, winged column.

The turtle orchid, *Onc. ampliatum,* named for the shape of the pseudobulbs that grow flat against the tree, has one to three leathery leaves, up to 15 inches long, growing from the apex of the pseudobulb. An erect or arching stalk bears a spray of 1-inch flowers up to 4 feet long mostly in the spring. The spreading petals and sepals are yellow with reddish-brown spots; the very large lip has three lobes. *Onc. cheirophorum,* a dwarf plant, has flattened, oval pseudobulbs up to 1½ inches long and 1 inch wide. They wrinkle with age. Leaves are thin and short. In autumn and winter, fragrant lemon-scented yellow flowers, up to ½ inch in diameter, bloom in a dense spray.

Onc. jonesianum has long, tapering cylindrical leaves that resemble those of an onion plant. In the fall, a 2-foot stalk bears 10 to 15 ruffled flowers 2 to 3 inches across; they are cream colored with scattered reddish-brown spots. The divided lip is very broad and has two brilliant yellow ears. *Onc. lanceanum* has very small pseudobulbs but heavy rhizomes. The burro-eared leaves—stiff, leathery and wide—grow up to 20 inches long. In summer 1½-foot branching stalks bear 2- to 3-inch scented flowers whose sepals and petals are yellow with brown spots and have slightly ruffled edges; the long two-lobed lip is magenta or rosy purple.

The butterfly orchid, *Onc. papilio,* which was first shown in England in 1823, is said to have roused a worldwide passion for orchids. This plant is one of the few oncidiums that blooms a single flower at a time, the flowers appearing in succession throughout most of the year. Displayed at the top of a 4-foot stalk, the butterfly orchid blossom's top two petals and one sepal rise like long yellow-and-brown antennae above the rest of the flower. The other two sepals curve downward and are banded and ruffled; the lip is heart shaped and full. *Onc. pulchellum* has no pseudobulbs; its leaves overlap each other to form a fan, much like those of an iris. The leaves are vaguely toothed on the edges, fleshy, rigid and pointed, reaching a length of 3 to 5 inches. In spring and summer, slender branched 15-inch stalks support sprays of 1-inch flowers. Small wedge-shaped sepals and petals, generally white tinged with rose or lilac, contrast with a large skirtlike lip.

Onc. pusillum bears leaves in a spreading fan shape. A stalk grows between folds in the leaves and brings forth five or six bright yellow flowers one after the other through the year. A long, erect top sepal with narrow ones on the sides distinguish this flower; the spreading petals sometimes have bars of reddish-brown. The center of the lip is blotched with brown, and the white column often has orange spots. *Onc. sphacelatum* is notable for a branching flower stalk that can grow as long as 5 feet, bearing great numbers of 1-inch brown-and-golden-yellow blossoms in spring. A fiddle-shaped lip graces each of these flowers.

Onc. splendidum is another species of the burro-eared group; it has a single 12-inch leaf growing from the apex of each pseudobulb. Erect flower spikes, up to 3 feet tall, bloom

Oncidium jonesianum

BUTTERFLY ORCHID
Oncidium papilio

Oncidium pusillum

in spring and early summer. On the 2- to 3-inch bright yellow flowers, both sepals and petals are blotched with reddish-brown; a large lip flares out from a narrow midsection, a vivid golden yellow. *Onc. stramineum,* small and burro-eared with 6- to 8-inch leaves, produces dense, pendant sprays of many tiny flowers in spring. White or straw-colored, these have slightly cupped sepals and petals so the whole flower is rounded in appearance.

HOW TO GROW. Oncidiums grow best in bright sun except at midday, or in 2,000 to 3,500 foot-candles of artificial light spread over a 14 to 16 hour day. These plants require an intermediate temperature level, between 55° and 60° during the night and between 65° and 75° in the daytime. Maintain humidity between 40 per cent and 60 per cent. Plant oncidiums in a mixture of 7 parts fir bark to 1 part redwood bark, 1 part perlite and 1 part coarse peat moss, or mount them on slabs of cork bark or tree fern. Adjust watering to the plant's growth cycle, giving it more water during the growing and flowering season and less at other times of the year. Wait until the bark feels dry underneath the surface, then water thoroughly. Fertilize during active growth every third watering, using a high-nitrogen formula such as 30-10-10 for potted plants, or a balanced formula such as 18-18-18 for slab-mounted plants; dilute either formula to half the strength recommended on the label. Propagate new plants by dividing into clumps of at least four pseudobulbs each.

ORNITHOCEPHALUS
O. bicornis (bird's-head orchid)

This dwarf species is called bird's-head orchid because the pollen-bearing column looks like the head of a bird with a long beak. Small bees pollinate the tiny flowers, and the odd shape of the column helps the bees do their work. Flexible stalks, 1 to 6 inches long, bear the cup-shaped flowers, which are sheathed at their bases by tiny modified leaves called bracts. The true leaves are fleshy and grow in stiff gray-green fans up to 3½ inches long. Usually the flower spike of this tree-dweller hangs downward, but it may grow upright or sideways. A tropical plant, it generally blooms twice a year in spring and fall. Its many pearly flowers, ¼ inch across, are either white with a greenish tinge or pale yellow-green. The green lips are fleshy.

HOW TO GROW. This easy-to-grow miniature needs intermediate to warm temperatures, 55° to 60° at night and 65° to 75° in the daytime. Indirect sunlight, the equivalent of 1,000 to 1,500 foot-candles, suits them best. Keep humidity at 40 to 60 per cent. Grow in a potting mixture of 7 parts fir bark to 1 part redwood bark, 1 part perlite and 1 part coarse peat moss, or mount on cork bark or tree-fern slabs. Susceptible to root rot, these plants should be kept moist but not wet; good drainage is essential. If the plant is potted, use a high-nitrogen fertilizer, such as 30-10-10 formulated for orchids, diluted to half the strength recommended on the label, applied with every third watering. If the plant is on a slab, use a balanced fertilizer such as 18-18-18, also diluted to half the recommended strength, at the same frequency. If accessory leaf fans appear, you can remove and repot them as soon as they have established roots.

P

PANSY ORCHID See *Miltonia*

PAPHIOPEDILUM
Paph. bellatulum; Paph. chamberlainianum; Paph. F. C.

BIRD'S-HEAD ORCHID
Ornithocephalus bicornis

Puddle; *Paph. fairrieanum; Paph.* Hellas 'Westonbirt'; *Paph. insigne; Paph.* Maudiae 'Magnificum'; *Paph.* McLaren Park; *Paph. niveum; Paph. spicerianum; Paph. sukhakulii; Paph. venustum* (all called lady's-slipper orchids)

Most of these Asiatic earth-dwelling orchids are at home on shaded mountain ledges or on the forest floor and therefore adapt well to indoor light and temperature conditions; only a few require the warmth and light of a greenhouse. The leaves are fleshy; those of warm-growing species often are mottled green, while the leaves of cool-growing plants are usually plain green. The flowers grow singly or in clusters on hairy stalks of varying lengths. Blossoms are typically combinations of strong colors, and each has a large top sepal standing high and wide over a slipper-shaped lip, or pouch. The remaining petals spread stiffly to the sides or droop slightly downward; the two other sepals are frequently joined behind the lip. *Paph. bellatulum* has mottled green leaves 6 to 10 inches long with purple underneath; in spring it produces 2½-inch flowers, white to pale yellow with purplish spots. The top sepal and petals are similar in shape, wide and only slightly pointed at the tips.

Paph. chamberlainianum may bloom year round. Its pale green leaves are up to 12 inches long, rather blunt at the tips, and its flower stalk rises 1½ feet, producing four to eight flowers in succession over a long period. The blossom has an upper round sepal that is yellowish-green with brown markings; the petals, twisting and undulating, are greenish-rose and speckled with small brown spots; the pouch is green spotted with red. The hybrid *Paph.* F. C. Puddle has very subtle mottling on the 5-inch leaves, which at first seem solid dusty green. The 3-inch flower is a glistening white with the faintest yellow veining; its top sepal and petals are softly undulating, while the surface of the egg-shaped pouch is smooth. This hybrid blooms twice a year, in early winter and irregularly thereafter.

Paph. fairrieanum is characterized by pale green leaves and a single 2½-inch flower, which is white or green-white veined with purple. The upper sepal undulates high and wide above the curving petals. A network of purple veins covering the pouch resembles the markings of a briar pipe. The plant blooms in fall. *Paph.* Hellas 'Westonbirt,' another hybrid, has solid green leaves about 7 inches long and a single light-amber flower measuring 4 inches across, blooming generally in winter. Both the top sepal and the inward-curving petals are marked with brown-orange veining.

Paph. insigne has 8- to 12-inch-long pale green leaves and produces four or five flowers, one per stalk, notable for their glistening surfaces; it blooms from autumn to early spring. The top sepal is narrow at the base but flares out widely at its undulating white tip; below the tip it is green with brown-purple spots. The fused lower sepals behind the pouch are smaller and pale green in color. The spreading petals twist slightly and droop downward; they are yellow-green with brown veins. The pouch is similarly marked.

In the hybrid *Paph.* Maudiae 'Magnificum,' the leaves are mottled and the solitary 3- to 4-inch flower, which blooms in the winter and irregularly thereafter, has a rounded upper sepal, white or pale green with green veins. The petals are green, blending into white at the tips, and the pouch is pale green. *Paph.* McLaren Park, also a hybrid, has 7- to 8-inch green leaves and a greenish-yellow blossom, 4 inches across, with a chartreuse pouch. It blooms during late fall or winter.

Paph. niveum has 4- to 6-inch mottled gray-green leaves, which are dark purple on the undersides. On erect stalks from 6 to 8 inches tall, its one or two small snowy-white

LADY'S-SLIPPER ORCHID
Paphiopedilum bellatulum

LADY'S-SLIPPER ORCHID
Paphiopedilum chamberlainianum

LADY'S-SLIPPER ORCHID
Paphiopedilum F. C. Puddle

LADY'S-SLIPPER ORCHID
Paphiopedilum sukhakulii

blossoms with slightly ruffled edges flower in the spring. The upper sepal and petals of each flower are marked with minute purple dots on the front, toward the base, and are red to purple in back. The sepal curves inward, while the rounded petals curve back.

Paph. spicerianum, with dark green 6- to 9-inch leaves, produces a solitary flower 3 inches wide in autumn and early winter. The upper sepal is high, curving backward to form two floating white butterfly wings; a crimson band streaks the center, and the slender base is green spotted with red. The narrow petals are pale green spotted and striped with purple and curve over a purple, green-edged pouch. *Paph. sukhakulii,* a species that was first described botanically in 1967, has mottled foliage about 5 inches long. The green-and-white upper sepal is sharply ribbed and pointed; the wide-spreading flat petals are speckled with red. The lip is rose-purple. This species blooms in the fall.

Paph. venustum has mottled gray-green leaves 4 to 6 inches long, which are purple on the underside. In winter and early spring it bears a solitary flower 3 inches wide. The rounded upper sepal is white with green veins; the spreading petals are green, darkened with blackish warts near the margins and with purple at the tips; the pale yellowish-green pouch is tinged with rose and veined with green.

HOW TO GROW. Green-leaved paphiopedilums need night temperatures of 50° to 55° and day temperatures of 60° to 70°, but mottled-leaved plants need warmer night temperatures of 60° to 65° and day temperatures of 70° to 80°. (The two types will adjust when grown together.) These low-light orchids require indirect sunlight except for the direct sun of very early morning, or 800 to 900 foot-candles of artificial light from spring through fall, raised to 1,000 to 1,500 foot-candles in the winter. Humidity of 40 to 60 per cent is sufficient. Grow paphiopedilums in a mixture of 8 parts fine fir bark to 2 parts fine gravel. Add a pinch of ground limestone to each pot to reduce acidity. Water thoroughly and keep the mixture damp but not wet; paphiopedilums' intake of water will vary according to the species, temperature and time of the year.

Fertilize the plants at every fourth watering, using a high-nitrogen fertilizer, such as 30-10-10, diluted to one half the strength recommended on the label. If the leaf tips turn brown, fertilize the orchids less frequently. When the plant has outgrown its pot or when the growing medium begins to deteriorate and drain poorly, repot just after flowering, breaking the plant into groups of three or four leaf clusters each and potting them separately.

PHAIUS
Phaius tankervilliae, also called *Phaius grandifolius* (nun's orchid)

These orchids produce brilliantly colored flowers in combinations of yellow, white and red, often as large as 4 inches across, growing on a single stalk. Blossoms are characterized by tubular lips. Most species are earth dwellers, found in swampy soil, but some are tree-growing. The plants are notable for their leaves as well as flowers, since they may become 3 feet tall and add a tropical touch to a greenhouse or to a garden in a warm climate. Nun's orchid has short egg-shaped pseudobulbs; heavy, folded 3-foot leaves; and a 4-foot flower spike that bears 10 to 20 fragrant flowers in spring and summer. The sepals and petals are white on the outside and reddish inside, with yellow edges. Ruffled and tubular, with a short spur, the lip is white; it has a yellow throat and sides colored dark burgundy and purple.

HOW TO GROW. Intermediate to warm temperatures suit the nun's orchid. In winter it grows well if it is given temperatures of 65° to 75° in the daytime and 55° to 60° at night; in summer, if kept moist and shaded, it adjusts to higher temperatures. Provide filtered sunlight or 1,000 to 1,500 foot-candles of artificial light for 14 to 16 hours daily, with humidity of 40 to 60 per cent or higher. Pot plants in a mixture of 2 parts coarse peat moss, 2 parts sandy loam and 1 part each perlite and fine fir bark; this terrestrial plant requires liberal watering with good drainage. Fertilize the plants at every third watering with a balanced orchid fertilizer, such as 18-18-18, diluted to half the strength recommended on the label. Repot phaius orchids every two or three years. To propagate additional plants, divide plants at the end of a growing season so that you can place at least three pseudobulbs in each pot. Alternatively, after flowering has stopped, cut the flower stalks into 6-inch pieces, each with at least two jointlike nodes. Place these cuttings on moist sand to root.

PHALAENOPSIS

Phal. Alice Gloria; *Phal. cornu-cervi; Phal.* Diane Rigg 'Pink Mist'; *Phal. equestris,* also called *Phal. rosea; Phal.* Golden Sands 'Canary'; *Phal. lueddemanniana; Phal. mannii; Phal. parishii; Phal.* Peppermint; *Phal. stuartiana; Phal. violacea* (all called moth orchids)

The blossoms of the tropical, tree-dwelling phalaenopsises seem to hover like moths high in the branches of trees, mostly in the Philippines, Malaysia and Indonesia. Some species are found near the seacoast; others grow at higher altitudes near mountain streams. They are notable for their long, tenacious roots, which cling not only to trees but to the root systems of other tree-dwelling plants. The leaves vary widely in size and in color. The flowers are generally flat, with delicate three-lobed lips, and grow on long stalks in sprays of about 20 flowers. Species with white blossoms generally grow on unbranching stalks, but some colored species bloom in branching sprays.

Phalaenopsis species are generally divided into two groups for identification purposes. In group I the petals are broader than the sepals, and there are appendages on the lips; in group II, the petals and sepals are equal in size, and the lips have no appendages. Many hybrids have been developed within the phalaenopsis genus, which also can be crossed successfully with many other genera.

The hybrid *Phal.* Alice Gloria, group I, has unusually beautiful 4-inch white flowers, which grow 12 to 20 to a stalk. The petals are spreading, with rounded edges; the sepals are narrower and pointed. The lips are flecked with yellow and have delicate appendages flaring out. This hybrid blooms in winter and spring.

Phal. cornu-cervi, group II, has leathery green leaves less than 1 foot long and a flattened flower stalk. In greenhouses it blooms throughout the year, producing waxy flowers, one or more at a time, of greenish-yellow streaked with brown; the lip is white. *Phal.* Diane Rigg 'Pink Mist' bears up to nine 4-inch pink flowers at one time, the lower sepals spotted with a darker pink and the lip a dark rose; it flowers in the spring. *Phal. equestris,* group II, produces small green leaves that are notched at the end. Its flowers bloom several times a year on arching stalks up to 12 inches long. Each stalk bears 10 to 15 blossoms, which open successively, and each blossom is about 1 inch across, with rose-purple sepals and petals; the latter may be edged with white. The middle lobe of the lip is brown and has bright purple and rose

NUN'S ORCHID
Phaius tankervilliae

MOTH ORCHID
Phalaenopsis Alice Gloria

MOTH ORCHID
Phalaenopsis mannii

MOTH ORCHID
Phalaenopsis parishii

markings; the side lobes are pink. This species is a favorite plant for hybridization.

The hybrid *Phal.* Golden Sands 'Canary,' group I, bears eight to 12 flowers, 3¾ inches across, which are buttercup yellow to lime-yellow speckled with rose and have very dark yellow-orange lips. The entire flower is flat in form, with rounded, spreading petals and sepals. It blooms from spring to fall. *Phal. lueddemanniana,* group II, has rigid bright yellow-green leaves up to 10 inches long and over 30 different color variations in the flowers. Usually under 2 inches wide and growing two to seven on a stalk, the flowers bloom in spring, are very fragrant and last as long as two months. Many are in shades of rose-purple, sometimes with emphatic white stripes; others are commonly cream to yellow, mottled or barred with brown. The lip of this species has erect side lobes with two tips; the middle lobe is often brilliant amethyst with pale edges and white bristles. After pollination, the entire flower turns green.

Phal. mannii, group II, has leaves up to 10 inches long varying on each plant from flaccid to rigid. Each flower stalk produces 10 to 15 flowers any time from spring to fall. Each flower is 1½ inches across with slender yellow petals and sepals that are spotted and barred with brown; the anchor-shaped lip is white, often with purple markings. This species was important in the creation of the first yellow hybrids. *Phal. parishii,* group I, is a small spring-blooming plant with dark green oval leaves only 2 to 4 inches long. Its ¾-inch flowers, which are borne on 3- to 4-inch stalks, are white except for the middle lobe of their crescent-shaped lips, which are white banded with brown.

The hybrid *Phal.* Peppermint, group I, has broad gray-green leaves mottled dark green on the upper surface and purple underneath; they are about 12 inches long. The 2-inch-wide flowers, blooming on 24- to 30-inch stalks in winter and spring, have pale pink sepals and petals striped with bright rose, and a brilliant candy-pink lip.

The gray-green leaves of *Phal. stuartiana,* in group I, are somewhat flaccid, mottled with silver-gray on top and often with magenta underneath; they are 12 to 18 inches long. The flowers, which bloom from fall to spring, are borne on 24-inch branching stalks. They have white sepals and petals; those close to the lip are yellow with red speckles. The horn-tipped lip is golden yellow edged with white and dotted with purple. *Phal. violacea,* group II, has shiny leaves. One form, which comes from Borneo, has pale 2½-inch green flowers with purple lips; the lateral sepals curve inward. Another, from Malaya, is purple-pink with spreading lateral sepals 1½ to 2 inches long. There is also a pure white Malayan variety. *Phal. violacea* blooms in the spring and summer and sometimes in other seasons.

HOW TO GROW. Phalaenopsises grow best in night temperatures between 60° and 65° and from 70° to 85° during the day. Although they can stand temperatures of above 90° for short periods of time, they should be protected from excessive summer heat. Give them indirect sunlight or from 1,000 to 1,500 foot-candles of artificial light for 14 to 16 hours daily. Keep humidity between 50 and 70 per cent.

Plant phalaenopsises in pots or mount them on slabs of cork bark or tree fern. For potted plants, use a mixture of 7 parts fir bark, 1 part redwood bark, 1 part perlite and 1 part coarse peat moss. Keep the mixture barely damp until roots are established. Then water thoroughly, allowing the planting medium to become nearly dry between waterings. Fertilize potted phalaenopsises at every third watering with a high-nitrogen fertilizer such as 30-10-10; for mounted plants use a balanced fertilizer such as 18-18-18. Dilute both to half the strength recommended on the label. In general, phalaenopsises should be repotted only when the potting mixture begins to deteriorate and drains poorly; the plant grows best in containers that seem rather small for its size. Repot when the flowering season has finished, just as new roots are developing. Propagate by means of plantlets that sometimes form along its flower stalk.

PHRAGMIPEDIUM
Phrag. caudatum var. *sanderae* (mandarin, Fu Manchu or slipper orchid); *Phrag. schlimii* (slipper orchid)

These tropical earth-growing plants are unusual for their strange colors and shapes. Both species bear clusters of strap-shaped leaves and blossoms with slipper-like lips. *Phrag. caudatum* var. *sanderae* has half a dozen leaves up to 2 feet long arching upward from the base. Its flower stalks, 1 to 2 feet tall, bear one to four blossoms with spiraled ribbon-like petals up to 2½ feet long. Yellow for the most part, the petals are shaded with brown, especially near the tips, while the lip ranges from yellow to reddish-brown with purple veins and brownish-purple hairs fringing the opening. The flowers appear from spring through fall. *Phrag. schlimii* has leaves up to a foot long that are green on top and purple underneath and greenish-purple flower stalks. It bears five to eight 1½-inch flowers on stalks that grow up to 2 feet tall. The blossoms, which are covered by a velvety down, are white stained with pink. The lips are rose streaked with white. This orchid may bloom twice a year, first in the spring and again in autumn.

HOW TO GROW. These plants will thrive in intermediate night temperatures between 55° and 60° and day temperatures of 65° to 75°. Give them medium indirect sunlight or 1,500 to 2,000 foot-candles of artificial light for 14 to 16 hours a day. Keep humidity between 50 and 60 per cent. Grow plants in a mixture of 8 parts fine fir bark and 2 parts fine gravel, plus a pinch of ground limestone to lower the acidity of the mix. Since neither plant has water-storing pseudobulbs, keep the mixture damp at all times, but be careful not to let water stand around the roots or at the base of the foliage. Fertilize at every third watering, using a high-nitrogen formula such as 30-10-10 diluted to half the strength recommended on the label. Repot in the spring. Propagate after plants bloom by dividing the leaf fans, with three or four new growths in each division.

PINK LADY'S SLIPPER See *Cypripedium*
PINK MOCCASIN FLOWER See *Cypripedium*
PLATYCLINIS FILIFORMIS See *Dendrochilum*

PLEIONE
Pln. maculata; Pln. praecox

The growth cycle of earth-dwelling pleione is unique, occurring in two stages. Each pseudobulb lasts only a year, bearing one or more folded leaves, 6 to 12 inches long. At the end of the year the leaves fall, and the pseudobulb is dormant until a new shoot sprouts from its base. This new shoot sends forth both roots and a flower stalk, and then rests after flowering until the following season, when a second shoot forms a new pseudobulb and leaves, and the whole cycle is repeated. *Pln. maculata* produces two fragrant white flowers 2 inches across on each 3- to 6-inch stalk and blooms in the fall. The petals are often streaked with purple and the side lobes of the lips often have purple spots. *Pln. praecox* bears one or two fragrant rose-purple blossoms on each 3- to

MANDARIN ORCHID
Phragmipedium caudatum var. *sanderae*

Pleione praecox

Pleurothallis grobyi

Polystachya luteola

4-inch stalk and also blooms in the fall. The lip of each blossom ends in a frilly edge.

HOW TO GROW. Pleione orchids grow best in cool greenhouse temperatures of 50° to 55° at night and 60° to 70° in the daytime, with humidity maintained close to 70 per cent. They need bright indirect or filtered sunlight or between 1,500 and 3,000 foot-candles of artificial light for 14 to 16 hours daily. Grow them in a mixture of 2 parts coarse peat moss, 2 parts sandy loam, 1 part perlite and 1 part fine fir bark. Water the plants liberally during active growth, then sparingly after flowering. At every third watering, fertilize with a balanced formula such as 18-18-18 diluted to half the strength recommended on the label. Repot when necessary after the flowers fade.

PLEUROTHALLIS
P. grobyi; P. rubens

More than a thousand species are found in this large and varied genus of New World orchids. All are multistemmed, growing not from pseudobulbs but rather from slender stems that grow out of primary horizontal stems. At the top of each secondary stem is a solitary leaf, and flowers rise from the leaf base. Most are tree dwelling, but they range in size from low-growing mosslike plants to bushy plants several feet high. The flowers are also variable in form, but usually the sepals are larger than the petals. *P. grobyi* has almost no stem and its leathery leaves with purple undersides are less than 3 inches long. The flower stalk is dull red, 5 inches tall, and bears widely spaced ¼-inch green-white or yellow flowers, often marked with red-purple stripes. The flowers bloom in spring and summer. *P. rubens,* another small species, produces slender sprays of ¼-inch yellow flowers that grow only from one side of the stem, like lilies-of-the-valley. The plant is 6 inches tall, with 4-inch leaves, and it too flowers in spring and summer.

HOW TO GROW. These two species of pleurothallis grow best in night temperatures of 55° to 60° and day temperatures of 65° to 75°. Keep them in semishade or grow them under 1,000 to 1,500 foot-candles of artificial light for 14 to 16 hours daily. Maintain humidity of 40 to 60 per cent. Grow in a mixture of 7 parts fir bark, 1 part redwood bark, 1 part perlite and 1 part coarse peat moss; or mount plants on slabs of cork bark or tree fern. Water liberally during active growth, and somewhat less afterward, never allowing the medium to dry out. At every third watering, fertilize pot-grown plants with a high-nitrogen formula such as 30-10-10 diluted to half the strength recommended on the label; for plants mounted on slabs use a balanced fertilizer such as 18-18-18, also diluted to half the recommended strength.

Repot as new growth starts only if necessary to relieve crowding or to change potting mixture that has begun to deteriorate and drain poorly. Propagate by dividing plants, allowing four or more leaves per division.

PLEUROTHALLIS GUTTULATA See *Restrepia*
PLEUROTHALLIS OSPINAE See *Restrepia*

POLYSTACHYA
Pol. luteola; Pol. pubescens

Although the flowers of tree-dwelling polystachyas come in many combinations of colors, one characteristic is common to most of them: the lip is at the top of the flower and opens downward, and the sepals swell around it to form a shielding hood. On most species the foliage is bright yellow-green. *Pol. luteola* produces leaves that may grow to 12 inches long out of pseudobulbs no more than ½ inch tall. Its fragrant ¼- to ½-inch-wide yellow-green flowers are borne in clusters of two to eight on 6- to 10-inch stalks. They may bloom year round. *Pol. pubescens* also has small pseudobulbs, but its leaves are only 3 to 4 inches long. The flower stalk rises no more than 5 inches, and in late spring 12 to 20 bright yellow bearded flowers, each ¾ inch across, form a cluster on top. Both sepals and lips are streaked with red.

HOW TO GROW. Polystachyas grow best when they are given intermediate night temperatures between 55° and 60° and day temperatures between 65° and 75°. Give them filtered sunlight or from 1,400 to 1,600 foot-candles of artificial light spread over a 14 to 16 hour day. The ideal humidity is 70 per cent, but orchid hobbyists have managed to grow polystachyas under average home conditions, with the humidity level between 40 and 60 per cent.

Grow polystachyas in small pots, using a mixture of 7 parts fir bark, 1 part redwood bark, 1 part perlite and 1 part coarse peat moss; or mount them on slabs of cork bark or tree fern. Keep the medium moist while plants are growing, but allow them to become almost dry when plants are at rest. Fertilize at every third watering with a high-nitrogen formula such as 30-10-10 for a bark mixture or with a balanced formula such as 18-18-18 for slab-mounted plants. Dilute to half the strength recommended on the label. Repot when the growing mixture begins to deteriorate and drain poorly, or when plants become crowded. Propagate when repotting by separating pseudobulbs into groups of three or four.

POTINARA
Pot. Carrousel 'Crimson Triumph'; *Pot.* Gordon Siu 'Red Radiance'

A four-way cross between the popular *Brassavola, Sophronitis, Laelia* and *Cattleya* genera, *Potinara* combines virtues inherited from all of its antecedents. Brassavola contributes a large, very ruffled lip; sophronitis and laelia account for bright and unusual flower tones that range from red to yellow, and laelia further gives this hybrid its free-flowering habit; cattleya determines the size and form of the blossoms and foliage. The plant's fleshy, swollen pseudobulbs sprout along a creeping horizontal stem, or rhizome, producing rather twisted thick leaves 6 to 8 inches long and 3- to 4-inch flower stalks that usually bear three 5-inch blossoms. *Pot.* Carrousel 'Crimson Triumph' blooms from winter to spring and bears clear deep-red blossoms with full lips; *Pot.* Gordon Siu 'Red Radiance' flowers in the spring, and produces red blossoms that have narrow sepals, triangular petals and full, very ruffled lips.

HOW TO GROW. Potinaras grow best when they are given intermediate temperatures of 55° to 60° at night and 65° to 75° during the day. Give the plants indirect or filtered sunlight or illuminate them for 14 to 16 hours a day with 1,500 to 2,500 foot-candles of artificial light. Keep the humidity at 40 to 60 per cent. Grow in a mixture of 7 parts fir bark, 1 part redwood bark, 1 part perlite and 1 part coarse peat moss. During the growing season drench the mixture and allow it to dry out before the next watering. At every third watering, fertilize plants with a nitrogen-rich formula such as 30-10-10 diluted to half the strength recommended on the label. Water less frequently during dormancy, just enough to keep the pseudobulbs from withering, and do not fertilize. Repot just as new growth starts, when plants outgrow the pots or potting mixture begins to deteriorate and drain poorly. Propagate new plants at the same time by dividing into clumps of three or four pseudobulbs each.

Potinara Carrousel 'Crimson Triumph'

Promenaea xanthina

Renanthera imschootiana

PROMENAEA

Prom. xanthina

Promenaea is a miniature tree-dwelling orchid with leaves and flower stalks between 2 and 4 inches long, and flowers proportionately larger, 1½ to 2 inches across. Its leaves grow from rounded pseudobulbs only 1 inch high, and its flower stalks rise from the bases of the pseudobulbs. It blooms in summer, producing one to three fragrant yellow flowers with reddish-brown spotted lips, whose combined weight causes the stalk to bend into an arc.

HOW TO GROW. *Prom. xanthina* requires warm greenhouse temperatures of 60° to 65° at night and 70° to 85° in the daytime, combined with 70 per cent humidity. It grows easily in indirect sunlight or under 1,500 foot-candles of artificial light for 14 to 16 hours a day.

Plant this orchid in small pots or in small suspended pans using a mixture of 7 parts fir bark, 1 part redwood bark, 1 part perlite and 1 part coarse peat moss. During the summer growth season, keep the potting mixture constantly moist, and at every third watering fertilize the plants with a formula rich in nitrogen, such as 30-10-10, diluted to half the strength recommended on the label. As the flowers fade, allow the plant to rest for about three weeks without water; then water through the winter only when the potting mixture becomes dry. Repot *Prom. xanthina* in fresh bark mixture every second spring, just as new growth starts. At this time new plants can be propagated by division into groups of at least three or four pseudobulbs.

PUNCH-AND-JUDY ORCHID See *Gongora*

R

REED ORCHID, FIERY See *Epidendrum*

RENANTHERA

Ren. coccinea; Ren. imschootiana; Ren. monachica (fire orchid)

Renantheras are valued for easy flowering and brilliant masses of red flowers splashed or barred with orange-and-yellow or yellow blossoms spotted with red; the genus is used in the creation of hybrids to induce the same bright colors. The flowers of renanthera orchids are distinguished also by the slenderness of the upper sepal and petals, and the width of the lower lateral sepals, which broaden from narrow bases. Most are tree dwelling, and they range in size from miniatures to the vinelike *Ren. coccinea*, which grows up to 30 feet tall in the wild. *Ren. coccinea*, which often must be 6 to 12 feet high before it flowers, produces 100 or more long-lasting blood-red flowers, 2 to 3 inches across and sometimes 3 to 4 inches long, in loosely branched pyramidal clusters. The stalk starts opposite an upper leaf joint on the long, climbing, freely rooting stem. It blooms from spring to fall.

Ren. imschootiana, which is a dwarf version of *Ren. coccinea*, grows from 6 inches to almost 3 feet high, and for this reason is preferred by most gardeners. It blooms in late spring and summer, bearing up to 20 scarlet blossoms 2 to 3 inches across on arching, branching flower stalks up to 1½ feet long. The flowers last more than a month. *Ren. monachica* blooms in spring, bearing between six and 25 yellow-to-orange blossoms with red spots. They grow 1 to 1½ inches wide on arching 18-inch flower stalks that grow along a 2-foot-tall stem. The leaves, which sheathe this stem, are stiff and remarkably fleshy, often ½ inch thick.

HOW TO GROW. *Ren. coccinea* and *Ren. monachica* grow

best in a warm greenhouse with night temperatures of 60° to 65° and day temperatures of 70° to 85° and a humidity of 70 per cent. *Ren. imschootiana* needs cooler temperatures of 55° to 60° at night and 65° to 75° in the daytime and a humidity of 40 per cent. Most renanthera orchids, including these three species, thrive in full sun or in artificial light equivalent to 3,000 or more foot-candles for 14 to 16 hours a day. But *Ren. imschootiana* and *Ren. monachica* will also bloom in diffused sunlight or under artificial lighting of 1,500 to 3,000 foot-candles.

Grow renantheras in a mixture of 7 parts fir bark, 1 part redwood bark, 1 part perlite and 1 part coarse peat moss, or plant them in baskets filled with osmunda or tree-fern chunks. The climbing *Ren. coccinea* can also be trained on tree-fern poles. Keep the plants constantly moist during their period of active growth but reduce watering and humidity slightly while the plant is dormant; *Ren. imschootiana* especially should have only enough water to keep the foliage firm. At every third watering fertilize potted plants with a nitrogen-rich fertilizer such as 30-10-10 diluted to half the strength recommended on the label; for plants grown in baskets use a balanced formula such as 18-18-18, also diluted to half the recommended strength.

Change the potting mixture every spring or early summer, pulling out the stale mixture and inserting fresh. *Ren. coccinea,* because of its rapid growth, may need cutting back, but that will delay flowering. Choose a time at the beginning of the growth period and cut the upper stem in 2- or 3-foot sections, each of which, with its aerial roots, can be used to propagate new plants. Renanthera can also be encouraged to produce new growth around the base of the plant by surrounding it with a layer of sphagnum moss.

RESTREPIA
R. antennifera, also called *Pleurothallis ospinae; R. guttulata,* also called *Pleurothallis guttulata*

The blossoms of these tree-dwelling orchids characteristically have threadlike upper sepals and enlarged, fused lower sepals, which are joined together for much of their length to form what appear to be single oblong tongues behind the lips. Usually the leaves of restrepias are longer than the flower stalks, and a sheath of papery bracts encloses each leaf and its accompanying flower stalk. *R. antennifera* has leaves about 1½ to 2 inches long and in spring produces a 1-inch-long flower on a 1- to 2-inch stalk; the flowers are yellow marked with purple. *R. guttulata* has similar markings, but it is a darker yellow and its flowers are larger, about 1½ to 2 inches long. Its leaves are 2 inches long and it blooms intermittently throughout the year. In either species, a single plant often produces several flowers at once, and a single stalk may produce a succession of blooms.

HOW TO GROW. Restrepias grow best in a cool greenhouse where night temperatures drop to between 50° and 55° and day temperatures range from 60° to 70°. Give them semishade or provide 1,000 to 1,500 foot-candles of artificial light for 14 to 16 hours a day. Keep the humidity high, 60 to 70 per cent, especially during summer.

Plant restrepias in a mixture of 7 parts fir bark, 1 part redwood bark, 1 part perlite and 1 part coarse peat moss. Water heavily, then let the potting mixture become moderately dry before the next watering. Fertilize at every third watering with a nitrogen-rich formula such as 30-10-10 diluted to half the strength recommended on the label. Repot when potting mixture begins to decompose and drains poorly. Propagate by dividing into clumps of three to five stems.

Restrepia antennifera

FOXTAIL ORCHID
Rhynchostylis gigantea

CORAL ORCHID
Rodriguezia secunda

RHYNCHOLAELIA DIGBYANA See *Brassavola*
RHYNCHOLAELIA GLAUCA See *Brassavola*

RHYNCHOSTYLIS
Rhy. gigantea (foxtail orchid)

Called foxtail orchid for its long, dense mass of 1-inch blossoms, *Rhy. gigantea* is a sturdy tree-dwelling plant that adapts equally well to warm or intermediate temperatures. It has a short, stout stem, less than 4 inches high, and fleshy tongue-shaped leaves, up to 1 foot long and 2½ inches wide. In fall and early winter, the 15-inch flower stalks are weighted with their fragrant burden of waxy blossoms, which are white with purple spots and elaborately shaped magenta lips with funnel-shaped spurs.

HOW TO GROW. *Rhy. gigantea* grows best when it is given intermediate temperatures between 55° and 60° at night and between 65° and 75° during the day, though temperatures up to 65° at night and 85° during the day will not harm it. A humidity of 70 per cent is ideal. Give it bright indirect sunlight or between 2,500 and 3,000 foot-candles of artificial light for 14 to 16 hours a day.

Grow the plants in baskets filled with osmunda or tree-fern chunks, or pot in a mixture of 7 parts fir bark, 1 part redwood bark, 1 part perlite and 1 part coarse peat moss. Keep the mixture evenly moist, watering less frequently in the winter, during cloudy periods and after repotting. At every third watering, fertilize basket-grown plants with a balanced formula such as 18-18-18; for potted plants use a high-nitrogen formula such as 30-10-10. Dilute to half the strength recommended on the label. Do not repot until the plants outgrow their pots, since rhynchostylis roots are very sensitive to being disturbed. Instead, when the potting mixture begins to deteriorate, lift the plants from the pots, remove the old mixture from around the roots and replace it with fresh mixture. Propagate when new stems take root around the base of a plant, separating them from the parent plant and repotting them individually.

ROCKET ORCHID See *Angraecum*

RODRIGUEZIA
Rdga. secunda, also called *Rdga. lanceolata* (both called coral orchid); *Rdga. venusta*

This tropical tree dweller bears extremely fragrant sprays of delicate, intricately shaped blossoms. They grow from small pseudobulbs, along with one or more leaves. *Rdga. secunda* blooms at any time of year; *Rdga. venusta* blooms in the autumn. The former has rigid, leathery 9-inch leaves growing from 1½-inch pseudobulbs; its flower stalks, up to 6 inches long, carry 20 to 30 pink blossoms ranked along one side of the stalk. *Rdga. venusta* has a single dark green leaf, 3 to 6 inches long, growing from each 1-inch pseudobulb along its creeping rhizome. Five to 10 flowers bloom on the plant's arching stalks, which are 7 to 12 inches long. The flowers are white, sometimes flushed with pink, and have lips mottled with yellow.

HOW TO GROW. Place the orchid in bright diffused sunlight or give it 2,000 foot-candles of artificial light for 14 to 16 hours a day. It needs intermediate night temperatures of 55° to 60°, day temperatures of 65° to 75° and a humidity of 50 to 60 per cent. Such a warm, moist atmosphere may best be achieved by cultivation in a greenhouse.

Grow rodriguezias in pots in a mixture consisting of 7 parts fir bark, 1 part redwood bark, 1 part perlite and 1 part coarse peat moss. Keep them evenly moist all year round. At every third watering, fertilize with a high-nitrogen formula such as 30-10-10 diluted to half the strength recommended on the label. Repot plants when they outgrow their pots or when the growing medium begins to deteriorate and drain poorly. Propagate at the same time by dividing the plants into clumps of three to four pseudobulbs each.

S

SACCOLABIUM

Saccm. hendersonianum, also called *Ascocentrum hendersonianum*; *Saccm. quisumbingii*, also called *Tuberolabium kotoense*

A compact growing habit and an abundance of brightly colored flowers make these tropical tree-growing plants favorites with collectors. They are generally no more than 6 inches tall, with four or five thick, leathery leaves, 5 to 6 inches long, and a lateral flower stalk of approximately the same length. During a single season one plant may produce 30 or more flowers.

Saccm. hendersonianum blooms in spring and summer, producing a cylindrical mass of flowers, each about ⅔ inch across. They range in color from pale pink to cherry red, with spurred lips of a slightly lighter color. *Saccm. quisumbingii,* only 4 inches tall, blooms in winter, its flower sprays of as many as 20 creamy white flowers standing out in sharp contrast against the heavy foliage. The flowers, ½ to ¾ inch wide, are marked with crimson or magenta, and the petals and sepals, slender and gently pointed, make the whole flower resemble a star.

HOW TO GROW. Saccolabiums grow best in a warm greenhouse where temperatures range from 60° to 65° at night and 70° to 85° during the day, and where humidity is kept between 60 and 70 per cent. They need bright diffused sunlight or more than 2,500 foot-candles of artificial light for 14 to 16 hours a day. These plants are mostly grown in baskets filled with osmunda. If potted, use a mixture of 7 parts fir bark, 1 part redwood bark, 1 part perlite and 1 part coarse peat moss. Keep the medium moist year round, but be careful to water less during cloudy periods. At every third watering, fertilize pot-grown plants with a high-nitrogen formula such as 30-10-10 diluted to half the strength recommended on the label; for plants in baskets use a balanced formula such as 18-18-18, also diluted to half the recommended strength. Repot when the growing medium begins to deteriorate and drains poorly. To propagate saccolabiums, remove and pot the rooted plantlets that may appear at the bases of the plants or along the stem.

Saccolabium hendersonianum

SAMURAI ORCHID See *Neofinetia*
SAN SEBASTIAN, FLOWER OF See *Cattleya*

SCHOMBURGKIA

Schom. lyonsii, also called *Laelia lyonsii; Schom. tibicinis,* also called *Laelia tibicinis; Schom. undulata*, also called *Laelia undulata* (cow-horn orchid)

A swollen elongated pseudobulb distinguishes this tree-dwelling orchid. Typically, schomburgkias have a reedlike unbranched flower stalk and flowers whose petals and sepals are deeply ruffled. However, though the genus grows well in moderate temperatures and humidity, it tends to bloom erratically until well established. *Schom. lyonsii* has 1- to 2-foot-tall pseudobulbs. It flowers in late summer and early fall, producing clusters of 10 to 20 blossoms 1½ to 2 inches wide on a stalk up to 5 feet tall. The sepals and petals are

Schomburgkia tibicinis

Scuticaria steelii

white spotted and barred with purple; the lip is white and is edged with yellow.

Schom. tibicinis, a spring- and summer-blooming species, is best known for its enormous pseudobulbs, up to 2 feet high and 3 inches in diameter. Each produces two to three leaves 5 to 14 inches long and a flower stalk up to 15 feet long, which ends in 10 to 20 blossoms 2 to 3 inches across, opening successively. Its flowers are in tones of purple and burnt orange, with cream-colored or deep purple lips. The flowers of *Schom. undulata* are waxy in texture, with narrow, twisting, ruffled petals colored wine-red to purplish-brown; the three-lobed rose-purple lips are marked with raised white ridges. The flowers are up to 2 inches across and cluster in dense heads of over 20 blossoms at the ends of 3- to 5-foot flower stalks, which rise from 1- to 2-foot-long pseudobulbs. They bloom in late winter and early spring.

HOW TO GROW. Schomburgkia orchids grow best in intermediate night temperatures of 55° to 60° and day temperatures of 65° to 75°. Give them full sunlight or provide 2,500 foot-candles of light for 14 to 16 hours a day. Provide 40 to 60 per cent humidity.

Plant in a mixture of 7 parts fir bark, 1 part redwood bark, 1 part perlite and 1 part coarse peat moss. Drench the mixture, then allow it to dry slightly before watering it again. At every third watering, fertilize with a high-nitrogen formula such as 30-10-10 diluted to half the strength recommended on the label. Decrease watering and humidity during the dormant period. Although stale potting mix should periodically be pulled out and fresh mix inserted among the roots, a plant should not be repotted until several pseudobulbs have grown over the edge of the pot. Propagate at this stage by dividing into groups of three or four pseudobulbs each.

SCORPION ORCHID See *Arachnis*

SCUTICARIA
S. steelii

The long, dangling, cylindrical leaves of scuticaria reach 2 to 6 feet in length and grow from small, clustered pseudobulbs. The flower stalks, which are much shorter than the leaves, spring laterally from the bases of the pseudobulbs and in summer and fall produce fragrant long-lasting 2- to 3-inch flowers, often in pairs. The flowers are pale yellow blotched with reddish-brown; the sepals and petals are similarly sized. The flaring lips are striped and speckled with brown, and have downy orange crests.

HOW TO GROW. *S. steelii* grows best in intermediate to warm night temperatures of 55° to 60° and day temperatures of 65° to 75°. Place the plants in bright diffused sunlight, taking care to protect their slender foliage from burning. Because of their size, scuticarias are not usually grown under artificial light. Maintain a humidity of 40 to 60 per cent.

Because of its pendulous leaves, *S. steelii* should grow suspended on tree-fern or cork-bark slabs or in hanging baskets filled with osmunda or tree-fern chunks. During the growing season, keep the medium constantly moist. At every third watering, fertilize plants with a balanced formula such as 18-18-18 diluted to half the strength recommended on the label. After flowers fade, keep the plants barely moist for a two-week period while they rest. Propagate by dividing each plant into groups of three or four pseudobulbs.

SHOWY LADY'S SLIPPER See *Cypripedium*
SLIPPER ORCHID See *Cypripedium, Paphiopedilum* and *Phragmipedium*

SOBRALIA
Sob. macrantha

Unlike most orchids that grow in the wild on rocks or on trees, this earth-dwelling orchid, a native of Central America, sends its many roots directly into the soil; it has no pseudobulbs. A large plant, it grows in closely set clumps, sending up flower stalks to a height of 4 to 7 feet. Each stalk bears three to nine large blossoms, each up to 9 inches across. The flowers bloom singly in spring and summer and last for several days; as each flower fades another comes into bloom. The ruffled petals and curving sepals are rose-purple; the lip, whose base forms a narrow tube around the column, has a creamy yellow throat. The leaves are rigid lances growing to 1 foot long at intervals along the flower stalk.

HOW TO GROW. *Sob. macrantha* grows best in intermediate temperatures of 55° to 60° at night and 65° to 75° during the day, with humidity at 50 per cent. Give the plant bright sun or from 1,500 to 2,500 foot-candles of artificial light 14 to 16 hours a day. Grow in 2 parts coarse peat moss, 2 parts sandy loam and 1 part each perlite and fine fir bark, or use a commercial cymbidium mix. Keep the soil moist but not soggy during the growing period, but reduce watering for a month or more when leaves have finished growing. Do not, however, allow soil to dry out completely. At every third watering, fertilize with a balanced fertilizer such as 18-18-18 diluted to half the strength recommended on the label. *Sob. macrantha* blossoms most freely when the plant is large. Therefore only specimens with eight to 12 stems should be divided in order to obtain new plants.

SOPHROLAELIOCATTLEYA
Slc. Anzac 'Orchidhurst'; Slc. Jewel Box 'Scheherazade'; Slc. Paprika 'Black Magic'

A crossing of three well-known genera, the epiphytic, or tree-dwelling, *Sophrolaeliocattleya* draws on the strengths of each parent: *Sophronitis* contributes its flower colors—bright reds and dramatic rose-purples, *Laelia* its free-flowering nature and fleshy substance, and *Cattleya* the size and form of the foliage and flowers. Seldom more than 1 foot tall, with thick, somewhat twisted leaves, the plants bear 3- to 6-inch-wide blossoms, normally in the winter and spring. *Slc.* Anzac 'Orchidhurst' has 4- to 6-inch reddish-purple blossoms, two to three to a stalk, and is frequently used as a parent plant in the breeding of red cattleya varieties. Its depth of color varies with its environment: one that is cool and bright produces the deepest reds. *Slc.* Jewel Box 'Scheherazade' yields three to five dark red 3- to 4-inch blossoms. A hardy orchid, ideal for window-sill gardening, it sometimes blooms twice a year. *Slc.* Paprika 'Black Magic,' another hardy hybrid, produces four to five dark red 3-inch flowers on a stalk, often twice annually.

HOW TO GROW. These hybrids generally grow best in temperatures ranging from 55° to 60° at night and 65° to 75° during the day. Give the plants bright indirect sun or illuminate 14 to 16 hours a day with 1,500 to 2,500 foot-candles of artificial light. Maintain humidity at 50 to 60 per cent.

Plant in a mixture of 7 parts fir bark to 1 part redwood bark, 1 part perlite and 1 part coarse peat moss. When watering, drench the potting mixture, but allow it to become almost dry between waterings. At every third watering, fertilize with a nitrogen-rich formula such as 30-10-10 diluted to half the strength recommended on the label. Repot sophrolaeliocattleyas every other spring to renew the potting medium; at this time additional plants may be propagated by division into clumps of three or four pseudobulbs.

Sobralia macrantha

Sophrolaeliocattleya Jewel Box 'Scheherazade'

Sophronitis coccinea

SOPHRONITIS
Soph. coccinea, also called *Soph. grandiflora*

This handsome tree-dwelling dwarf orchid compensates the grower for its difficulty of cultivation by producing solitary outsized scarlet blossoms up to 3 inches across on a plant that is at most only 4 inches tall. The sepals are narrow, the petals are broad ovals and the lip is scarlet streaked with yellow. The flowers appear in fall and winter on short slender stalks that grow from the tips of clustered pseudobulbs 1 inch in height. Each pseudobulb also bears one fleshy, rigid, lance-shaped dark green leaf, 2 to 3 inches long. *Sophronitis* has often been crossed with *Cattleya* and *Laelia* orchids to obtain the same vivid red on a less demanding plant.

HOW TO GROW. *Soph. coccinea* grows best in a cool night temperature of 55°, increasing to 60° to 65° during the day, and in a humidity of 60 to 70 per cent. It needs diffused sunlight or 1,500 to 2,000 foot-candles of artificial illumination for 14 to 16 hours a day.

Plant *Soph. coccinea* in baskets filled with chunks of tree fern or osmunda or in small pots, using a mixture of 7 parts fir bark, 1 part redwood bark, 1 part perlite and 1 part coarse peat moss. Keep the mixture evenly moist throughout the year. Fertilize basket-grown plants at every third watering with a balanced formula such as 18-18-18; for pot-grown plants use a nitrogen-rich fertilizer such as 30-10-10. Dilute to half the strength recommended on the label. Repot when the potting mixture begins to deteriorate and drains poorly. Propagate when new growth begins by separating pseudobulbs into groups of three or four.

SPICE ORCHID See *Epidendrum*
SPIDER ORCHID See *Brassia*

STANHOPEA
Stan. wardii (El Toro orchid)

The fantastic shape of stanhopea's 3- to 5-inch blossom is allied to its pollination system. Insects visiting this tree-dwelling plant land on the flower's smooth lip and fall into the long beaklike column that curves to meet the lip. In leaving the column the insects brush against the flower's sex organs, transferring pollen from male anther to female stigma. The flowers of *Stan. wardii* are 3 to 5 inches wide with spreading sepals and narrower, wavy petals; both petals and sepals are usually golden yellow, often spotted with reddish-brown. The base of the complex lip is orange-yellow with a red spot on either side. Three to nine blossoms crowd at the ends of trailing stalks that sprout from the bases of 2- to 3-inch pseudobulbs. Each pseudobulb also bears one leathery, pleated leaf, up to 18 inches long and tapering from a width of 6½ inches. The fragrant flowers appear in summer and fall and last only a few days. The plant's other oddity, apart from its flower, is its habit of sending its flower stalks down through the growing mix to bloom from the basket's bottom.

HOW TO GROW. Stanhopeas grow best when they are given intermediate temperatures of 55° to 60° at night and 65° to 75° in the daytime, although during the growing season temperatures may rise without harm to 65° at night and 85° in the daytime. They need filtered sunlight or 1,500 to 2,000 foot-candles of artificial light for 14 to 16 hours a day. Provide 40 to 60 per cent humidity.

Grow stanhopeas on slabs of tree fern or in hanging baskets that will allow the flower stalks to grow through the potting mixture and out the bases of the containers. Fill the baskets with osmunda or sheet moss. Water abundantly during growth, then suspend watering for a month after new

EL TORO ORCHID
Stanhopea wardii

pseudobulbs are formed, watering only enough to keep foliage firm. During growth, fertilize with a balanced formula such as 18-18-18 diluted to half the strength recommended on the label. To propagate, divide the plant periodically into groups of three to five pseudobulbs; overly large clumps of pseudobulbs will inhibit flowering.

STAR-OF-BETHLEHEM ORCHID See *Angraecum*

STELIS
S. bidentata; S. ciliaris; S. micrantha

The tiny tricorn flowers of stelises, often only ⅛ inch across, can usually be identified as to species only by studying them under a microscope. Composed of proportionately long rounded sepals, small fleshy petals and barely visible fleshy lips, the blossoms cluster along the top half of 1- to 6-inch-long flower stalks. The leathery leaves of these tree-dwelling plants grow singly on stems that rise in clumps from a creeping rhizome; the tips of the leaves are generally serrated, with two or three teeth. *S. bidentata* varies in color from purple to white suffused with green, purple or reddish-brown. The leaves are 1¼ to 3 inches long and the slender erect flower stalks are up to 4½ inches high. The species blooms in summer, the flowers opening usually at night. *S. ciliaris* is named for the hairlike growth, or cilia, that fringes its maroon to purple sepals. This species produces 1¼- to 6-inch leaves and 2- to 7-inch flower stalks that in spring are laden with up to 50 or more blooms. *S. micrantha* often blooms throughout the year; its flower stalks, which grow up to 6 inches tall, bear ⅜-inch blossoms with pale green sepals and dark purple or red petals and lips. The leaves are 4 to 6½ inches long.

HOW TO GROW. Stelises grow best in intermediate temperatures of 55° to 60° at night, rising to 65° to 75° during the day. Give them diffused sunlight or 1,500 to 2,000 foot-candles of artificial light for 14 to 16 hours a day. Maintain a humidity of 40 to 60 per cent. Plant in a mixture of 7 parts fir bark, 1 part redwood bark, 1 part perlite and 1 part coarse peat moss. Keep the mixture evenly moist but not soggy. At every third watering, fertilize with a nitrogen-rich formula such as 30-10-10 diluted to half the strength recommended on the label. Repot when the potting mix begins to deteriorate and drain poorly. Propagate by dividing the rhizomes into groups of at least four leafy stems.

SWAN ORCHID See *Cycnoches*

T

THUNIA
Thu. alba; Thu. marshalliana

Tall earth-dwelling plants with abundant, attractive foliage, thunias bear flowers that are similar in form to those of the cattleya. The canelike stems grow close together and each cane sprouts numerous alternating papery wax-covered leaves along its length; the leaves drop off at the end of the flowering season. White flowers, which last seven to 14 days, bloom in the summer on nodding stalks at the tips of the canes. The flower's sepals and petals are thin and lance shaped; the lip is ruffled and fringed, streaked with purple or veined with yellow. *Thu. alba* has robust stems 2 feet long, pale green leaves 6 to 8 inches long and stalks of five to 10 flowers 2½ to 3 inches across. *Thu. marshalliana,* an even more robust species, has stems that grow up to 3 feet long and produces blossoms as large as 5 inches wide.

Stelis ciliaris

Thunia marshalliana

Trichoglottis philippinensis var. *brachiata*

Trichopilia suavis

HOW TO GROW. Thunias do best in intermediate temperatures of 55° to 60° at night and 65° to 75° during the day while the plant is growing but should be kept slightly cooler while in flower. Afterward, while the stems continue to thicken, return to the warmer temperature range; then when the foliage drops, reduce the temperatures to 50° to 55° at night and 60° to 70° in the daytime. Maintain a humidity throughout the year of 60 per cent. Give the plant diffused sunlight, taking care not to burn the delicate leaves, or illuminate 14 to 16 hours a day with 1,500 to 2,000 foot-candles of artificial light. A greenhouse environment may best ensure these rather special conditions.

Grow thunias in pots in a mixture of 2 parts coarse peat moss, 2 parts sandy loam and 1 part each perlite and fine fir bark. Keep evenly moist during the growing season; suspend watering after the leaves fall until new growth starts. At every third watering, fertilize with a balanced fertilizer such as 18-18-18 diluted to half the strength recommended on the label. Repot every spring to renew potting mix. Propagate at this time by dividing the stem cluster at the base.

TIGER ORCHID See *Odontoglossum*

TRICHOGLOTTIS

Trgl. philippinensis var. *brachiata,* also called *Trgl. brachiata*

This tree-dwelling orchid has short oval leaves that spring alternately, at close intervals, from a sturdy stem. On most species the flower stalk rises from the base of the leaves, and each stalk usually produces a single flower in spring or summer. The stem of the variant *brachiata* is 2 feet tall; its leaves are 2 inches long, and its blossoms, 2 inches wide, are generally a rich red edged with yellow or white. The lip is white with wine-colored streaks and a brilliant yellow throat.

HOW TO GROW. *Trgl. brachiata* grows best in bright sunlight or under artificial illumination of 2,500 or more foot-candles for 14 to 16 hours a day. It requires warm temperatures of 60° to 65° at night and 70° to 85° during the day and a humidity between 40 and 50 per cent. Plant it in a mixture of 7 parts fir bark, 1 part redwood bark, 1 part perlite and 1 part coarse peat moss. Water abundantly during the growing season, but less frequently when the plant is resting. At every third watering fertilize with a high-nitrogen formula such as 30-10-10 diluted to half the strength recommended on the label. Repot when the plants become overcrowded or the growing medium begins to decay. Propagate additional plants by dividing stems so that each division contains several leaf nodes, or bases.

TRICHOPILIA

Trpla. suavis; Trpla. tortilis

These small tree-dwelling orchids are admired for their large flowers and their dark evergreen leaves. The latter grow singly from compact pseudobulbs that rise from creeping rhizomes. Large fragrant flowers with slender sepals and petals and wavy lips are borne on stalks that arch from the base of the pseudobulb to hang below the pot. The spring-flowering *Trpla. suavis* has white 3- to 4-inch-wide blossoms with very large ruffled lips spotted with rose-purple. Highly fragrant, they bloom in clusters of two to five flowers per stalk. *Trpla. tortilis* produces its flowers singly or in pairs in the winter. Also very fragrant, they have narrow sepals and petals twisting into spirals; these measure 2 to 4 inches wide, but if laid flat they extend to 6 inches. Their color is in shades of purple with a border of yellow-green. The lip is white with red-brown spots near its tubular base.

HOW TO GROW. Trichopilias grow best in intermediate night temperatures of 55° to 60° and day temperatures of 65° to 75°. Give them at least four hours of filtered sunlight a day or 1,500 to 2,000 foot-candles of artificial light for 14 to 16 hours. Provide 40 to 60 per cent humidity.

Pot plants in a mixture of 7 parts fir bark, 1 part redwood bark, 1 part perlite and 1 part coarse peat moss; mound the mixture slightly in the center so the plant is higher than the rim. Trichopilias also grow well attached to hanging slabs of cork bark or tree fern. Keep the growing medium evenly moist during the growing season, but when pseudobulbs have matured, allow the mixture to dry out slightly between waterings. With every third watering, fertilize pot-grown plants with a high-nitrogen formula such as 30-10-10; give slab-mounted plants a balanced fertilizer such as 18-18-18. Dilute either formula to half the strength recommended on the label; do not feed plants when they are dormant.

These orchids flower best when grown in small clumps, so they should be repotted yearly. Propagate in early spring or immediately after flowering by dividing into clumps of at least three pseudobulbs each.

TUBEROLABIUM KOTOENSE See *Saccolabium*
TULIP ORCHID See *Anguloa*
TURTLE ORCHID See *Oncidium*

V

VANDA

V. coerulea (blue orchid); *V.* Hilo Queen; *V.* Onomea; *V.* Rothschildiana; *V. sanderiana,* also called *Euanthe sanderiana; V. teres*

The popular vandas are easy to grow. Their beautiful flowers grow on long fluttering stalks, arching or erect, that emerge from among the leaves along the plant's sturdy stem. Each stalk bears from five to as many as 80 blossoms, which last from three to six weeks. Their sepals and petals, usually rounded and similarly sized, surround a short fleshy lip and give the blossom as a whole an open-faced appearance. The evergreen leaves may be one of three shapes: cylindrical, strap shaped or V shaped, though most are strap shaped. All grow alternately on opposite sides of a main stem where aerial roots develop as well. Vanda has been used in many hybrid crosses with other genera, including *Aerides, Ascocentrum* and *Neofinetia.*

V. coerulea, the blue orchid, grows 1½ to 3 feet tall with 8-inch strap-shaped leaves. From late summer through late winter its 18-inch flower stalks bear from five to 15 flowers, 3 to 4 inches across, in varying shades of blue, usually with darker blue veins.

V. Hilo Queen is a cross between *V.* Jennie Hashimoto 'Spire' and *V.* Eisenhower 'Mamie.' It has large pink flowers 4 inches across, that bloom in dense clusters of eight to 14 blossoms at various times throughout the year on stalks that are 12 inches long; the leaves are strap shaped. *V.* Onomea, another strap-leaved hybrid, is a cross between *V. sanderiana* and *V.* Rothschildiana; its pin-wheel-shaped, 3- to 5-inch flowers are light purple with darker mottling. Its season of bloom is variable.

V. Rothschildiana is a hybrid between *V. coerulea* and *V. sanderiana.* It produces 3- to 6-inch blossoms in dense clusters throughout the year. The flowers are lavender checkered with dark blue. The leaves are strap shaped.

V. sanderiana has strap-shaped leaves up to 1 foot long. About 15 flowers 3 to 4 inches across appear on 12-inch long

BLUE ORCHID
Vanda coerulea

Vanda teres

VANILLA ORCHID
Vanilla planifolia

stalks in the fall. The upper sepal and petals are a fairly uniform white to rose; the lower sepals are yellow-green, heavily veined with reddish-brown. *V. teres,* with its slender many-branched stem and erect 4- to 8-inch-long cylindrical leaves, grows several feet high. Its flower stalks, 6 to 12 inches long, produce three to six blossoms in spring and summer; they are pale rose in color, with orange-tinted lips.

HOW TO GROW. Vandas do best in a warm temperature range of 60° to 65° at night and 65° to 75° or higher during the day. Cylindrical-leaved varieties need at least six hours of very bright sun a day; strap-leaved varieties need at least four hours of direct sunlight but should be shielded from the intense midday sun. Because of their light requirements, vandas do best in greenhouses or very sunny windows. The smaller vanda hybrids, the ascocendas, do well under lights, requiring 2,500 to 3,000 foot-candles for 14 to 16 hours a day. All vandas need humidity of 40 to 60 per cent.

Grow vandas in a mixture of 7 parts coarse fir bark, 1 part redwood bark, 1 part perlite and 1 part coarse peat moss. Keep the medium constantly moist but not soggy, watering less frequently in cloudy weather or during periods when plants are not actively growing. At every third watering fertilize with a high-nitrogen formula such as 30-10-10 diluted to half the recommended strength. Vandas should be repotted as little as possible. When the potting mix begins to deteriorate and drains poorly, simply replace the top layer. If the lower stem loses its leaves, cut off just below living aerial roots and repot. To propagate, allow the plantlets growing at the base to develop roots; then remove and pot them.

VANILLA
V. planifolia (vanilla orchid)

The seed pods of this orchid, which provide vanilla extract for flavoring food, grow on a vining stem that may reach more than 100 feet in length. The vine sends out aerial roots at most of the leaf nodes, along with the fleshy evergreen leaves and the flower spikes, which eventually support the vanilla beans. Each leaf is 6 to 8 inches long and 2 inches wide. The flower spikes, only 3 inches long, produce 20 or more buds, which open singly and last for several days. The fragrant flowers, 2½ to 3 inches across, often do not open completely. The blossom has long yellow-green sepals and petals and a 2-inch white lip with a ruffled edge and an orange-yellow throat. They bloom intermittently throughout the year. Only very large plants produce flowers, however, and then only when given ideal growing conditions. Flowers must be hand-pollinated to produce the 6-inch-long vanilla beans, which take eight to nine months to mature.

HOW TO GROW. *V. planifolia* grows best in warm moist air. It needs night temperatures of 60° to 65°, day temperatures of 70° to 85° and a humidity of 40 to 60 per cent. Give the plant at least four hours of bright sunlight a day.

Plant vanilla in a mixture of 2 parts coarse peat moss, 2 parts sandy loam, and 1 part each perlite and fine fir bark. Provide the vine with some sort of support to climb on. Keep the soil evenly moist all year round and feed at every third watering with a balanced fertilizer such as 18-18-18 diluted to half the strength recommended on the label. When the potting medium deteriorates and drains poorly, replace the top layer instead of repotting the plant. Propagate from stem cuttings that include three to five leaf nodes, and insert the cuttings in potting mixture until new plants develop.

VIOLET ORCHID See *Ionopsis*
VIRGIN ORCHID See *Diacrium*

VUYLSTEKEARA

Vuyl. Cambria 'Plush'

Vuylstekeara is a hybrid of three other orchids: *Cochlioda,* *Miltonia* and *Odontoglossum*—and *Vuyl.* Cambria 'Plush' is a cross between *Vuyl.* Rudra and *Odm.* Clonius, giving it a complex ancestry. This epiphytic or tree-dwelling orchid grows from small, flattened pseudobulbs 3 to 4 inches high, each of which produces four to five 6- to 10-inch-long narrow evergreen leaves. Its flowers are 3 inches wide, with undulating wine-red petals and sepals lined with white and a 2-inch-long white lip lined with red and yellow at the throat. Seven or eight flowers bloom on each arching stalk and last for several weeks. It blooms from winter through spring.

HOW TO GROW. *Vuyl.* Cambria 'Plush' grows best in intermediate to cool night temperatures of 55° to 60° and day temperatures of 65° to 75°. Provide 50 to 70 per cent humidity, and give the plants bright filtered sunlight or 1,500 to 2,000 foot-candles of artificial light 14 to 16 hours a day.

Pot in a mix of 7 parts fir bark, 1 part redwood bark, 1 part perlite and 1 part coarse peat moss. Keep the mixture evenly moist during active growth, but let it dry slightly between waterings while the plant is resting, after new growth has matured. Fertilize at every third watering with a high-nitrogen formula such as 30-10-10 diluted to half the recommended strength. Repot every two to four years when the pseudobulbs start to grow over the edge of the container or the potting mix starts to deteriorate and drains poorly. To propagate when repotting, divide the rhizome, keeping three or four pseudobulbs in each division.

Y

YELLOW LADY'S SLIPPER See *Cypripedium*

Z

ZYGOPETALUM

Z. intermedium

This pleasantly scented earth-dwelling orchid produces as many as five leaves, up to 18 inches long, from the top of each pseudobulb. The leaves are narrow and pleated, and in winter a 24-inch-long stalk carries four to six dappled blossoms 2½ inches across. The narrow, undulating sepals and petals are light green heavily splotched with brown, and the broad flaring lip is white with radiating lines of fine purple hairs. The flowers last for at least four weeks.

HOW TO GROW. *Z. intermedium* grows best in intermediate temperatures of 55° to 60° at night and 65° to 75° in the daytime. Give it filtered sunlight or 1,500 to 2,500 foot-candles of artificial light for 14 to 16 hours a day and provide 40 to 60 per cent humidity. Grow in a mix of 2 parts coarse peat moss, 2 parts sandy loam and 1 part each perlite and fine fir bark. During active growth, keep plants evenly moist; afterward, allow the potting mix to dry slightly between waterings until new growth begins. Do not let water stand around the base of the leaves, especially of young plants, since their close growing habit makes them vulnerable to rotting. Fertilize at every third watering with a balanced formula such as 18-18-18 at half the recommended strength.

If a plant has outgrown its container, repot when new growth begins. But if flower spikes appear simultaneously with new growth, wait to repot until flowering is completed. Zygopetalum has fragile roots, which must be handled gently in repotting. Propagate at the same time, dividing the rhizome into clumps of three or four pseudobulbs.

Vuylstekeara Cambria 'Plush'

Zygopetalum intermedium

Appendix

Orchid pests and diseases

The chart below identifies types of plant damage and their causes; the last column prescribes treatments. Chemicals recommended for roses are usually safe for orchids. For sucking insects, a systemic insecticide that circulates within the plant is preferable. Vary the kinds of insecticides and fungicides you use to prevent pests and diseases from developing resistance. Read chemical labels carefully and observe all cautions.

PEST	SYMPTOM
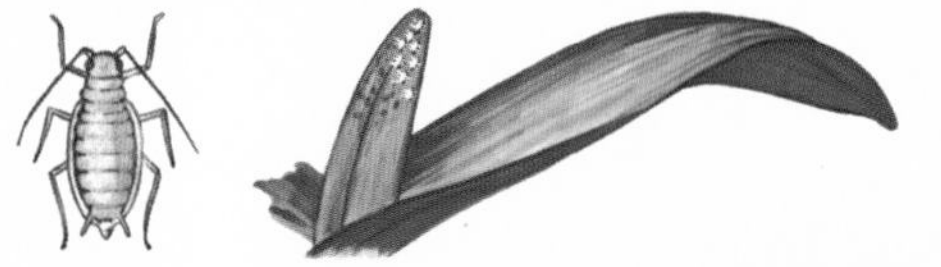	**APHIDS** Leaves and stems appear stunted; flowers may be malformed or fail to open. Aphids are visible, particularly on new growth. At left, green peach aphids infest a young phalaenopsis leaf. MOST VULNERABLE: CATTLEYA, ONCIDIUM, PHALAENOPSIS
	**MEALY BUGS** Cottony masses especially infest points of juncture such as the crook between two leaves of a phalaenopsis orchid at left. Plants may appear stunted or shriveled. MOST VULNERABLE: CATTLEYA, DENDROBIUM, PHALAENOPSIS
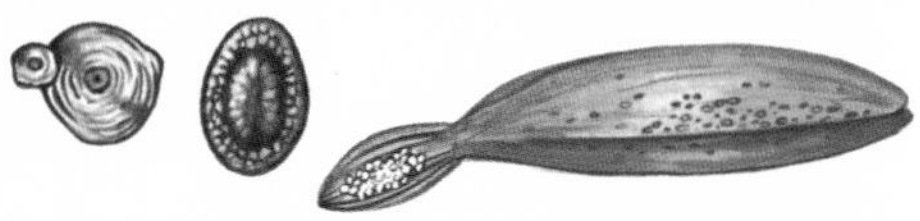	**SCALES** Round or oval shells in brown, gray or white, often accompanied by a sooty mold, appear on the plant, as on the cattleya leaf and pseudobulb at left. The plant may be stunted, with leaves yellowing and falling off. MOST VULNERABLE: CATTLEYA, CYMBIDIUM, PAPHIOPEDILUM
	**SLUGS AND SNAILS** The plant is punctured with ragged holes, and a slimy trail is visible where pests have passed. At left, a snail has chewed a vanda root and a slug has damaged its leaves. VULNERABLE: ALL ORCHIDS, ESPECIALLY SEEDLINGS
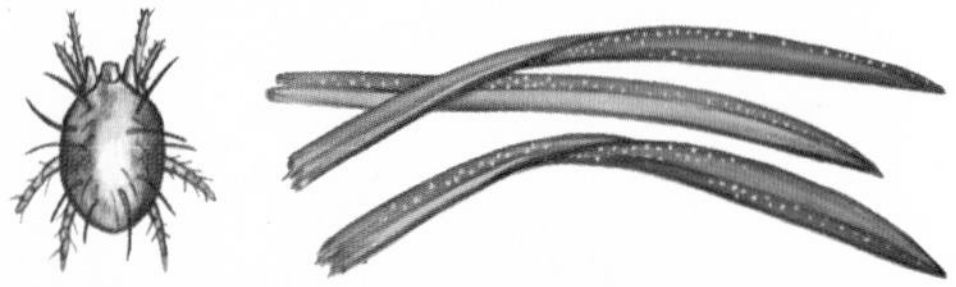	**SPIDER MITES** Leaves appear pitted or stippled with white, as on the cymbidium leaves infested by the two-spotted spider mite at left. A white webbing may show on undersides of leaves. MOST VULNERABLE: CYCNOCHES, CYMBIDIUM, DENDROBIUM, PHALAENOPSIS

DISEASE	SYMPTOM
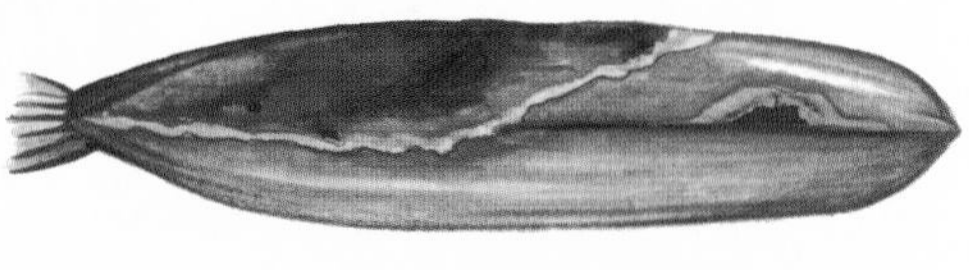	**BLACK ROT** Purplish blotches edged with yellow appear on leaves and new leads. Rotting may work downward from leaves or upward from roots and rhizomes. At left, a cattleya leaf shows black rot. MOST VULNERABLE: CATTLEYA-TYPE ORCHIDS, PHALAENOPSIS
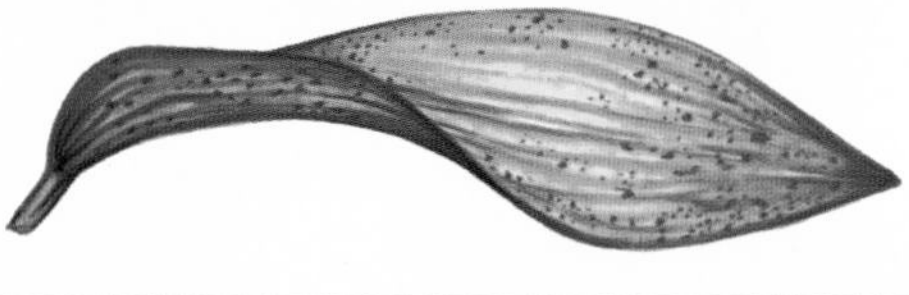	**LEAF SPOT** Raised or sunken spots in yellow, brown or purplish shades spread quickly over leaves, as on the odontoglossum leaf at left. In advanced stages, leaves turn yellow or brown and die. MOST VULNERABLE: ONCIDIUM, DENDROBIUM, MILTONIA, ZYGOPETALUM
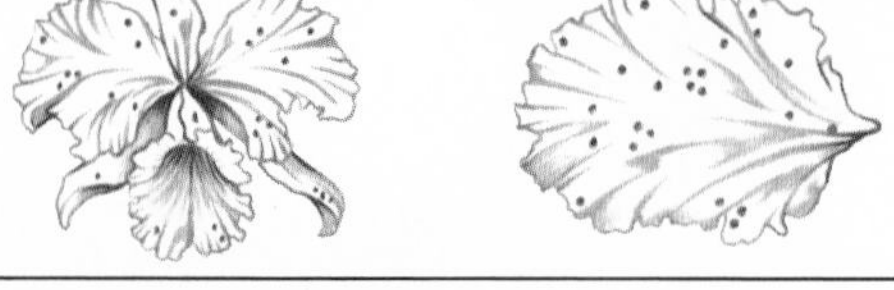	**PETAL BLIGHT** Small brown circles, often with pink edges, appear on sepals and petals, as on the cattleya blossom and separate petal at left. MOST VULNERABLE: CATTLEYA-TYPE ORCHIDS, DENDROBIUM, ONCIDIUM, PHALAENOPSIS, VANDA
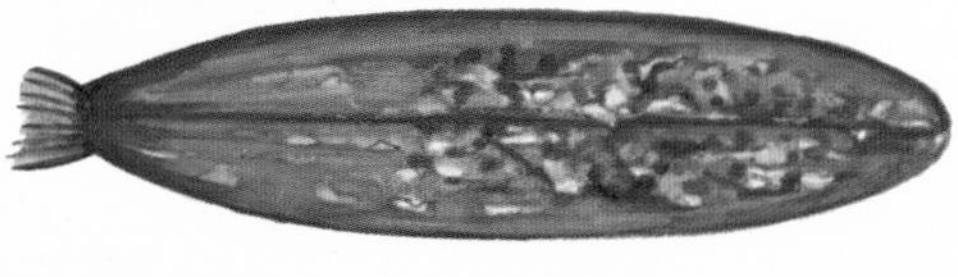	**VIRUS** Leaves may show yellow or brown pitting, mottling and streaking. Flowers too may be streaked or mottled. At left, a cattleya leaf suffers from cymbidium mosaic virus. VULNERABLE: ALL ORCHIDS

A clean plant environment is the best defense against pests and diseases: sterilize pots and tools and dispose of old leaves and potting mixes. Isolate or destroy afflicted plants. Provide enough air circulation so that leaves sway gently, and water plants early on sunny days when they will dry quickly. Careful weekly inspection with a strong magnifying glass may alert you early to illness and infestations.

CAUSE	REMEDY
Aphids are soft-bodied plant lice less than ⅛ inch long. Disease carriers that suck sap, they have plump bodies, narrow heads and a broad range of colors. Many are flying pests. All aphids secrete a shiny, sticky fluid known as honeydew that invites ants and an unsightly black fungus.	Wash off black fungus with water and mild kitchen detergent. Use an insecticide containing the systemic poison acephate (Orthene), diazinon or malathion.
Soft-bodied insects less than ¼ inch long, mealy bugs have a white, powdery coat. They suck sap from stems, leaves and buds. The pests produce a sticky honeydew that attracts ants and plays host to a harmless but ill-appearing black fungus.	Remove small infestations with a cotton swab dipped in alcohol. On heavy infestations use an insecticide containing the systemic poison acephate (Orthene), diazinon or malathion.
Many species of scale insects infest orchids, sucking their sap. Soft scales are $1/12$ to $1/3$ inch long and produce honeydew. Armored scales are less than ⅛ inch long and have a tough shell but do not produce honeydew. Scales crawl to one spot where they remain.	Pick off small infestations with tweezers or knife, or swab with alcohol. Spray adult scales with an insecticide containing the systemic poison acephate (Orthene), carbaryl, diazinon or malathion.
Snails are ½ to 2 inches long; slugs may reach 5 inches. Both are legless mollusks (though slugs have no shells) that generally hide during the day and emerge at night to feed on foliage, buds, flowers and root tips. The pests generally lay their eggs in damp areas or in the potting mix. Bush snails are only ⅛ to ¼ inch long.	A tuft of cotton wool around the stem will protect flowers. Trap snails and slugs with pesticide bait containing metaldehyde or Mesurol. Or lure slugs at night into a saucer of beer to drown.
Less than $1/50$ inch long, spider mites may be seen by tapping a leaf over a piece of paper so they fall off. Or touch a leaf with cellophane tape, then examine the tape with a magnifying glass. Normally, spider mites suck sap only from undersides of leaves, but microscopic false spider mites, which spin no webs, infest both sides.	Scrub and rinse foliage with warm water to break up webs. Spray heavy infestations with pesticide containing diazinon, dicofol (Kelthane) or malathion.
CAUSE	REMEDY
Black rot is caused by two types of fungi that favor high humidity, cool temperatures and standing water. Damping off, which affects seedlings, is caused by one of the black rot fungi and occurs most readily in community pots.	Treat infected plants with a fungicide such as Truban or Banrot. Remove infected parts—cut an inch into healthy tissue—and seal cuts with fungicide. Destroy badly diseased plants.
Leaf spot is usually caused by those species of cercospora fungus that thrive in high humidity. It is especially destructive to seedlings but rarely fatal to mature plants.	Reduce humidity and increase air circulation. Cut off diseased leaves; spray cuts with fungicide. Apply a systemic fungicide containing benomyl (Benlate) weekly until infection is controlled.
Petal blight, also known by the name of the fungus that causes it, botrytis, generally appears in cool, damp weather when there is inadequate air circulation. Microscopic spores are carried by insects, water or human hands. Fungus tends to attack old and fading flowers.	Cut off and destroy infected blossoms. Spray plants with a fungicide containing benomyl (Benlate), ferbam or zineb.
Two main types of viral diseases, cymbidium mosaic and tobacco mosaic, spread through the vascular systems of plants. Highly infectious, viruses may be transmitted by infected plants, hands, tools or aphids. Some infected plants show no symptoms.	There is no cure. Destroy infected plants. When dividing, flame-sterilize the knife between cuts, dip potting sticks in a 10 per cent household bleach solution. Buy plants certified virus-free.

Characteristics of 223 orchids

	FLOWER COLOR					OTHER TRAITS						NIGHT TEMP.			LIGHT			HUMIDITY		BLOOMING SEASON				
	White-green	Yellow-orange	Pink-red	Blue-purple	Multicolor	Epiphytic	Terrestrial	Sympodial	Monopodial	Deciduous	Evergreen	Cool (50°-55°)	Intermediate (55°-60°)	Warm (60°-65°)	Under 1,500 foot-candles	1,500-3,000 foot-candles	Over 3,000 foot-candles	Medium (40%-60%)	High (over 60%)	Spring	Summer	Fall	Winter	Intermittent
AERANGIS CITRATA		●				●		●			●		●		●			●		●			●	
AERANGIS RHODOSTICTA	●					●		●			●		●		●			●		●		●	●	
AERANTHES GRANDIFLORA	●					●		●			●		●		●			●	●		●	●	●	
AERIDES JAPONICUM	●					●			●		●				●		●		●	●				
AERIDES ODORATUM	●		●			●			●		●				●		●		●	●				
ANGRAECUM DISTICHUM	●					●			●		●		●	●		●						●		●
ANGRAECUM SESQUIPEDALE (star-of-Bethlehem orchid)	●					●			●		●		●	●		●							●	
ANGULOA CLOWESII (tulip orchid)		●					●	●		●		●			●				●	●				
ANGULOA RUECKERI (tulip orchid)	●	●					●	●		●		●			●				●	●				
ANSELLIA AFRICANA (leopard orchid)		●		●	●	●		●			●			●		●	●	●					●	
ARACHNIS FLOS-AERIS (scorpion orchid)		●		●	●	●			●		●			●		●	●	●				●		
ASCOCENDA MEDA ARNOLD		●	●		●	●			●		●			●		●		●						
ASCOCENDA TAN CHAI BENG			●		●	●			●		●			●		●		●						
ASCOCENDA YIP SUM WAH		●	●		●	●			●		●			●		●		●						
ASCOCENTRUM AMPULLACEUM		●				●			●		●			●		●		●						
ASCOCENTRUM MINIATUM		●	●			●			●		●			●		●		●						
ASCOCENTRUM SAGARIK GOLD		●				●			●		●			●		●		●						
ASPASIA EPIDENDROIDES	●		●		●	●		●			●	●	●	●		●			●					
BIFRENARIA HARRISONIAE	●		●		●	●		●			●		●			●			●					
BRASSAVOLA CORDATA	●					●		●			●		●			●			●		●			
BRASSAVOLA DIGBYANA	●	●				●		●			●		●			●			●					
BRASSAVOLA GLAUCA	●					●		●			●		●			●				●				
BRASSAVOLA NODOSA (lady-of-the-night orchid)	●					●		●			●		●			●						●	●	
BRASSIA CAUDATA (spider orchid)	●	●		●	●	●		●			●		●			●			●					
BRASSIA LANCEANA (spider orchid)	●			●	●	●		●			●		●			●			●					
BRASSIA MACULATA (spider orchid)	●			●	●	●		●			●		●			●			●				●	●
BRASSOCATTLEYA DAFFODIL		●				●		●			●		●			●		●						
BRASSOLAELIOCATTLEYA ERMINE 'LINES'		●				●		●			●		●			●		●						
BRASSOLAELIOCATTLEYA FORTUNE		●	●			●		●			●		●			●		●		●				
BRASSOLAELIOCATTLEYA MALWORTH 'ORCHIDGLADE'		●	●			●		●			●		●			●		●						
BRASSOLAELIOCATTLEYA NORMAN'S BAY			●			●		●			●		●			●		●						
BROUGHTONIA SANGUINEA			●			●		●			●		●		●		●		●			●		●
BULBOPHYLLUM LOBBII		●		●	●	●		●			●		●		●		●		●	●				
BULBOPHYLLUM LONGISSIMUM			●	●	●	●		●		●	●			●		●		●					●	
BULBOPHYLLUM MEDUSAE		●			●	●		●			●		●		●		●					●	●	
BULBOPHYLLUM ORNATISSIMUM		●		●	●	●		●			●		●		●		●							
CALANTHE VESTITA	●		●		●		●	●		●			●		●		●						●	
CATASETUM FIMBRIATUM	●	●		●	●	●		●		●			●			●		●				●		
CATTLEYA AURANTIACA		●	●		●	●		●			●		●			●		●			●			
CATTLEYA BOB BETTS	●			●		●		●			●		●			●		●						●
CATTLEYA BOWRINGIANA		●	●			●		●			●		●			●		●				●	●	
CATTLEYA CITRINA		●				●		●		●	●		●			●		●			●			
CATTLEYA GASKELLIANA	●		●			●		●			●		●			●		●			●			
CATTLEYA INTERMEDIA	●		●	●		●		●			●		●			●		●			●			
CATTLEYA LOUISE GEORGIANNA	●					●		●			●		●			●		●			●			
CATTLEYA LUTEOLA	●	●		●		●		●			●		●			●		●					●	●
CATTLEYA MOSSIAE (Easter orchid)			●	●	●	●		●			●		●			●		●		●				
CATTLEYA PERCIVALIANA			●	●		●		●			●		●			●		●					●	
CATTLEYA SKINNERI			●	●		●		●			●		●			●		●		●	●			
CATTLEYA TRIANAEI (Christmas orchid)	●			●	●	●		●			●		●			●		●					●	

150

	FLOWER COLOR					OTHER TRAITS						NIGHT TEMP.			LIGHT			HUMIDITY		BLOOMING SEASON				
	White-green	Yellow-orange	Pink-red	Blue-purple	Multicolor	Epiphytic	Terrestrial	Sympodial	Monopodial	Deciduous	Evergreen	Cool (50°-55°)	Intermediate (55°-60°)	Warm (60°-65°)	Under 1,500 foot-candles	1,500-3,000 foot-candles	Over 3,000 foot-candles	Medium (40%-60%)	High (over 60%)	Spring	Summer	Fall	Winter	Intermittent
CHYSIS AUREA		●		●	●	●		●		●			●		●		●			●				
COELOGYNE CRISTATA	●			●		●		●			●	●			●			●	●	●			●	
COELOGYNE GRAMINIFOLIA	●	●		●	●	●		●			●		●		●			●		●				
COELOGYNE MASSANGEANA		●		●	●	●		●			●		●		●			●	●					
COELOGYNE PANDURATA (black orchid)	●	●		●	●	●		●			●		●		●			●						●
COMPARETTIA COCCINEA		●	●		●	●		●			●		●		●		●	●		●	●	●		
CYCNOCHES CHLOROCHILON (swan orchid)	●	●			●	●		●		●			●		●			●	●					
CYMBIDIUM DEVONIANUM	●			●	●	●		●			●	●			●	●		●		●				
CYMBIDIUM FINLAYSONIANUM		●			●	●		●			●		●		●	●		●		●				
CYMBIDIUM GERAINT	●				●	●		●			●		●		●	●		●		●				
CYMBIDIUM HAWTESCENS		●			●	●		●			●	●			●	●		●		●				
CYMBIDIUM JUNGFRAU	●				●	●		●			●	●			●	●		●						
CYMBIDIUM MARY PINCHESS		●			●	●		●			●		●		●	●		●						
CYMBIDIUM PETER PAN 'GREENSLEEVES'	●				●	●		●			●		●		●	●		●						
CYMBIDIUM PUMILUM			●		●	●		●			●	●	●		●	●		●						
CYPRIPEDIUM ACAULE (pink lady's slipper)				●			●	●			●	●		●			●		●	●				
CYPRIPEDIUM CALCEOLUS (yellow lady's slipper)		●			●	●	●	●			●	●		●			●		●	●				
CYPRIPEDIUM REGINAE (showy lady's slipper)	●		●		●		●	●			●	●		●			●		●					
CYRTORCHIS ARCUATA	●				●		●		●		●		●		●			●					●	
DENDROBIUM AGGREGATUM		●			●	●		●		●	●	●			●			●	●	●				
DENDROBIUM BIGIBBUM			●	●		●		●			●			●	●			●	●	●				
DENDROBIUM CUCUMERINUM	●		●			●		●		●	●	●			●			●	●					
DENDROBIUM GATTON SUNRAY		●			●	●		●			●		●		●			●	●	●				
DENDROBIUM KINGIANUM	●		●			●		●		●	●	●			●	●	●	●						
DENDROBIUM LODDIGESII			●		●	●		●			●		●		●	●	●	●				●		
DENDROBIUM NOBILE	●		●		●	●		●		●	●	●			●	●	●	●				●		
DENDROBIUM PULCHELLUM				●	●	●		●			●		●		●	●	●	●				●		
DENDROBIUM X SUPERBIENS			●	●		●		●			●			●	●	●	●					●		
DENDROCHILUM FILIFORME (chain orchid)	●	●			●	●		●			●		●			●		●	●					
DIACRIUM BICORNUTUM (virgin orchid)	●				●	●		●			●			●		●		●	●					
DORITAENOPSIS JERRY VANDE WEGHE	●		●				●		●		●		●	●	●			●						●
DORITAENOPSIS MEMORIA CLARENCE SCHUBERT			●				●		●		●		●	●	●			●						●
DORITIS PULCHERRIMA			●	●	●		●		●		●			●	●		●					●	●	
EPIDENDRUM ATROPURPUREUM (spice orchid)				●	●	●		●			●		●		●	●	●	●		●	●			
EPIDENDRUM CILIARE	●	●			●	●		●			●		●		●	●		●					●	
EPIDENDRUM COCHLEATUM (clamshell orchid)				●	●	●		●			●		●		●	●		●						●
EPIDENDRUM IBAGUENSE (fiery reed orchid)		●	●		●	●		●			●		●		●	●		●						●
EPIDENDRUM MARIAE	●	●			●	●		●			●		●		●	●		●		●				
EPIDENDRUM NOCTURNUM	●	●			●	●		●			●	●	●		●	●		●		●	●			
EPIDENDRUM POLYBULBON				●	●	●		●			●		●		●	●	●	●				●		
EPIDENDRUM PSEUDEPIDENDRUM				●	●	●		●			●		●		●	●		●		●	●			
EPIDENDRUM STAMFORDIANUM				●	●	●		●			●		●		●	●	●	●				●		
EPIDENDRUM TAMPENSE				●	●	●		●			●		●		●	●		●						●
EPIDENDRUM VITELLINUM		●	●			●		●			●		●		●	●		●				●		
ERIA JAVANICA	●				●	●		●			●		●	●	●			●	●	●	●			
GONGORA ARMENIACA (Punch-and-Judy orchid)		●	●		●	●		●			●		●		●			●			●	●		
GONGORA GALEATA (Punch-and-Judy orchid)		●			●	●		●			●		●		●		●				●	●		
HAEMARIA DISCOLOR (jewel orchid)	●					●	●	●			●		●	●	●			●				●	●	
HEXISEA BIDENTATA			●			●		●			●		●		●		●	●	●	●				
IONOPSIS SATYRIOIDES (violet orchid)	●				●	●		●			●		●		●	●	●	●	●				●	

	FLOWER COLOR					OTHER TRAITS						NIGHT TEMP.			LIGHT			HUMIDITY		BLOOMING SEASON				
	White-green	Yellow-orange	Pink-red	Blue-purple	Multicolor	Epiphytic	Terrestrial	Sympodial	Monopodial	Deciduous	Evergreen	Cool (50°-55°)	Intermediate (55°-60°)	Warm (60°-65°)	Under 1,500 foot-candles	1,500-3,000 foot-candles	Over 3,000 foot-candles	Medium (40%-60%)	High (over 60%)	Spring	Summer	Fall	Winter	Intermittent
IONOPSIS UTRICULARIOIDES (violet orchid)	●		●	●		●		●			●		●			●		●	●	●			●	
ISOCHILUS LINEARIS	●		●			●		●			●		●		●			●						●
LAELIA ANCEPS		●		●		●		●			●		●			●		●					●	
LAELIA AUTUMNALIS			●	●		●		●			●		●			●		●				●	●	
LAELIA CINNABARINA		●	●			●		●			●		●			●		●				●	●	
LAELIA CRISPA	●			●		●		●			●		●			●		●			●			
LAELIA LUNDII	●			●		●		●			●		●			●		●					●	
LAELIA PUMILA			●	●		●		●			●		●			●		●				●		
LAELIOCATTLEYA CASSANDRA			●	●		●		●			●		●			●		●					●	
LAELIOCATTLEYA DERNA		●	●			●		●			●		●			●		●					●	
LAELIOCATTLEYA JAY MARKELL			●	●		●		●			●		●			●		●					●	
LAELIOCATTLEYA SOUTH ESK 'JUDY DOIG'			●			●		●			●		●			●		●				●	●	
LEPTOTES BICOLOR	●			●		●		●			●		●			●		●		●			●	
LOCKHARTIA ACUTA (braided orchid)		●	●			●		●			●		●			●		●				●		
LOCKHARTIA LUNIFERA (braided orchid)		●	●			●		●			●		●			●		●				●	●	
LOCKHARTIA OERSTEDII (braided orchid)		●	●			●		●			●		●			●		●						●
LYCASTE AROMATICA		●				●		●		●		●			●			●		●				
LYCASTE VIRGINALIS	●		●			●		●		●		●			●			●				●	●	
MASDEVALLIA BICOLOR		●		●	●	●		●				●	●			●		●	●				●	●
MASDEVALLIA CHIMAERA	●	●		●	●	●		●				●	●			●		●	●					●
MASDEVALLIA COCCINEA			●			●		●				●	●			●		●	●	●	●			
MASDEVALLIA ERYTHROCHAETE		●		●	●	●		●				●	●			●		●	●					
MASDEVALLIA INFRACTA	●	●		●	●	●		●					●			●		●	●					
MASDEVALLIA TOVARENSIS	●					●		●				●				●		●	●			●	●	
MAXILLARIA CRASSIFOLIA		●		●		●		●			●		●			●		●				●		●
MAXILLARIA PICTA		●		●		●		●			●		●			●		●			●		●	
MAXILLARIA SANDERIANA	●		●			●		●				●	●			●		●			●	●		
MILTONIA X BLUNTII (pansy orchid)				●	●	●		●			●		●			●		●			●	●		
MILTONIA CANDIDA (pansy orchid)				●	●	●		●			●		●			●		●				●		
MILTONIA CUNEATA (pansy orchid)				●	●	●		●			●		●			●		●		●				
MILTONIA ROEZLII (pansy orchid)				●	●	●		●			●	●				●		●		●		●		
MILTONIA SPECTABILIS (pansy orchid)	●		●	●	●	●		●			●		●			●		●			●	●		
MORMODES IGNEUM (goblin orchid)				●	●	●		●		●				●		●		●			●		●	
MORMODES VARIABILIS (goblin orchid)		●			●	●		●		●				●		●		●			●		●	
MYSTACIDIUM CAPENSE	●					●			●		●			●		●		●		●	●			
NEOFINETIA FALCATA (samurai orchid)	●					●			●		●		●			●		●			●	●		
NOTYLIA BARKERI	●					●		●			●		●		●			●		●	●			
NOTYLIA XYPHOPHOROUS			●			●		●			●		●		●			●		●				
ODONTOGLOSSUM GRANDE (tiger orchid)		●		●	●	●		●			●		●			●		●				●	●	
ODONTOGLOSSUM PULCHELLUM (lily-of-the-valley orchid)	●					●		●			●		●			●		●					●	
ONCIDIUM AMPLIATUM (turtle orchid)		●	●			●		●			●		●			●		●		●				
ONCIDIUM CHEIROPHORUM (Colombia buttercup)		●				●		●			●		●			●		●				●	●	
ONCIDIUM JONESIANUM	●			●		●		●			●		●			●		●				●		
ONCIDIUM LANCEANUM		●		●		●		●			●		●			●		●		●				
ONCIDIUM PAPILIO (butterfly orchid)		●		●	●	●		●			●		●			●		●						●
ONCIDIUM PULCHELLUM	●			●	●	●		●			●		●			●		●		●	●			
ONCIDIUM PUSILLUM		●		●	●	●		●			●		●			●		●						●
ONCIDIUM SPHACELATUM		●		●	●	●		●			●		●			●		●		●				
ONCIDIUM SPLENDIDUM		●		●	●	●		●			●		●			●		●		●	●			
ONCIDIUM STRAMINEUM	●	●						●			●		●			●		●		●				

Name	White-green	Yellow-orange	Pink-red	Blue-purple	Multicolor	Epiphytic	Terrestrial	Sympodial	Monopodial	Deciduous	Evergreen	Cool (50°-55°)	Intermediate (55°-60°)	Warm (60°-65°)	Under 1,500 foot-candles	1,500-3,000 foot-candles	Over 3,000 foot-candles	Medium (40%-60%)	High (over 60%)	Spring	Summer	Fall	Winter	Intermittent
FLOWER COLOR →										**OTHER TRAITS**		**NIGHT TEMP.**			**LIGHT**			**HUMIDITY**		**BLOOMING SEASON**				
ORNITHOCEPHALUS BICORNIS (bird's-head orchid)	•	•				•		•			•		•	•		•			•		•		•	
PAPHIOPEDILUM BELLATULUM (lady's-slipper orchid)	•	•		•			•	•			•	•	•			•			•		•			
PAPHIOPEDILUM CHAMBERLAINIANUM (lady's-slipper orchid)				•			•	•			•		•	•		•			•					•
PAPHIOPEDILUM F. C. PUDDLE (lady's-slipper orchid)	•						•	•			•	•	•			•			•				•	•
PAPHIOPEDILUM FAIRRIEANUM (lady's-slipper orchid)	•		•	•	•		•	•			•	•	•			•			•			•		
PAPHIOPEDILUM HELLAS 'WESTONBIRT' (lady's-slipper orchid)		•		•			•	•			•		•	•		•			•				•	•
PAPHIOPEDILUM INSIGNE (lady's-slipper orchid)				•			•	•			•		•			•			•			•	•	•
PAPHIOPEDILUM MAUDIAE 'MAGNIFICUM' (lady's-slipper orchid)	•						•	•			•		•			•			•				•	•
PAPHIOPEDILUM MCLAREN PARK (lady's-slipper orchid)				•			•	•			•		•			•			•				•	•
PAPHIOPEDILUM NIVEUM (lady's-slipper orchid)	•						•	•			•			•		•			•		•			
PAPHIOPEDILUM SPICERIANUM (lady's-slipper orchid)				•			•	•			•		•	•		•			•				•	•
PAPHIOPEDILUM SUKHAKULII (lady's-slipper orchid)				•			•	•			•	•	•			•			•		•			
PAPHIOPEDILUM VENUSTUM (lady's-slipper orchid)				•			•	•			•	•	•			•			•	•		•		
PHAIUS TANKERVILLIAE (nun's orchid)	•		•				•	•		•			•			•			•	•	•			
PHALAENOPSIS ALICE GLORIA (moth orchid)	•				•	•			•		•		•	•	•			•	•	•		•		
PHALAENOPSIS CORNU-CERVI (moth orchid)				•	•	•			•		•			•	•			•	•					•
PHALAENOPSIS DIANE RIGG 'PINK MIST' (moth orchid)			•		•	•			•		•			•	•			•	•	•				
PHALAENOPSIS EQUESTRIS (moth orchid)			•	•	•	•			•		•			•	•			•	•					•
PHALAENOPSIS GOLDEN SANDS 'CANARY' (moth orchid)		•			•	•			•		•			•	•			•	•	•	•	•		
PHALAENOPSIS LUEDDEMANNIANA (moth orchid)				•	•	•			•		•			•	•			•	•		•			
PHALAENOPSIS MANNII (moth orchid)				•	•	•			•		•			•	•			•	•	•	•	•		
PHALAENOPSIS PARISHII (moth orchid)	•			•	•	•			•		•			•	•			•	•	•	•			
PHALAENOPSIS PEPPERMINT (moth orchid)			•		•	•			•		•			•	•			•	•				•	
PHALAENOPSIS STUARTIANA (moth orchid)				•	•	•			•		•			•	•			•	•			•	•	
PHALAENOPSIS VIOLACEA (moth orchid)				•	•	•			•		•			•	•			•	•					•
PHRAGMIPEDIUM CAUDATUM VAR. SANDERAE (mandarin orchid)				•			•	•			•		•			•		•		•	•			
PHRAGMIPEDIUM SCHLIMII (slipper orchid)	•		•				•	•			•		•			•		•		•		•		
PLEIONE MACULATA	•		•				•	•		•		•				•		•				•		
PLEIONE PRAECOX			•	•			•	•		•		•				•		•				•		
PLEUROTHALLIS GROBYI	•	•		•		•		•			•		•			•		•			•	•		
PLEUROTHALLIS RUBENS		•				•			•		•		•			•		•	•		•	•		
POLYSTACHYA LUTEOLA	•	•				•		•			•	•	•			•	•	•	•					•
POLYSTACHYA PUBESCENS		•			•	•		•			•	•	•			•	•	•	•		•			
POTINARA CARROUSEL 'CRIMSON TRIUMPH'			•			•		•			•		•			•	•	•			•			
POTINARA GORDON SIU 'RED RADIANCE'			•			•		•			•		•			•	•	•			•			
PROMENAEA XANTHINA		•				•		•			•	•	•			•		•			•			
RENANTHERA COCCINEA		•			•				•		•			•			•	•	•	•	•	•		
RENANTHERA IMSCHOOTIANA		•							•		•		•				•	•	•	•	•			
RENANTHERA MONACHICA (fire orchid)		•		•	•				•		•		•				•	•	•	•	•			
RESTREPIA ANTENNIFERA		•	•	•		•		•			•	•	•			•		•						•
RESTREPIA GUTTULATA		•				•		•			•		•			•		•						•
RHYNCHOSTYLIS GIGANTEA (foxtail orchid)	•			•					•		•		•	•		•		•				•	•	
RODRIGUEZIA SECUNDA (coral orchid)			•			•		•			•		•			•		•						•
RODRIGUEZIA VENUSTA	•	•		•		•		•			•		•			•						•		
SACCOLABIUM HENDERSONIANUM		•							•		•			•		•		•	•	•	•			
SACCOLABIUM QUISUMBINGII	•	•							•		•			•		•		•					•	
SCHOMBURGKIA LYONSII				•		•		•			•		•			•		•			•	•		
SCHOMBURGKIA TIBICINIS				•		•		•			•		•			•		•			•	•		
SCHOMBURGKIA UNDULATA				•		•		•			•		•			•		•		•			•	
SCUTICARIA STEELII		•	•			•		•			•		•			•	•	•			•	•		

153

	White-green	Yellow-orange	Pink-red	Blue-purple	Multicolor	Epiphytic	Terrestrial	Sympodial	Monopodial	Deciduous	Evergreen	Cool (50°-55°)	Intermediate (55°-60°)	Warm (60°-65°)	Under 1,500 foot-candles	1,500-3,000 foot-candles	Over 3,000 foot-candles	Medium (40%-60%)	High (over 60%)	Spring	Summer	Fall	Winter	Intermittent
SOBRALIA MACRANTHA			●	●			●	●			●		●			●			●	●	●			
SOPHROLAELIOCATTLEYA ANZAC 'ORCHIDHURST'			●	●		●		●			●		●			●			●				●	
SOPHROLAELIOCATTLEYA JEWEL BOX 'SCHEHERAZADE'			●			●		●			●		●			●			●					●
SOPHROLAELIOCATTLEYA PAPRIKA 'BLACK MAGIC'			●			●		●			●		●			●			●					●
SOPHRONITIS COCCINEA			●			●		●			●	●	●			●		●				●	●	
STANHOPEA WARDII		●	●			●		●			●		●			●			●		●	●		
STELIS BIDENTATA			●	●		●		●			●		●			●			●					
STELIS CILIARIS				●		●		●			●		●			●		●						●
STELIS MICRANTHA			●	●		●		●			●		●			●			●					
THUNIA ALBA	●						●	●		●		●	●			●			●		●			
THUNIA MARSHALLIANA	●						●	●		●		●	●			●			●		●			
TRICHOGLOTTIS PHILIPPINENSIS VAR. BRACHIATA			●				●		●		●			●		●			●		●			
TRICHOPILIA SUAVIS	●		●			●		●			●		●			●		●						
TRICHOPILIA TORTILIS			●	●		●		●					●			●			●				●	
VANDA COERULEA (blue orchid)				●		●			●		●			●		●			●			●	●	
VANDA HILO QUEEN			●			●			●		●			●		●			●					●
VANDA ONOMEA				●		●			●		●			●		●			●					●
VANDA ROTHSCHILDIANA				●		●			●		●			●		●			●					●
VANDA SANDERIANA			●	●		●			●		●			●		●			●			●		
VANDA TERES			●			●			●		●			●		●			●		●	●		
VANILLA PLANIFOLIA	●	●				●	●		●					●				●	●					●
VUYLSTEKEARA CAMBRIA 'PLUSH'	●		●			●		●				●				●		●	●				●	
ZYGOPETALUM INTERMEDIUM				●			●	●			●		●			●			●				●	

Bibliography

Allan, Mea, *Darwin and his Flowers*. Faber and Faber, Ltd., 1977.

American Orchid Society, Inc., *Growing Orchids Indoors*. AOS, 1969.

American Orchid Society, Inc., *Handbook on Orchid Culture*. AOS, 1976.

American Orchid Society, Inc., *Handbook on Orchid Pests and Diseases*. AOS, 1975.

American Orchid Society, Inc., *Handbook on Judging and Exhibition*. AOS, 1969.

American Orchid Society, Inc., *Meristem Tissue Culture*. AOS, 1969.

American Orchid Society, Inc., *An Orchidist's Glossary*. AOS, 1974.

Bailey, Ralph, *The Good Housekeeping Illustrated Encyclopedia of Gardening*. The Hearst Corp., 1972.

Blowers, John W., *Pictorial Orchid Growing*. John W. Blowers, 1966.

Bowen, Leslie, *The Art and Craft of Growing Orchids*. G. P. Putnam's Sons, 1967.

Boyle, Louis M., *Cymbidium Orchids for You*. Louis M. Boyle, 1950.

Briscoe, T. W., *Orchids for Amateurs*. W. H. & L. Collingridge, Ltd., 1948.

Brooklyn Botanic Garden, *Handbook on Orchids*. BBG, 1967.

Burnett, Harry C., *Orchid Diseases*, Bulletin 10. Florida Department of Agriculture and Consumer Services, 1974.

Chittenden, Fred J., ed., *The Royal Horticultural Society Dictionary of Gardening*, 2nd ed. Clarendon Press, 1974.

Craighead, Frank, *Orchids and Other Air Plants*. University of Miami Press, 1963.

Crockett, James U., *Greenhouse Gardening as a Hobby*. Doubleday, 1961.

Dodson, Calaway H., and Gillespie, Robert J., *The Biology of the Orchids*. The Mid-America Orchid Congress, Inc., 1967.

Dunsterville, G. C. K., *Introduction to the World of Orchids*. Doubleday & Co., 1964.

Eigeldinger, O., and Murphy, L. S., *Orchids: A Complete Guide to Cultivation*. John Gifford, Ltd., 1971.

Everett, T. H., *New Illustrated Encyclopedia of Gardening*. Greystone Press, 1960.

Fennell, T. A., Jr., *Orchids for Home and Garden*, rev. ed. Rinehart and Co., Inc., 1959.

Freed, Hugo, *Orchids and Serendipity*. Prentice-Hall, Inc., 1970.

Graf, Alfred Byrd, *Exotic Plant Manual*. Roehrs Co., Inc., 1974.

Graf, Alfred Byrd, *Exotica*, Series 3, 8th ed. Roehrs Co., Inc., 1976.

Hawkes, Alex D., *Encyclopaedia of Cultivated Orchids*. Faber and Faber, Ltd., 1965.

Hawkes, Alex D., *Orchids: Their Botany and Culture*. Harper and Brothers, 1961.

International Orchid Commission, *Handbook on Orchid Nomenclature and Registration*. IOC, 1976.

Irvine, William, *Apes, Angels and Victorians*. McGraw-Hill Book Co., Inc., 1955.

Kijima, Takashi, *The Orchid*. Kodansha, 1975.

Kramer, Jack, *Growing Orchids at your Windows*. D. Van Nostrand Co., Inc., 1963.

Kramer, Jack, *Orchids: Flowers of Romance and Mystery*. Harry N. Abrams, Inc., 1975.

Logan, Harry B., and Cosper, Lloyd C., *Orchids are Easy to Grow*. Ziff-Davis Publishing Co., 1949.

Luer, Carlyle, *The Native Orchids of the U.S. and Canada*. New York Botanical Garden, 1975.

Noble, Mary, *Florida Orchids*. Florida State Department of Agriculture, 1951.

Noble, Mary, *You Can Grow Cattleya Orchids*. Mary Noble, 1968.

Noble, Mary, *You Can Grow Orchids,* 4th rev. ed. Mary Noble, 1975.

Noble, Mary, *You Can Grow Phalaenopsis Orchids*. Mary Noble, 1971.

Northen, Rebecca Tyson, *Home Orchid Growing*. Van Nostrand Reinhold Co., 1970.

Northen, Rebecca Tyson, *Orchids as House Plants*, 2nd rev. ed. Dover Publications, Inc., 1976.

Oregon Orchid Society, Inc., *Your First Orchids and How to Grow Them,* 6th rev. ed. OOS, 1977.

Pacific Orchid Society of Hawaii, *Handbook for the Growing of Orchids in Hawaii*. POS of Hawaii, 1962.

Parkinson, John, *Theatrum Botanicum: The Theater of Plants*. Thomas Cotes, 1640.

Paul, Michel, *Orchids, Care and Growth*. Universe Books, Inc., 1964.

Ratcliffe, Edna, *The Enchantment of Paphiopedilums*. Leach's of Abington, 1977.

The Reader's Digest Association, Ltd., *Reader's Digest Encyclopaedia of Garden Plants and Flowers*. RDA. 1971.

Reinikka, Merle A., *A History of the Orchid*. University of Miami Press, 1972.

Richter, Walter, *Orchid Care: A Guide to Cultivation and Breeding*. The Macmillan Co., 1969.

Richter, Walter, *The Orchid World*. E. P. Dutton & Co., Inc., 1965.

Sander, David, *Orchids and Their Cultivation,* 7th ed. International Publications Service, 1969.

Sander, C. F., F. K. and L. L., *Sanders' Orchid Guide*. Sanders, 1927.

Sanders, Ltd., *Sanders' Complete List of Orchid Hybrids*. Gibbs & Bamforth, Ltd., 1946.

Shuttleworth, Floyd S., Zim, Herbert S., and Dillon, Gordon W., *Orchids*. Golden Press, 1970.

Staff of the L. H. Bailey Hortorium, Cornell University, *Hortus Third: A Dictionary of Plants Cultivated in the United States and Canada*. Macmillan Publishing Co., Inc., 1976.

Sunset Editors, *How to Grow Orchids*. Lane Publishing Co., 1977.

Swinson, Arthur, *Frederick Sander: The Orchid King*. Hodder & Stoughton, 1970.

Van der Pijl, L. and Dodson, Calaway H., *Orchid Flowers: Their Pollination and Evolution*. University of Miami Press, 1966.

Veitch and Sons, *A Manual of Orchidaceous Plants*. H. M. Pollett and Co., 1887.

Williams, Henry, *The Orchid Grower's Manual*. Victoria and Paradise Nurseries, 1894.

Withner, Carl, *The Orchids, Scientific Studies*. Wiley and Sons, 1974.

Picture credits

The sources for the illustrations in this book are listed below. Credits from left to right are separated by semicolons, from top to bottom by dashes. Cover: Tom Tracy. 4: William Skelsey. 6: Derek Bayes, courtesy Lindley Library, Royal Horticultural Society, London. 8, 9: Steve Tuttle, from *Theatrum Botanicum* by John Parkinson, 1640, courtesy U.S. National Agricultural Library. 11: Derek Bayes, courtesy Lindley Library, Royal Horticultural Society, London. 13: Drawings by Kathy Rebeiz. 17: Edward S. Ross. 18: Kjell B. Sandved, Smithsonian Institution—Edward S. Ross. 19: Kjell B. Sandved, Smithsonian Institution—Z. Leszczynski, © Earth Scenes. 20, 21: Kjell B. Sandved, Smithsonian Institution. 22: Enrico Ferorelli. 25: Richard Jeffery. 29, 31, 32: Drawings by Kathy Rebeiz. 35 through 46: Enrico Ferorelli. 48 through 61: Drawings by Kathy Rebeiz. 63: John Zimmerman. 64: Enrico Ferorelli. 65: Tom Tracy. 66, 67: John Zimmerman. 68, 69: Tom Tracy. 70, 71: Linda Bartlett. 72, 73: Henry Groskinsky. 74: Enrico Ferorelli. 77, 79: Drawings by Kathy Rebeiz. 81: Courtesy R. & E. Ratcliffe (Orchids) Ltd. (2)—Patrick Thurston, courtesy R. & E. Ratcliffe (Orchids) Ltd.; courtesy R. & E. Ratcliffe (Orchids) Ltd.—courtesy R. & E. Ratcliffe (Orchids) Ltd.; courtesy Orchid Society of Great Britain. 82: Courtesy R. & E. Ratcliffe (Orchids) Ltd.—Patrick Thurston, courtesy R. & E. Ratcliffe (Orchids) Ltd. (2)—courtesy R. & E. Ratcliffe (Orchids) Ltd.; courtesy R. & E. Ratcliffe (Orchids) Ltd.—Patrick Thurston, courtesy R. & E. Ratcliffe (Orchids) Ltd. 83: Courtesy R. & E. Ratcliffe (Orchids) Ltd. 85, 86: Drawings by Kathy Rebeiz. 88: Illustration by Richard Crist. 90 through 147: Illustrations by artists listed in alphabetical order: Adolph E. Brotman, Richard Crist, Susan M. Johnston, Mary Kellner, Gwen Leighton, Trudy Nicholson, Carolyn Pickett, Eduardo Salgado, Ray Skibinski. 148: Illustrations by Susan M. Johnston.

Acknowledgments

The index for this book was prepared by Anita R. Beckerman. For their help in the preparation of this book, the editors wish to thank the following: Robinson P. Abbot, Silver Spring, Md.; Clive Atyeo, Vienna, Va.; Roy Bogan, Finksburg, Md.; Tony Bos, Jones and Scully, Inc., Miami, Fla.; Dr. O. Wesley Davidson, North Brunswick, N.J.; Curtis T. Ewing, Clarksville, Md.; Emily Friedman, Los Angeles, Calif.; Dr. Allan Fusonie, Rare Book Collection, National Agricultural Library, Beltsville, Md.; John and Nancy Gardner, Ellicott City, Md.; Andy Gay, Jones and Scully, Inc., Miami, Fla.; Hillwood Orchid Collection, Washington, D.C.; Mr. and Mrs. Richard Hoffman, Springfield, Va.; Ilgenfritz Orchids, Great Lakes Orchids, Inc., Monroe, Mich.; Mr. and Mrs. Chet Kasprzak, Rockville, Md.; Chester Kawakami, South River Orchids, Edgewater, Md.; Mr. and Mrs. Howard W. King, Baltimore, Md.; Dr. Roger Lawson, plant virologist, USDA Beltsville Agricultural Research Center, Beltsville, Md.; Louis and Sophia Martin, Fulton, Md.; Mary Noble McQuerry, Jacksonville, Fla.; Mr. Edward J. Neuberger, Clarksville, Md.; staff at the Propagation Range, New York Botanical Garden, Bronx, N.Y.; Orchids by Hausermann, Inc., Elmhurst, Ill.; Jim Pendelton, The Good Earth Nursery, Falls Church, Va.; Richard Peterson, American Orchid Society, Inc., Cambridge, Mass.; Edna Ratcliffe, R. & E. Ratcliffe, Ltd., Chilton, England; Don Richardson, Greentree, Manhasset, N.Y.; Harold Ripley, San Francisco, Calif.; Bob Russo, Propagation Range, New York Botanical Garden, Bronx, N.Y.; S. & G. Exotic Plant Co., Beverly, Mass.; Mr. and Mrs. Gordon Sawyer, Los Angeles, Calif.; Elinor S. Yocom, Naples, Fla.

Index

Numerals in italics indicate an illustration of the subject mentioned.